MEDIA PARASITES IN THE EARLY AVANT-GARDE

Avant-Gardes in Performance

Series Editors
Sarah Bay-Cheng, University at Buffalo, The State University of New York
Martin Harries, University of California, Irvine

Media Parasites in the Early Avant-Garde: On the Abuse of Technology and Communication
By Arndt Niebisch

Media Parasites in the Early Avant-Garde

On the Abuse of Technology and Communication

Arndt Niebisch

MEDIA PARASITES IN THE EARLY AVANT-GARDE
Copyright © Arndt Niebisch, 2012.
Softcover reprint of the hardcover 1st edition 2012 978-1-137-27685-8
All rights reserved.

First published in 2012 by
PALGRAVE MACMILLAN®
in the United States—a division of St. Martin's Press LLC,
175 Fifth Avenue, New York, NY 10010.

Where this book is distributed in the UK, Europe and the rest of the
World, this is by Palgrave Macmillan, a division of Macmillan Publishers
Limited, registered in England, company number 785998, of Houndmills,
Basingstoke, Hampshire RG21 6XS.

Palgrave Macmillan is the global academic imprint of the above
companies and has companies and representatives throughout the world.

Palgrave® and Macmillan® are registered trademarks in the United
States, the United Kingdom, Europe and other countries.

ISBN 978-1-349-44684-1   ISBN 978-1-137-27686-5 (eBook)
DOI 10.1057/9781137276865

Library of Congress Cataloging-in-Publication Data

Niebisch, Arndt.
    Media parasites in the early avant-garde : on the abuse of
  technology and communication / Arndt Niebisch.
      pages   cm

    1. Communication and the arts.   2. Technology and the arts.
    3. Arts—Experimental methods—History—20th century.   I. Title.
    NX180.C65N54 2012
    700'.411—dc23   2012024716

A catalogue record of the book is available from the British Library.

Design by Integra Software Services

First edition: December 2012

10 9 8 7 6 5 4 3 2 1

Transferred to Digital Printing in 2013

For Leo

Contents

List of Illustrations	ix
Foreword	xi
Acknowledgments	xv
Introduction: An Avant-Garde Parasitology	1
1 The Press and the Parasites	17
2 Poetic Media Effects	45
3 Parasitic Media	81
4 Parasitic Noise	109
5 Ether Parasites	143
Conclusion: Odradek and the Future of the Parasite	175
Notes	181
Bibliography	215
Index	225

Illustrations

2.1 The poem "Karawane" from Richard Huelsenbeck, *Dada Almanach* (1920) — 67

2.2 Front page of *Der Dada 1* (1919) — 71

2.3 "OFFEA" by Raoul Hausmann (1918), Berlinische Galerie — 75

2.4 "K'perioum" by Raoul Hausmann (1920), Berlinische Galerie — 77

3.1 "Jump" Chronophotograph (1888), College de France — 84

3.2 "Suonatore di violoncello" (1913–14) by A. and A. G. Bragaglia — 90

3.3 "Dada-Rundschau" (1919) by Hannah Höch, Berlinische Galerie — 100

3.4 "Der Dadaist Wieland Herzfelde" by John Heartfield from *Der Dada 3* (1920) — 104

4.1 Photograph of Russolo and *intonarumori* from *l'arte dei rumori* (1916) — 113

4.2 "Sveglio di una città" score from *l'arte dei rumori* (1916) — 118

Foreword

Despite the many acts of denial and resistance embodied in the phrase "death of the avant-garde," interest in experimental, innovative, and politically radical performances continues to animate theatre and performance studies. For all the attacks upon tradition and critical institutions (or perhaps because of them), the historical and subsequent avant-gardes remain critical touchstones for continued research across media and disciplines. We are, it seems, perpetually invested in the new.

Avant-Gardes in Performance enables scholarship at the forefront of critical analysis: scholarship that not only illuminates radical performance practices, but also transforms existing critical approaches to those performances. By engaging with the charged phrase "avant-garde," the series considers performance practices and events that are *formally* avant-garde, as defined by experimentation and breaks with traditional structures, practices, and content; *historically* avant-garde, defined within the global aesthetic movements of the early twentieth century, including modernism and its many global aftermaths; and *politically* radical, defined by identification with extreme political movements on the right and left alike.

Arndt Niebisch's *Media Parasites in the Early Avant-Garde* argues for a renewed understanding of the politics of two of the formative movements in the early historical avant-garde, Futurism and Dada. Niebisch unsettles expectations about form, history, and politics alike by insisting on the importance of media to both of these foundational movements. In this context, Futurism and Dada were irritants in media systems that, by refusing the straightforward circuit of communication, made the underlying mode of those systems visible: the "noise" of the avant-garde revealed the code underlying all standard communication. As the avant-garde harnessed available media to its own ends, the medium of media, so to speak, became more readily accessible.

The importance of Niebisch's argument becomes clear in comparison with what remains one of the foundational texts in the study of the avant-garde, Peter Bürger's *Theory of the Avant-Garde*. Bürger argues that the avant-garde's aim "is to reintegrate art into the praxis of life..."[1] Further, Bürger claims, the avant-garde attempts "to organize a new life praxis from a basis in art" (49). Niebisch's emphasis on the avant-garde's engagement with media troubles the divide essential to Bürger's formulation. Bürger's Marxist phrase, "praxis of life," might promise a new order of living undamaged by modern alienation. Niebisch's focus on media is, however, also at a fundamental level a focus on mediation. If life is lived through newspapers and gramophones, then the renewal of the "praxis of life" cannot happen independent of these media. And what life comes before or after them? In Niebisch's account, the avant-garde makes the peculiar nature of the mediated nature of modern life distinctly visible.

In his introduction Niebisch stresses the avant-garde's role in what he calls, on the book's first page, "a synesthetic reeducation of humankind." Rather than an additional stream in the flows of communication, the force of the avant-garde, here, lies largely in the way it makes the stuff of these codes apparent. The newspaper's need for news, for example, becomes apparent when the avant-garde uses the newspaper as a forum for nonsense that cannot pass as news. *Media Parasites* presents the avant-garde in a resolutely social light: far from the formations of self-enclosed coteries, Futurism and Dada here are constantly at work on, and at work with, the growingly dominant mass cultural codes of a common culture. His title announces his central figure to describe this relationship between media and the avant-garde: the parasite. Drawing on the work of Michel Serres, Niebisch rethinks the parasite as a way to theorize the avant-garde's combination of dependence upon and "irritation" of mass media loops. "Irritation" is another of the book's crucial terms: Niebisch never makes inflated claims for avant-garde revolution. Rather than an overturning of the mass media that serve as its hosts, Niebisch's parasitic avant-garde intervenes through education, by marking what might otherwise pass unnoticed. The shock of the new, here, is the shock of an art that makes its audience aware of what it has already taken for granted. Avant-garde irritation makes the force of media newly graspable.

Another of the great strengths of this book is that it does not assimilate these two important early avant-garde movements to one another: throughout, Niebisch is careful to stress that while Futurism and Dada worked within roughly similar media environments, their modes of parasitic irritation were distinct. In Chapter 3's discussion of the different disruptions of poetic language in Futurism and Dada, for instance, he argues that, where Marinetti sought a "language resistant to noise," Dada poets wanted to generate "noise through poetry." A larger distinction between what one might call Futurism's communicative strategy and

Dada's anti-communicative stance is central to the book's understanding of the two movements. Niebisch is also careful not to reduce the disparate members of one or the other movement to a false unanimity of practices: differences inside the movements are as important here as the general projects Futurists or Dadaists had in common. Certain figures emerge here with special force. As the editor of a volume of the technical and scientific writings of Raoul Hausmann, Niebisch is particularly alert to the extraordinary corpus of this fascinating and complex figure. Throughout *Media Parasites*, however, there are detailed and compelling readings of the work of a wide range of figures from Marinetti to Hugo Ball—readings that include verbo-visual materials, photographs, and other forms, as well as somewhat more straightforwardly literary productions.

Media Parasites initiates a new series, *Avant-Gardes in Performance*, by placing the formal innovations of two exemplary early avant-garde movements in relation to the media that made these innovations possible. Skeptical of claims about the revolutionary force of the avant-garde, *Media Parasites* is nevertheless a book about its political work. If life is lived in part through media, this is a book about the politics of everyday life.

Sarah Bay-Cheng and Martin Harries

Acknowledgments

A project like this could never have been accomplished without the help of many others. I especially thank David Marshall for his continuous interest and support for this project from its beginning many years ago in Florence. My great gratitude goes to the Berlinische Galerie, especially to Ralf Burmeister and Wolfgang Erler, for giving me access to Hausmann's unpublished technical and scientific writings. William Dodson was an extraordinary help in editing the final version of the manuscript, and everything would not have come together without Julia's support.

Introduction:
An Avant-Garde
Parasitology

AT THE END OF FEBRUARY 1932, the intellectual leader of Dada Berlin and so-called "Dadasoph" Raoul Hausmann received a brief message from his friend the engineer Daniel Broido.[1] Broido asked him in this letter for some journals that he would like to send to his sister in Leningrad for leisure reading. Broido made this request because he knew that Hausmann owned a plethora of lifestyle magazines that dealt with the newest inventions and scientific discoveries of the day. Broido, however, clearly underestimated and misunderstood the importance of these journals for Hausmann. Popular magazines from the Weimar period such as *Die Koralle, Wissenschaft und Fortschritt,* among others, were not simply leisure reading for the Dadaist. Their numerous reports about the theory of relativity, quantum physics, solar cells, or astonishing prosthetic devices provided the fuel for his ideas about an "optophonetic" worldview that implied a synesthetic reeducation of humankind.[2] Even more significant for the engineer Broido, these journals constituted the main sources for Hausmann's knowledge about photo cells and patent law that Hausmann contributed to his and Broido's collaboration on a photoelectrically switched calculating machine, which they tried to design from 1930 on.[3]

Broido's little note shows that in 1932, a good ten years after the high point of the Dada movement, Hausmann was still surrounded by mass-media-produced information—this time not for reassembling pictures and letters in a visual collage, but for inventing media technologies. In fact, the engineering work of the Dadasoph carried traces of Dadaistic practices. Hausmann and Broido's calculating machine, which Hausmann in 1966 still misrepresented as the first modern computer,[4] had a central issue: it was not a real invention. Certainly, Hausmann had some experience in designing technological equipment—he even developed improvements for the gramophone, an endoscope and a sound–light converter,[5] and the famous *optophone*,[6] but all the technologies that the Dadaist assembled were not particularly new and merely reflected the established technological standard of the twenties. Dr. Bormuth, the patent clerk in Berlin who constantly rejected Hausmann and Broido's patent applications, apparently knew this very well and realized that what the engineer and the Dadaist tried to assemble was merely a collage of Hausmann's notes about technical devices that he collected from his journals.[7]

The struggle with the patent office indicates that Hausmann's technical work was based on an exploitation of the media—a practice that Hausmann developed in his Dada time, when he and his fellows radically cut-and-pasted everything that they were able to collect and reassemble. They inhabited like parasites the media discourses of their time, constantly irritating and taking from them. This parasitic attitude, however, did not start with Dada, but was already present in 1909, when F. T. Marinetti published his Futurist Manifesto[8] that strategically abused the front page of the French newspaper *Le Figaro* for creating a new art movement rather than for informing the public about the news of the day. It is typical for Dada and Futurism that they did not merely reject the contemporaneous discourse of the media, but that they exploited the new communicative possibilities that opened up before their eyes.

The artistic scene of the early twentieth century saw the birth and further development of many new technologies. Several of them had a more or less direct impact on the aesthetic production of the avant-garde. The telegraph turned under the regime of the British-Italian engineer Guglielmo Marconi into the radio that soon was able to transmit not only Morse code, but voices, inspiring Dadaists and Futurists to conceptualize a new poetics. The phonograph enabled the recording of voices, and the gramophone record started a new form of mass marketing of sounds and noises, which fueled the sonic experiments of the avant-garde. Cinema developed from a magic trick in the variety theater of the French trickster Georges Méliès into an industrially produced mass illusion, which Dadaists and Futurists used and abused for their own visual works. Airplanes, at first dangerous and unreliable machines handled by individual heroes, were adored by Futurists and became logistic and military key factors even before the Second World War. In many ways, the technological development mirrored and even surpassed the avant-garde call for changing and accelerating the world. The artists of the early twentieth century lived in a completely new and unknown media ecology, and the avant-garde was the first to formulate a program that attempted to inhabit, irritate, and shape this environment.

Although the term "media ecology" has a history that is associated with the work of media theorists such as Marshall McLuhan and Neil Postman,[9] it gained new theoretical traction especially after Matthew Fuller's book *Media Ecologies*.[10] This field of inquiry is very vibrant, and an attempt to specify a clear definition of what media ecology is would be too deterministic and disregard the complexity and diversity of this discussion. Michael Goddard and Jussi Parikka edited an issue of the *Fibreculture Journal* on the topic "Unnatural Ecologies," in which they presented a series of essays addressing media ecologies. In their introduction they emphasized the diversity of approaches, but also acknowledged that a media ecological perspective highlights the complex interaction of nature and technology.[11]

> Technology is not only a passive surface for the inscription of meanings and signification, but a material assemblage that partakes in machinic ecologies. And, instead of assuming that "ecologies" are by their nature natural (even if naturalizing perhaps in terms of their impact or capacities of sensation and thought) we assume them as radically contingent and dynamic, in other words as prone to change.[12]

The notion of media ecology that I am adopting throughout this book follows largely this line. Media ecologies are technologically created spheres of interaction that a society inhabits. These ecologies are no passive tools, but active in shaping communication and rules of a society; however, these ecologies are also influenced by its inhabitants, so that a dynamic and complex exchange occurs that leads to a continuous transformation of this media ecology. In my understanding, the term "media ecology" suspends simple inside/outside dichotomies and implements a dynamic fusion of the environment and its inhabitants.

The avant-garde movements engaged intentionally in such an exchange and contributed to the development of their media ecology: they simultaneously used and abused, criticized and celebrated the emerging forms of communication and technology in the early twentieth century. They were closely connected to the technological, social, political, aesthetic, and scientific discourses of their time. However, they created a position from where they did not simply affirm the status quo, but were able to constantly subvert and intervene into it. I suggest that this position can be described as parasitic.

The Greek root of *parasite*, consisting of *para*, meaning "beside," and *sitos*, meaning "grain," indicates that the parasite exists next to its nourishing host. Biology uses the term for describing an organism that inhabits and lives from another organism, and although the parasite constitutes a permanent irritation, it will rarely destroy the host. The parasite creates an intricate adaptation that is based on a supporting organism.[13] The avant-garde adopted such a parasitic relationship. The media environment that consisted of telegraph messages, daily newspapers, all kinds of advertisements, gramophone recordings, and numerous other gadgets was the fertile ground for the imagination of avant-garde artists. They were fascinated by these technologies and embraced the language and concepts of modern sciences such as Hermann von Helmholtz' acoustics,[14] Bohr and Rutherford's atom model,[15] and Albert Einstein's relativity.[16] Of course, they engaged with these ideas without obeying the laws of the university or the rigidity of engineering. The avant-garde arbitrarily took from these discourses and reassembled such fragments in order to proclaim the dawn of a new man or era that would emerge from an accelerated modernity.

THE PARASITE AND COMMUNICATION

The emphasis on the parasite links this study to a model of communication, developed by the French theorist Michel Serres. Serres is a philosopher and historian of science who brings sciences and humanities together in a unique way. His works reread mathematical and communication theoretical theorems through a lens that is informed by mythology and anthropology.[17] He thereby develops approaches that do not attempt to circumvent complexities but focus on the productive impact of noise and derivations. Accordingly, he identifies irritations and distortions as an unavoidable part of every communication. Errors and disruptions are not recognized as merely destructive, but as genuinely productive, because they generate a new complexity.[18] Serres develops this notion in *The Parasite*.[19] This book hardly provides a clear and discursive theory of communication, but it contains several meditations about myths and fables that re-describe the central elements of information theory.[20] More precisely, Serres rethinks the position and importance of noise in communication and relates the parasite to the notion of noise in communication theory as developed by the American mathematician Claude E. Shannon.[21]

Shannon described communication based on a sender-receiver model that is neutral to the semantic content transmitted through the channel. Shannon developed this theory during the Second World War through his work in cryptography.[22] To conceal an important message, Shannon attempted to disguise the transmitted message as the noise that contaminates every communication. This way, enemy interceptors would ideally not be able to distinguish between the channel's white noise and the message. Shannon played two parasites of the communication system against each other. First, there is the uninvited interceptor that feasts on every signal transmitted through the communication lines of the enemy. Second, there is the environmental noise that is created by and impacts every actually operating communication system. The strategy for securing a message is to simulate for the parasitic interceptor a parasitic noise, so that a message appears as nothing else than the static of the channel. The cryptographic techniques demand that the interceptor filter noise (i.e., decipher a message), because in all communication, noise needs to be separated from the signal in order to receive the message. Thus, Shannon's cryptographic camouflage did not only describe communication in wartime, but would quickly after the Second World (in 1949) emerge as a general mathematical theory of all human and nonhuman forms of communication. Its most central lesson is not only that communication can be described independent of the meaning of the message, but also that noise is an unavoidable part of every communication that forces military channels as well as all civil communication to decipher messages contaminated by parasites inhabiting the channel.

Shannon does not conceptualize noise explicitly as parasitic; Serres uses the term parasite for explicating the creative force of noise. The parasite is for Serres the emblem for a small interruption in a communicative flow. He draws this consideration from the linguistic particularity that "parasite" not only refers to a biological entity that depends on its host, but that "parasitic" is also used in electrical engineering to describe irritations or the static in a transmission channel.[23] Serres emphasizes that such interruptions in communication systems are not only destructive, but creative elements that force the system to react to the disturbance and to create a new complexity.[24] An example of such compensation is a conversation in a noisy environment. The noises that continually interfere in a dialogue I am having with a friend in a café, for example, make it harder to communicate. The noises are uninvited guests, intervening in our conversation. These noises, however, force me to speak more loudly, to repeat myself, and so on. This redundancy in speech is what the parasite triggers. The parasite is not in itself productive, but it forces its host to react and produce. Serres describes this dynamic with the following theorem: "noise gives rise to a new system, an order that is more complex than the simple chain. This parasite interrupts at first glance, consolidates when you look again."[25] Serres deduces from this dynamic between system and parasite that the parasite is not simply an outside intruder, but the index for the complexity in a system. This is an ecological turn, because Serres no longer separates a communication system from its disturbing outside but describes noise as an integral part of the ecology of communication. Complex systems, for Serres, always include irritations; therefore, the parasite is a necessary inhabitant of complex processes. The parasite does not enter into an exchange, but rather takes without giving.[26] It distorts and irritates an exchange of equal values and thereby generates a new communicative situation. A parasite irritates its host, but also forces it to compensate for this perturbation. The term "irritation" is central to this understanding, because it implies not only a disturbance, but also stimulation: an irritation evokes a reaction—a strategy to cope with this impact. An irritation is thus not simply disturbing, but also stimulating, that is, productive.

The avant-garde interventions in the early twentieth century can be read in analogy to this model. Their tactics to irritate media discourses constitute an integral factor in the development of an emerging media ecology that involves every inhabitant and constantly demands a reaction.

AVANT-GARDE PARASITES

Dadaist and Futurist parasites did not provoke the bourgeois society of their time from the outside, but contributed to the modern media ecology that they inhabited and used as their host. The avant-garde artists were not simply freaks at the periphery, but constituted an integral part of the media economy of the early twentieth century. Marinetti, who created an enormous marketing campaign, is probably the most famous publicist of the avant-garde, but also Dada was very successful in integrating itself in the mass media channels of its time. The avant-garde artists, however, were not satisfied with occupying established media channels. They soon realized that modern media art was more than literature, music, drama, and visual works and recognized the potential of new technologies such as the radio or photo cells to construct a completely new form of *Gesamtkunstwerk*. In fact, the avant-garde artists envisioned their works as extremely powerful and imagined that their art would be able to overwrite the military-industrial complex of the time. For example, the Futurist composer Luigi Russolo predicted that factories would be built only to perform noise symphonies,[27] Marinetti wanted to cancel out the moonshine with electrical lights,[28] and Hausmann dreamed in a similar fashion about sound-light symphonies on an industrial scale.[29] However, all these attempts of taking over media discourses ended up being nothing more than small irritations to the hegemonic communication systems. Ironically, the irritating and subversive impact of collages, performances, and media experiments was the most important ally of Futurism and Dada, because the avant-garde injected their media transformations in a subversive and ubiquitous way into aesthetic and social discourses that enabled the persistent development of the avant-garde over decades.

The subversive engagement with media as an omnipresent irritation in the channel constitutes the avant-garde's parasitic nature. Serres points out that the parasite does not occupy a fixed position. The parasite is no simple isolatable element in a diagram. It is something that inhabits a system, that occupies the relationships between the single parts of a system, and it does not dwell in clearly defined places.[30] A noise source in a system is not clearly identifiable. Noise, errors, and interruptions can come from everywhere. To occupy this "everywhere" is precisely the project of the avant-garde. The artistic practices were—at least at first—designed to be surprising and unpredictable. The noise they generated could intrude at every moment and everywhere. Taking art to the street was not an attempt to liberate it from its institutional context, but incorporated the parasitic strategy to abuse the public discourse. The avant-garde artists created for themselves a special position by not occupying a certain fixed place. Especially the Dada movement tried to constantly change and transform its program, but also Futurism attempted a continuous metamorphosis in order to stay flexible and innovative. Although many avant-garde artists dreamed about taking over communication channels, they ultimately succeeded by contaminating the discourse networks of their time with small irritations that were based on a creative abuse of media technologies and practices.

THE ABUSE OF MEDIA AND TECHNOLOGY

The avant-garde artists recognized the importance of media for their purposes and started to experiment with and to exploit emerging technologies. The modes that they applied to use or abuse media technologies resemble in some ways the developments that the German media theorist Friedrich Kittler diagnosed for the invention of entertainment electronics.[31] Kittler became famous for emphasizing the importance of war and the military as the driving force for the development of media technologies. According to him, technologies such as the radio, the hi-fi record, electromagnetic tape recording, and stereophony were originally designed for military purposes such as tank warfare, as guiding systems for bomber pilots, or as enemy recognition. Only later, they were "abused" through the entertainment industry for civil purposes, thereby putting society in a constant state of military mobilization, which he summarized in the *bon mot* that our "discos are preparing our youths for a retaliatory strike."[32] This position is highly debatable,[33] but Kittler provides significant examples that show how the entertainment business profited from military developments like a parasite by transferring these technologies into the public realm to serve commercial purposes. For my reading of the avant-garde the question of the military origin of media is not of primary concern, but the parasitic abuse, that is, decontextualization of technologies through Futurism and Dada. The media strategies and technologies of the avant-garde do not necessarily emerge from the military field, but also constitute grotesque transformations and distortions of already existing practices and devices. The avant-garde abused media technologies; they not only manipulated the meaning transmitted through mass media circuits, but hacked into all kinds of data streams from the messages of the newspaper and the signals of radio broadcasting to the impulses of the human nervous system. Marinetti exploited in his poetics the film, the telegraph, telephone circuits, and the radio for manipulating the human psyche. The noise composer Luigi Russolo mocked and amputated the gramophone to construct his noise intoners and to recalibrate human sensibility. Hausmann imagined human perception on the basis of a misapprehension of photo cells and radio stations. They all did not engage in a contemplative, slow reflection on media, but delved into the blooming media fantasies of their time.

The understanding that the avant-garde project consisted in an abuse of contemporaneous media finds its support in Walter Benjamin's essay "The Work of Art in the Age of Mechanical Reproduction."[34] Benjamin recognizes a crucial difference between how Dada and Futurism dealt with the technologies of their time. The essay closes with the famous accusation of Futurism that it would generate a fascist aesthetization of politics.[35] Benjamin saw in Marinetti's orgiastic celebration of technological cruelties of the modern battlefield an "unnatural" or "inadequate" use of modern technologies.[36] Benjamin portrays Dada in contrast as a movement that ironically adopts, filters, and reassembles all the trash and garbage that technology produces.[37] While Futurism constantly affirms technology and war, Dada provides a simple but sophisticated strategy to educate the senses of modern humans. Although I believe that Benjamin draws a much too strict line between these two movements in regard to their adoption of technology, I agree with the basic assumption that Futurism and Dada used completely different strategies to irritate the public discourse. Futurism tried to establish a megalomaniacal metanarrative that attempted to turn the world into a technological fantasy, and Dada intended to subvert the very possibility for such a narrative. However, Dada as well as Futurism hacked into the media circuits of their time in order to create constant irritations. As Benjamin outlined, Futurism did that because it intended to block the potential of modern media channels to liberate the people, or, as I show in this study, to use communication technologies as devices for psychophysiological control. Dada did not attempt a control through media technology. Artists like

Raoul Hausmann and Richard Huelsenbeck deconstructed the potential of newspapers to disseminate information and distorted the ability of language to contribute to communication in order to enhance the perceptual and communicative abilities of humans.

All these irritations are connected to an abuse of media, because they all try to expand and transform established practices. This is also what Kittler means with his "misuse of military equipment." In *Gramophone Film Typewriter*, he develops the notion of "abuse" on the basis of the anecdote about how the engineer Hans Bredow used radio tube equipment dedicated for military purposes for broadcasting news and music. This use was prohibited by a superior command post, because it constituted an "abuse of military equipment."[38] Thus, "abuse" implies not a "true" or "natural" use of media, but (ab)use of media technologies by parasites in the system in a way not intended by hegemonic powers. This is exactly what the avant-garde did. Futurists and Dadaists have in common that they experimented with media practices and technologies in order to extend the possibilities of contemporaneous media discourses. They were not satisfied with the intended functioning of media systems and attempted to expand the possibilities of the newspaper, radio, film, or whatever media they encountered. Such a manipulation is parasitic, because it depends on the supply of new media gadgets through science and technology and it does not intend to engage in a dialogue or equal exchange with these fields. The avant-garde artists were not interested in a discursive dialogue with media engineers. Russolo's rejection of contemporaneous physics and the constant arguments between Hausmann and Broido demonstrate that clearly. They rather fed on the knowledge and technologies provided by the host in order to irritate the powers that be. These irritations did not vanish in the silence of history, but constantly reemerged throughout the twentieth century, as Caleb Kelly documents in his book *Cracked Media*.[39] The avant-garde broke, cracked, and expanded technologies not only to find new forms of aesthetic performances, but also to challenge conventional media practices. The work of more contemporary artists such as Nam June Paik or John Cage, who made the technique of the "prepared piano" famous, carries on this tradition of media subversion by parasitically abusing all kinds of technological equipment. Perhaps the most impressive example for such an abuse is Karlheinz Stockhausen's *Helicopter String Quartet*, which used four helicopters as mere sound sources.

The parasitic abuse of technology is thus not simply a destructive rejection of hegemonic discourses, but a creative intervention that exploits, bends, and shows the limits of established practices. The avant-garde exploitations did not demolish existing forms of communication but irritated media discourses and forced these systems to generate new creative transformations.

The Avant-Garde and Media Theory

The avant-garde targeted established media practices and intended to transform them into self-referential loops that left hermeneutic content behind. The outer appearance of their art works as a meaningless collection of syllables, objects, sounds, noises, or images is, however, not simply a provocation of bourgeois aesthetics but rather a mimicry of information processed by modern media channels and psychophysical laboratories. In *Discourse Networks 1800/1900*[40] Friedrich Kittler recognizes the absence of meaning as central to emerging media technology and emphasizes that in the late nineteenth and early twentieth century the production of random noises in modern psychology coincided with the development of the ability to record complex phenomena with newly invented media technology. "In the discourse network of 1900," Kittler argues, "discourse is produced by RANDOM GENERATORS. Psychophysics constructed such sources of noise; the new technological media stored their input."[41] As an example of these "Random Generators," Kittler refers to the memory experiments of the psychologist Hermann Ebbinghaus.[42] Ebbinghaus tried to measure the human brain's ability to store (i.e., memorize) different amounts of random data. In order to generate a stream of meaningless—and in its appearance Dadaesque—syllables, he used a random calculus that ensured no conscious intervention would charge the test material with meaning. The avant-garde learned from these technologies and psychological laboratories. Hausmann produced poetry based on stochastic systems, Russolo disassembled phonographic devices, and Marinetti adopted in his poetry the unpredictable rhythm of Brownian motion. Their art was no longer based on hermeneutic meaning but on the entropy of the medium. They produced feedback loops that fed the products of modern media systems back into the emerging media channels in order to parody, irritate, and accelerate established media practices. This aesthetic of feedback is fundamental for the avant-garde's parasitic nature, because feedback is parasitical. It is not an original production, but feeds something already existing back into the point of origin, thereby amplifying or modifying this event without adding anything new to it. As Serres also underlines, feedback is a parasitic or mediating circular function.[43]

However, the intention of the avant-garde was not merely to vanish in the feedback loops of this new mediality. They recognized their art as devices to educate the physiology of modern man. In his art of noises

Russolo abused experimental equipment to train soldiers for the auditory challenges of coming wars, Marinetti wanted to implement more efficient communication standards that fused military protocols and human physiology, the Dadaist Huelsenbeck accelerated in his manifestos the data streams of the press, and Hausmann finally conceptualized the human brain as universal electromagnetic receiver. Such abuse of scientific equipment, military communication systems, and public interaction was not only meant as provocation, but intended to expand the possibilities of media and was more fundamentally geared toward a reinvention of the human being.

In his *Theory of the Avant-Garde*[44] Peter Bürger is critical of approaches that strongly emphasize the importance of media. Although he acknowledges that the exploration of technological conditions is certainly central for an understanding of modernity, he also asserts that this cannot sufficiently explain the transformation of art through the avant-garde.[45] He argues that a focus on the technical preconditions of artistic production invites mono-causal explanations and undercuts the complex interplay between art, society, and technology. In a similar way Jonathan Sterne, in his media archaeological study of sound reproducing technologies, *The Audible Past*,[46] argues that technological "[i]mpact narratives have been rightly and widely criticized as a form of technological determinism; they spring from an impoverished notion of causality."[47] This criticism targets posthumanist interpretations that formulate a hegemony of machines over humans. For example, Kittler polemically marginalized in an interview[48] the role of human activity in the creation of technology: "Silicon is nature! Silicon is nature calculating itself. If you leave out the part of engineers who write little structures on silicon you see one part of matter calculating the rest of matter."[49] Such radical posthumanist statements can appear as an exaggeration, or as mere science fiction[50]; however, it also cannot be denied that the gap between human beings and machines is becoming smaller and smaller. From the nineteenth century on, with the rise of the nation-state that registered its citizens, and increasingly conceptualized a society based on statistical data, up to today where our identity becomes more and more configured through computable data sets, the ability to interact as a free subject in the networks of modernity becomes less and less. Regaining autonomy over one's own subjectivity would entail a destruction of all data-processing systems that construct our subjectivity as citizen, employee, Internet user, or whatever data record connects us to communication circuits. Such a revolution is in fact impossible, because it would mean that we cut ourselves out of the communication channels that form our identity.

The avant-garde movements of the early twentieth century were the first to recognize this communicative situation and simultaneously affirmed and subverted the media channels of their time. Their project was to reprogram social interaction, and they realized that they had to use the established codes of communication in order to change these structures—that is, they needed to alter and abuse existing technologies. This did not trigger a great revolution, but was forceful as minor irritations that spread like a virus over the culture of the early twentieth century. An investigation of this parasitic manipulation of the discourse network of modernity depends on a close reading of communicative practices and technologies of this time, because only in this way does it become apparent how the avant-garde modified established media practices.

Parasitic Subversion

Marinetti, Hausmann, and the others constantly intervened in the media networks of the early twentieth century. This development, which began with linguistically coded media, turned into the exploration of the information entropy of the human body and ended in the white noise of radio transmissions. Such a history testifies to the media theoretical awareness of the avant-garde, because it demonstrates how they realized more and more what actually determined communication. They attempted to undermine—to use a disputed term by Friedrich Kittler—the *media a priori* that determined their situation. Friedrich Kittler uses the notion of "Discourse Networks"/"Aufschreibesysteme" in order to describe the procedures and rules that determine the exchange and communications in a society.[51] According to Kittler, these discourse networks form a *media a priori* that is the technical precondition for interactions, and thus determines all communication in a culture. This approach radically challenges the notion of the subject as an individually acting agent and ascribes technologies an enormous power. It is not that culture produces technologies, but rather that technologies determine culture. This position, of course, attracted criticism[52]; however, it also pointed out the great importance that technologies have on the formation of subjects.

Although my approach also focuses on the discursive power of communicative practices and media technologies, my reading diverges from Kittler's position through a focus on the parasite as an irritant to the media system. I show that the parasite erodes Kittler's media deterministic prophecy. Kittler's claim that "media determines our situation"[53] asserts the power of established media discourses, but it can also be reinterpreted as a media ecological statement that describes media users as parasites who inhabit and irritate their environment, that is, the discourse network. The media parasite subverts the strong deterministic trait of Kittler's *media a priori*; the parasite that occupies the channel will not be able to overwrite the established simulation of reality, but nonetheless it is a constant irritation to the media system. It has the subversive power to contaminate communicative channels and thus forces the host to adjust to the parasite's demands. The parasitic contamination transforms media circuits from a clearly calculating system into a dynamic organism that is open to the intrusion of unpredictable behavior. In this sense, I am able to write a media history that focuses on the materiality of communication and describes how the avant-garde artists as parasites engage in media discourses and are not simply determined by media technology. The parasite has the ability to subvert Kittler's insistence on the ruling power of integrated circuits without falling back into a discourse that centers on hermeneutic understanding and establishes the human being as an omnipotent actor.

The parasite liquefies media determinism by implementing the avant-garde artists as noise that is able to infuse minimal irregularities into communication channels. These contaminations can lead to transformations, because—although they do not overwrite the hegemonic media discourses—they create minimal shifts that in the long run have a potential to impact the emergence of new media practices.[54] Surely, Hausmann and Marinetti toyed around with ideas to produce a new master narrative that would implement a new human being into an ultramodern, high-speed media environment. However, these ideas ended up being nothing more than minor irritations to the media industries of their time. Nonetheless, these projects fueled media technological and theoretical discourses that ultimately continued the avant-garde project in the age of digital sampling and electrical amplification.

An Avant-Garde Parasitology

This book develops a parasitology of the avant-garde. This means that it displays how Futurism and Dada abused media technologies and how they occupied the communication channels of the early twentieth century.[55] The chapters of this book retrace these tactics from the abuse of conventional media such as print and speech to more technical media that emerged around 1900 such as film, photography, phonography, radio broadcasting, and photo cells. The first chapter highlights how Marinetti created Futurism as a media event and attempted to fill the mass media with his technological mythology. The Dada manifestos abused the continuous thirst of the press for news by providing a polyvalent set of incomprehensible messages that called, because of their amorphous structure, for constant press coverage. The second chapter investigates how avant-garde poetry is consciously designed as manipulation of established communicative practices and technologies. I reflect on how Marinetti reconstructed language as an abuse of the media of film and telegraphy and how Dadaists explored and deformed the media of the printing press and human articulation. In the third chapter I discuss the media of film and photography. The indexicality of photography demands that it represents something that is external to itself and therefore implies a parasitic relationship to reality. I show how Futurist and Dada abstract film discarded the representative aspects of film and photography to create a new order of seeing that undermined the parasitic structure of these media. Berlin Dada, however, with its widespread use of photocollage, did not exclude the parasite, but amplified the parasitic abuse of a mass-media-produced reality. They did not only accept photographs as a means of aesthetic expression but reassembled mass-produced images circulating through the press. The parasitic irritation and abuse of media coincided in the creation of a sophisticated satirical art that was most importantly represented in the works of Hannah Höch and John Heartfield. In the fourth chapter, I analyze Luigi Russolo's art of noises and demonstrate how Russolo incorporated different phonographic technologies and psychoacoustic theorems in order to transform sound into something that he called "sound-noise." Dada conceptualized its own vitalistic understanding of noise in a misappropriation of Russolo's experiments that excluded media technology, and this understanding was highly successful in creating feedback loops between audience and stage that greatly amplified the noise. Raoul Hausmann turned the creation of noisy feedback loops back into media technology. In his design of a mechanical amplification system he alluded to new technological possibilities that manifested in the radio tube. The final chapter discusses the media technological transformation of the avant-garde that became especially apparent in Marinetti's and Hausmann's work. Both artists developed a program for reeducating the senses based on a model of tactility that had the ultimate goal to switch human beings as sender-receiver stations into the radio ether. Marinetti and Hausmann imagined the creation of a new media technological environment that embedded the media users as parasites into the endless media loops of avant-garde networks. These media experiments are very interesting because they try to invert the host-parasite relationship and attempt to establish avant-gardistic technologies as dominant discourses. The fact that these projects failed underlines the fundamentally subversive and parasitic structure of the avant-garde.

The comparative juxtaposition of Futurism and Dada has, however, not the goal to point out simple influence patterns or to identify a set of similarities and differences of these movements, but to show that the parasitic abuse of media was central to their practices and explains their constant attractiveness for media theoretical questions.[56] The parasitological perspective also attempts to complicate a comparative analysis of Futurism and Dada. My aim is not only to show that these movements were parasites, that is, subversive irritants, but also that they constantly attempted to renegotiate the parasite-host relationship. The intentions to create own sonic, tactile, or radiophonic media ecologies is precisely such an attempt to step out of the parasite's role and to assume the host's position. Significantly, these intentions were never fully realized and rather threw the avant-garde artists back in their role as parasites, thereby emphasizing that their true creative power consisted in subversive tactics.

CHAPTER 1

THE PRESS AND THE PARASITES

THE GENRE OF THE MANIFESTO, the most important means of the avant-garde movements to communicate their ideas, invoked the parasite. The *Communist Manifesto*, which according to the literary critics Marjorie Perloff[1] and Martin Puchner[2] constitutes the pre-form of the artistic manifestos of the twentieth century, opened with the portrayal of a parasite: "A spectre is haunting Europe—the spectre of communism."[3] Like Michel Serres's parasite, the specter of communism had no fixed discursive position, but contaminated communicating channels. In the famous preamble of the manifesto, Marx and Engels described how communism was not a real entity, but a curse without a specific quality that was used as an empty concept to defame the enemy: "Where is the party in opposition that has not been decried as communistic by its opponents in power? Where is the opposition that has not hurled back the branding reproach of communism, against the more advanced opposition parties, as well as against its reactionary adversaries?"[4] At that moment communism was nothing more than a parasite that occupied communicative relations; it had no specific meaning, it could be injected into every discourse, and its sole function was to disturb an ongoing dialogue. Communism was at that moment not so much a political worldview as a provocation. Marx and Engels's text had the intention to neutralize the parasitic appearance of communism and to turn it into a historical force that would no longer haunt Europe, but create a new political order. The difference between Marx and Engels's text and the avant-garde manifestos is that avant-garde authors such as F. T. Marinetti, Richard Huelsenbeck, Hugo Ball, and Raoul Hausmann tried to conserve such a spectral quality. Futurist and Dada manifestos continued to raise the specter that was portrayed in the

Communist Manifesto. While Futurism installed a new narrative that constantly invoked new spirits through a technological mythology, the Dada manifestos manipulated the daily press by injecting meaningless messages into the mass media circuits, thereby replicating the ghostly appearance that Marx and Engels ascribed to communism at the beginning of their founding text.

This spectral tactic of avant-garde manifestos was an innovative element. The avant-garde proclamations were more complex in their structure than their historical predecessors such as political declarations or other forms of social or aesthetic propaganda. In general, the word "manifesto" was used from the seventeenth century on in order to denote public announcements. Up to the nineteenth century, "manifesto" referred principally to a written declaration by a head of state or a state representative.[5] These texts did not carry subversive messages; they were intended to establish sovereignty.[6] Only in the nineteenth century did the term "manifesto" acquire a broader meaning—referring to political as well as artistic proclamations that opposed an established status quo and called for a new alternative.

Accordingly, the avant-garde manifesto transcended its character as a merely mediating text that stated political or artistic goals and aims. The avant-garde manifestos constituted complex rhetorical constructs that, although they contained explicit utterances about goals and artistic techniques, cannot be reduced to their programmatic content. Dada even openly announced the absurdity of their manifestos, and Futurist proclamations celebrated a hyperbolic rhetoric that can hardly be taken on face value. Dada and Futurist manifestos founded a practice that transcended their mediating use and established them as irritating and provoking elements that fed on the sensationalism of modern mass media.

The idiosyncratic features of avant-garde manifestos do not so much represent their aesthetic quality as they embody part of the avant-garde tactics to irritate the media ecology of the early twenties. I discuss in this chapter how the avant-garde abused the genre of the manifesto to irritate its audience and to manipulate mass media channels. The experimental qualities of the manifestos do not simply transform them into poetical texts, but also have to be seen as techniques for a subversion of mass media networks. The manifesto had the power to irritate, disturb, and intervene in public discourses, and it functioned as a deliberate manipulation of the public sphere.[7] The avant-garde movements simultaneously irritated and shaped the media ecology of their time; they did, however, not cancel out the press, but created a complicated form of cohabitation. The journalists waited for new irritations produced by the avant-garde parasites, so that they could report about them, and thus the press engaged in a relationship with Dada, in which the distinction between host and parasite became increasingly blurred.

Manifestos had such an important communicative function because they were widely distributed through flyers, posters, and newspapers. The first Futurist Manifesto, for example, appeared in the French newspaper *Le Figaro* and most clearly testified to the collaboration between the avant-garde and mass media. The avant-garde text emerged in a modern mass media environment and has to be discussed within changing paradigms in mass media production—most importantly, journalistic writing and the invention of the news of the day. As I argue, the continuous production of manifestos in the avant-garde corresponded to the newspaper's need to generate such news at a frequent rate. What the media theorist Neil Postman said about the news holds true for the avant-garde manifesto: "The news of the day is a figment of our technological imagination. It is, quite precisely, a media event."[8] In regard to Futurism and Dada, this means that manifestos occupied the mechanics of news coverage in order to become a part of the reality created by the mass media.

The manifesto assimilated itself to the news of the day transmitted through the mass media. The medium of the news does not follow the rhythm of events, but rather imposes the rhythm of its own demands for a daily reporting of events. The news of the day does not so much represent an actual picture of the world, as it satisfies the thirst of the medium. More radically formulated, the news does not exist because something happened in the world; rather it exists because something has to be reported. Theorists such as Umberto Eco,[9] Neil Postman,[10] and Niklas Luhmann[11] underscore this feature of mass media. The avant-garde groups, with their constant attempts to publish programmatic news about their movements, abused this demand of mass media to exhibit information. In what follows, I show how the newspaper became the willing host for the manifesto production. Such medial implications elevated the manifesto above the status of merely explicatory texts and transformed them into functional devices that corrupted the daily press by mimicking its media industrial mechanisms.

FUTURIST NEWS

Marinetti had already circulated in literary circles his programmatic proclamations before the publication of the Futurist Manifesto in the French newspaper *Le Figaro*;[12] also, the term "Futurism" made a great public appearance outside of the founding manifesto, in the title of Marinetti's novel *Mafarka the Futurist*,[13] which caused a public outrage but did not establish the foundation of the new movement of Futurism.

Only the manifesto published in *Le Figaro* was finally able to root the avant-garde project in the public discourse. Marinetti documented the great success of the manifesto by claiming that he had received thousands of responses to his text.[14] Regardless of whether this is true, the Futurist Manifesto had a lasting effect on the international art scene. Forty-two years later, the German poet Gottfried Benn still praised the initial impact of the Futurist Manifesto in his speech "Problems of Poetry."[15]

> The event that established modern art in Europe was the publication of the futurist manifesto by Marinetti that was issued on February 20th, 1909 in the "figaro" in Paris. "Nous allons assister à la naissance du Centaure—we will witness the birth of centaurs"—he wrote, and: "a roaring automobile is more beautiful than the Nike of Samothrace."[16]

Benn refers to the Futurist Manifesto as a foundational historical event that would change poetry and establish artistic modernism. Benn did not forget that this text was published as a newspaper article. He even identified the publication in *Le Figaro* as the central event that changed literary production. When Benn praises Marinetti's innovation, he refers not simply to the text, but also to the media technological dissemination through the press. This retrospective description understands the founding manifesto as part of the news of the day: it is not exclusively a literary moment but a mass media event: not only is the founding of Futurism an occurrence transmitted through the media, but its existence over and above its appearance is bound up with the media. The very act of being published in *Le Figaro* generated the founding of Futurism, not simply the text itself.[17]

This connection between manifestos and media cannot be emphasized enough. Although criticism often stresses that the Futurist manifestos have a strong performative dimension and were an integral part of the Futurist soirées,[18] the decisive structural feature of the manifestos was that they were distributed through mass media and not solely through a stage performance. That the manifestos played an important part in theatrical performances does not mean that this was their primary function. Manifestos were not solely presented in stage performances. They were also reproduced and distributed by mass media. In fact, Futurist self-staging gained the dimension of a European advertisement campaign in which the technological revolution was not only the main narrative but also the communicative precondition. Hansgeorg Schmidt-Bergmann, however, underscores the importance of happenings and performances for the advertisement of Futurist ideas and contends that such performances were more effective than merely publishing a polemical text in a journal or newspaper.¹⁹ Also, Claudia Salaris claims that the Futurist soirées were the most important instruments in Marinetti's attempt to create an all-encompassing mass audience.²⁰ Schmidt-Bergmann and Salaris are without doubt right to emphasize the importance of the Futurist *serate*, but they overlook the fact that Marinetti strategically targeted the attention of the press with these events. If they not had been reported through mass media, the *serate* would not have had such a great effect on other European art movements. Just like the founding manifesto, the performances have to be understood as mass media events that achieved their full power only through the newspaper.

This media focus of the manifesto becomes apparent by looking at how much attention Marinetti paid to the technology with which media disseminated and processed information and how he promoted his artistic movement by means ordinarily used for advertising commercial products.

The Futurist Manifesto not just appeared as cultural information in the feuilleton (the privileged place for cultural news) but established itself on the front page as the news of the day. The typographic outline clearly reveals this intention. Marinetti was a friend of Mohammad El Rashi Pasha, a major stock holder of *Le Figaro*, and through this channel he was able to arrange that his text would be placed prominently in the left column of the newspaper, exposing the headline "Le Futurisme."²¹ The information about the founding of Futurism is the first thing the *Le Figaro* reader registered on February 20, 1909. Indeed, Marinetti was deeply concerned about the moment of publication. Supposedly, Marinetti moved the publication of the first manifesto (planned for December 1908) to February, because in December an earthquake dominated the headlines. Apparently, Marinetti did not want the reader of *Le Figaro* to be distracted from the proclamation of Futurism by other news.²²

Marinetti completely subscribed to the operations of mass media culture and created a parasitic relationship to it. He recognized that the surprising character of the news was not simply determined by the event, but also dependent on the medium. The text was supposed to shock and irritate the reader. This impact could not be caused by the text itself; only its implementation into news programming was able to establish such an effect. The shock of the manifesto intended by Marinetti corresponds to the programming of the news of the day. Luhmann highlights this feature of the news of the day and claims that news media have to provide a constant stream of surprises. Otherwise, it would be impossible to announce the news daily.²³ To inform about such constant changes is the task of the news. The Futurist Manifesto as part of the daily news has thus the same intention: to surprise and irritate its readership through reporting changes and discontinuities in the world. Marinetti used this feature of the news to his advantage. However, he was not under time pressure, because the mass media had an endless hunger for news and would always be prepared to announce the founding of a new radical art movement.

Since the Futurist Manifesto only actualized itself in the medium of the newspaper, it did not demand an event outside the mass media. Marinetti even accepted cuts in the manifesto text so that it could be published on the first page of *Le Figaro*.[24] This makes clear that only the medium of the newspaper was able to satisfy Marinetti's thirst for a sensational start of his movement. The publication of his text in literary circles did not suffice. Marinetti not only wanted to proclaim radically new concepts, he wanted to make news. The opening scene replicates this longing for innovation by the mass media:

> We had stayed up all night, my friends and I, under hanging mosque lamps with domes of filigreed brass, domes starred like our spirits, shining like them with the prisoned radiance of electric hearts. For hours we had trampled our atavistic ennui into rich oriental rugs, arguing up to the last confines of logic and blackening many reams of paper with our frenzied scribbling....
>
> Suddenly we jumped, hearing the mighty noise of the huge double-decker trams that rumbled by outside, ablaze with colored lights, like a village on holiday suddenly struck and uprooted by the flooding Po and dragged over falls and through gorges to the sea.
>
> Then the silence deepened. But, as we listened to the old canal muttering its feeble prayers and creaking bones of sickly palaces above their damp green beards, under the windows we suddenly heard the famished roar of automobiles.
>
> "Let's go!" I said. "Friends, away! Let's go! Mythology and the Mystic Ideal are defeated at last. We're about to see the Centaur's birth and, soon after, the first flight of Angels!"[25]

The introduction of the Futurist Manifesto differs in many ways from what could be expected, for example, from a political manifesto.[26] The text does not open with a clear enumeration of programmatic points; it does not simply peddle propaganda or give shape to a political utopia. Rather, it starts out from a literary scene and has a high literary quality throughout that transcends the function of the manifesto to convey an artistic program.[27] It is not so much a unique creative form of expression as an attempt to create a founding myth of Futurism—the myth of a society about to wake up. This is radical news, because it tells the reader about the dawn of a new era. The instantaneous character of the scene is emphasized through ubiquitous presence of electric light. The lamps of the mosque light up Marinetti's apartment, the Futurists understand themselves as watchtowers, and finally there are the lights of the tram that break into the apartment. This final electric stimulus irritates the Futurists significantly. The Futurists jump because of the light stimuli, as if these irritations were electric shocks. This occurrence does not refer to a mystical experience of the Futurists but to a new and general mode of experience. It indicates the actuality of the manifesto and establishes the connection to one of the more significant changes in civilization, namely the electrification of cities.[28]

PARASITIC MYTHOLOGY

The Futurist Manifesto continues now in the following way: The awakened Futurists start their journey into a modern world, and Marinetti begins the narration of a myth—the story of the birth of Futurism. The car race that is now beginning and that ends in an accident is first introduced as a funeral or execution: "I stretch out on my car like a corpse on its bier, but revived at once under the steering wheel, a guillotine blade that threatened my stomach."[29] This sequence ends indeed in a ditch and honors the promise of a funeral. This ditch, where Marinetti ends up having lost control of his car,[30] is not only a metaphorical grave but also a uterus filled with liquid industrial muck that gives birth to Futurism. Marinetti even connects this mud to the black breast of his Sudanese nurse—emphasizing, in this way, birth and new beginning—and he emerges from the pit as a parasite nourished by the by-products of industrial production.

The scene of the accident in the first manifesto is marked by a religious index. The connection between death and birth connotes a resurrection from death, but this religious motive is immediately retranslated into a material foundation: "They thought it was dead, my beautiful shark, but a caress from me was enough to revive it; there it was, alive again, running on its powerful fins!"[31] This transformation from death to life is a typical feature of the Futurist machine—a machine that suspends the dichotomy of life and death.[32] The intertwining of mythology and technology is so typical of Futurism that Benn recalls it in his speech from 1951, when he cites the birth of the centaurs. With the publication of his manifesto, Marinetti intervened in the news production of the press and established a new mythology. According to Benn, the news of the day on February 20, 1909, was "la naissance du Centaure," and it entailed the substitution of ancient symbols (Nike of Samothrace) by the omnipotent power of modern engineering (automobile). Futurism translated mythology into technology: the angels, which—according to Marinetti—will be seen flying, were not sacral figures but airplanes.

This adaptation of mythological pictures reflects on Marinetti's ideology of the future in a problematic way. In fact, the Futurist constructs in his founding manifesto an antagonistic tension between mythical pictures and modern technology: "Mythology and the Mystic Ideal are defeated at last. We're about to see the Centaur's birth and, soon after, the first flight of Angels!"[33] On the one hand, Marinetti abolished mythology and mysticism as old and "passatistic." On the other hand, he celebrated the emergence of mythological creatures: centaurs and angels. Marinetti refers in the first sentence to the mythological memory of the Occidental world and in the second to the newly emerged technological imaginary that recognizes the man-machine hybrids of car drivers, pilots, or factory workers as centaurs, and airplanes as angels, and thus blends mythological figures into a mass industrial world—giving technology a divine power. Marinetti recklessly borrowed pictures from powerful social discourses such as the technological imaginary in order to promote his project. He intervened as a parasite in the repository of established cultural knowledge.

Giovanni Lista points out the ambivalence in Marinetti's project entailed in this adaptation of myth.[34] Lista attests that Marinetti radicalizes "his message to the point of giving it the dimension of mythology,"[35] while he also remarks that "'antitradition' was the means of bringing about a new Italian culture."[36] Marinetti apparently did not care much about any potential inconsistency by mixing mythology and technology, or history and innovation, but intentionally abused the fact that "myth" is etymologically as well as functionally connected to social communication. The Greek *mythos* means "word," and stands in contrast to *logos*. While *logos* denotes "word" in the context of a discursive logical argument, *myth* rather indicates "story," a narrative model for explaining human activity, society, wisdom, and knowledge.[37] Mythological stories are at the foundation of collective beliefs in a society that are transmitted over generations.

Myths represent the collective memory of a society. They are a mass medium that stores, transmits, and processes a collective knowledge. Roland Barthes's understanding of mythology that he developed in his essay "Myth Today"[38] goes a step further and is of special significance for an understanding of Marinetti's abuse of mythological images. Barthes does not understand mythology as a specific set of narratives that are rooted in a culture, but as a system of communication that (ab)uses the referential structure of language.[39] He describes mythology as a semiological system consisting of three elements: the signified, the signifier, and the sign (or myth).[40] The myth is a third or parasitic element in communication that distorts the original meaning of words and charges them with a mythological or ideological meaning.[41] Barthes did not develop this notion in reference to Serres, but there are significant similarities between Serres's parasite and Barthes's myth. Barthes explicitly calls myth a parasite and describes it as an omnipresent element that is able to invade all aspects of everyday life.[42] It is an abuse of the original referential structure of language.

Marinetti's strategies are related to such a communicative notion of myth. Not only does Marinetti transform technological images into a mythological speech, but he crossbreeds technology and mythological images in order to create an ideologized language. With his use of figures like centaurs and angels, Marinetti is up to more than mere ornamentation. Marinetti draws on traditional elements, but only to install an ideology of technology. It constitutes a clear communicative abuse of mythological images. A prominent example for this operation is Marinetti's adoration of speed.

Speed is the most integral feature of the Futurist worldview and denotes more than the power of trains, cars, or telegraphic communication. It is a central category in the Futurist mythology and imagination. Barthes recognizes that myth naturalizes a rhetorical expression, and Marinetti does precisely that with speed. As an omnipresent experience in modernity, speed is described not just as a technological innovation but as a natural force. Marinetti celebrates the beauty and importance of speed in points 4 and 8 of the founding manifesto:

> 4. We say that the world's magnificence has been enriched by a new beauty: the beauty of speed. A racing car whose hood is adorned with great pipes, like serpents of explosive breath—a roaring car that seems to ride on grapeshot—is more beautiful than the Victory of Samothrace.
>
> ...
>
> 8. We stand on the last promontory of the centuries!... Why should we look back, when what we want is to break down the mysterious doors of the Impossible? Time and Space died yesterday. We already live in the absolute, because we have created eternal, omnipresent speed.[43]

In point 4 Marinetti praises an aesthetic ideal, and in the other passage he claims an orientation in the future. However, both points are connected by their concentration on speed. Speed not only replaces the ideal of art with an aesthetic of technology, but also enables completely new dimensions of social interaction. For Marinetti, speed is not merely the symbol for technological progress per se, but a momentum shattering established understandings of time and space. Marinetti refers to the new possibilities for bridging spatiotemporal distances. Traveling and communication were transformed by the railway, the automobile, and the telegraph, which made it necessary to redefine the relationship between time and space.[44] However, speed is not only a technological fact, but a life-changing force that establishes a new media ecology.

Jeffrey Schnapp recognizes speed as the distinctive drug of modernity,[45] and Wolfgang Schivelbusch in his book *The Train Journey*[46] and Stephen Kern in his *Culture of Time and Space*[47] outline the specific changes that the acceleration of the modern transportation system had on human physiology as well as culture. Marinetti's claim accordingly testifies not only to these great technological but also to significant cultural transformations. Speed is not only a technological feature but also a condition that alters the everyday understanding of the world. The acceleration of the Industrial Revolution around 1900 through the extension of the transportation system and the increased use of electric communication systems also generated new hopes and ideas about the possibilities of technology. When Marinetti speaks about war, steam ships, cars, and other objects of the modern world, he uses them as emblematic features that do not describe the actual status quo; rather, they stand as abbreviations for a utopian realm in which man and machine merge. Speed is an important part of this utopia. Marinetti does not celebrate the velocity of a specific car. He celebrates the fact that, in general, cars are fast. Every newly developed car is for Marinetti a promise of a technological future to come.

Marinetti elaborates this position clearly in his manifesto "The New Religion-Morality of Speed."[48] Here, speed gains explicitly a mythical dimension. Marinetti understands high-speed travel in this text as communication with a divine reality, as a prayer: "If prayer means communication with the divinity, running at high speed is prayer."[49] The saints in his religion of high speed are the small meteorites that fall to the earth with a great velocity: "Our male saints are the numberless corpuscles that penetrate our atmosphere at an average velocity of 42,000 meters a second."[50] Marinetti takes elements from the world that are connected to high velocities, such as trains, high-speed travel, or meteorites, and fashions them into divine entities. This sacredness that leaves everything slow behind—treating it as profane—constructs a new "religion" of speed and creates a discursive context in which all these fast objects coalesce to an overall ideology of speed and technological progress.

Marinetti extends his ideology so much that no site of Futurist imagination—such as war or train stations—exists without an omnipresent velocity. The Futurist world is a scene of speed. The idea of Futurist speed is, therefore, not limited to a specific context such as a train or the speed of telegraphic communication, but signifies the complete infrastructure of industrial nations. In Futurist ideology, speed is not simply a new experience derived from technological innovations, but rather an omnipresent structure that determines reality. In other words, it is the foundation of the media ecology of modernity.

OCCUPYING THE CHANNEL

This obsession with speed constitutes perhaps only next to violence, the most important "value" in the Futurist ideology, and it also points to Marinetti's obsession with infrastructure. Marinetti adored not only cars, trains, and steamships, but also streets, railways, and power grids. The daily newspaper was another example for the infrastructure of an accelerated modernity. The Futurist Manifesto not only attempted to formulate a new aesthetic worldview, but displayed the intention to occupy the channels of mass media. The Futurist manifestos had the function to expand on this founding text and create a Futurist program in an aggressive fashion. Mostly under the regime of Marinetti, manifestos were authored that addressed every aspect of the modern life from politics, family, and war to painting, film, and food. The messages were thereby very similar. All these manifestos had one thing in common: they rejected the present state of society; they resented history and called for a violent and cleansing revolution. So, Marinetti did not want to communicate different ideas through the manifestos, but intended to occupy the total infrastructure of modernity. This involvement with infrastructure, however, was not only expressed through his aggressive media politics, but also resonates in the content of many manifestos.

It is, for example, significant that Marinetti targeted Venice as one of his favorite objects for polemics. For Marinetti, Venice was a symbol for the passatist attitude of Italy that adored the past but was blind to the future. However, there could have been another reason for why Venice was a prime object of his polemics. Venice is the city of canals, the town that incorporates a complex traffic network, and therefore has the potential to become the emblem of a Futurist city. Such a reading is supported through Marinetti's "Speech to the Venetians,"[51] because this text portrays Venice not simply as an old and outdated town but as the place from where a Futurist reorganization of society could start. For Marinetti, Venice is a town with enormous promises for a truly Futurist center of commerce and warfare: "Your Grand Canal, widened and dredged, must become a great commercial port. Trains and trams, launched on wide roads built over canals that have finally been filled in, will bring you mountains of goods and a shrewd, wealthy, busy crowd of industrialists and businessmen!"[52] Marinetti recognized developments toward the future primarily as an extension of infrastructure that would then accelerate the modern life even more. It is thus also not a big surprise that in a later text Marinetti celebrated electric power grids: "Nothing is more beautiful than a great humming central electric station that holds the hydraulic pressure of a mountain chain and the electric power of a vast horizon, synthesized in marble distribution panels bristling with dials, keyboards, and shining commutators."[53] This electric station is not only a symbol for the all-encompassing force of electricity, but an element in an enormous communication network. To integrate the human subject into these networks is the ultimate goal of Futurism. As he writes, "With us begins the reign of the man whose roots are cut, of the multiplied man who mixes himself with iron, who is fed by electricity and no longer understands anything except the lust for danger and daily heroism."[54] However, the Futurist is not the sovereign of modern infrastructures. He adores and lives in the increasingly accelerating media ecology, and profits from it like a parasite. The manifestos are Marinetti's first attempt to hook into and irritate these high-speed networks and to turn this media ecology into a Futurist media environment.

Thus, it also does not come as a surprise that one of the last manifestos signed with Marinetti's name was the Futurist radio manifesto "La Radia."[55] I will discuss the Futurist involvement with radio in the last chapter, but here I would like to emphasize that this manifesto also put an end to the Futurist process of occupying the communication channel, because Marinetti described the radio as the medium that rendered all other communication channels obsolete.[56] The radio was recognized as an electromagnetic system as the emblem of pure communication, in which Futurism ultimately dissolved as a mere parasite or specter.

Dada Media Subversion

> There is no toothpaste, no food product in existence in possession of an equivalent publicity apparatus with such a wide radius or with such willingness to perform every service, indeed without costing a cent. Whatever goals the newspapers are pursuing are wholly irrelevant: the papers are there to enhance the Dada boom.[57]

This quote from a 1920 article, "What Is Dada?" demonstrates impressively how Dada abused the press for advertising its program. It even acknowledges that the Dadaists manipulated the press as parasites by paying nothing for the unintentional publicity. A famous example for this form of Dada public relations was the report about a duel between the Dadaists Tristan Tzara and Hans Arp in 1919. This duel never happened; it was just a hoax, but the press released this message seemingly without hesitation, even emphasizing that it was a duel between Dadaists and thus advertising the movement.[58] The article was taken so seriously that it even triggered an official investigation of the Swiss government, which also involved Jakob Christoph Heer, an author of pastoral novels (*Heimatromane*), who now had to continuously release counterstatements, because his presence at this hoax event was, of course, not true, and because he had no affiliation with Dada.[59] This example not only emphasizes the spectral quality of the brand "Dada" that could be glued on everything, even on an established author of novels that focus on romanticized pastoral clichés, but also shows that Dada was—from its very beginning—an attraction that highly stimulated the press.

The question is, however, why was the mass media so interested in a noisy antibourgeois movement that had nothing more to offer than nonsense? I suggest that the reason for this lies in the similarity between the demand of the daily news to continuously report about new events, and the Dada desire to permanently reinvent itself. The amorphous structure of Dada manifestos, which I will discuss in what follows, was intentionally used to trigger and attract the mass media. The assertions of all avant-garde movements should be taken with a grain of salt, but Dada exhibits a particular ambivalent mode of presenting its ideas and program. Dada manifestos can hardly be taken at face value, because they convey conflicting ideas rather than a consistent content. While Marx and Engels used their manifesto to define communism, Dada manifestos continuously undermined all possibility to create a clear understanding of the movement. This has crucial consequences for the interpretation of the manifestos. Dadaistic forms of programmatic writing cannot be understood as keys for deciphering the Dada movement; they rather have to be recognized as texts that distorted and reflected contemporaneous discursive practices in a performative way.[60] They created a specter or parasite that fed on communicative expectations, but never satisfied the audience with an understandable message. I contend that the Dada strategies to mock their audiences and to inject meaningless nonsense in the mass media circuits were tactics employed to trigger the interest of media and to accelerate media production. "Dada" was created in the manifestos as an object of endless inquiry that satisfied the hunger of the press for rumors, speculations, and changes. The Dadaists created their movement as an entropic and transformative system that was similarly difficult to predict as the stock market and thus demanded, like financial developments, continuous press coverage.

In this part of the chapter, I will outline in detailed analyses of pivotal manifestos how Dada created such a transformative and entropic dynamic, and will relate it to Serres's understanding of a parasitic intervention. Provocations through the manifesto enabled Dada not only to irritate contemporaneous discourses but also to generate numerous responses that attempted to identify "Dada." The Dada movement contaminated mass media discourses through this method, and these media began to spread the paradoxical and nonsensical messages of the Dadaists over and over again. The press did not so much report about this art movement, as the media coverage itself was hijacked by Dadaists, who used the media to disseminate an infinite reiteration of empty and disturbing messages.

CREATING THE PARASITE

The parasitic implementation of Dada in public communication was already a main tactic of the first Dadaists in Zurich. A journalist even acknowledged that Dada emerged in Switzerland as a phenomenon that was of primary importance only to the press: "In the war, Zurich gave Dadaism to the world, the world was not very excited about that, only the editors of the feuilleton were thankful for the opportunity to be able to report about these funny guys."[61] This statement is critical of the true impact that Dada had by asserting that it was simply a passion of the press, and that it was hardly recognized outside of mass media. It is not without irony that this critique was published in a newspaper and demonstrates the ignorance of the author about the mechanics of his medium. Even if one does not assume that reality is a construct generated through the mechanism of media, it has to be stressed that in modernity art movements were fundamentally dependent on reports in the press in order to flourish and to develop, and thus the Dada relationship with the press was more than justified. However, putting this consideration aside, the quotation demonstrates that Dada was, already in its initial phase, highly successful in occupying mass media channels. The Dadaists were able to hack into news streams, because the press had a great and apparent interest in the movement. This attraction, however, was not simply based on numerous provocations and performances by the Dadaists, but prepared through a highly elaborate rhetoric of the Dada manifestos that simultaneously suggested and removed meaning from the audience. Such tactics triggered the interest of the press, because Dada promised to provide a continuous flood of always changing information.

One of the first manifestos that introduced the term "Dada"—Richard Huelsenbeck's "Erklärung," which he presented in the spring of 1916 at the Cabaret Voltaire—already incorporates such a tactic and invents "Dada" as a parasite that had the power to irritate and occupy public communication:

> Noble and respected citizens of Zurich, students, craftsmen, workers, vagabonds, aimless people of all countries, unite. In the name of the Cabaret Voltaire and in the name of my friend Hugo Ball, the grounding father and leader of this highly educated institute, tonight, I have a statement to make that will move you intensely. I hope that you will come to no bodily harm, but what I have to tell you now will hit you like a bullet. We have decided to sum up our various activities under the name Dada. We found Dada, we are Dada, and we have Dada. Dada was found in a dictionary; it means nothing. This is the meaningful Nothing, on account of which nothing means something. We want to change the world with Nothing, we want to change poetry and painting with Nothing, and we want to end the war with Nothing. We stand here without any intention; we do not even have the intention to entertain or to amuse you. Although all this is as it is, namely in that it is nothing, we do not have to end as enemies. At the moment when you, overcoming your bourgeois opposition, write Dada on your flag, we are again united and the best of friends. Please accept Dada as a present from us, because anybody who does not accept it is lost. Dada is the best medicine and helps you to have a happy marriage. Your children's children will thank you for it. I now say goodbye with the Dada greeting and a Dada bow. Long live Dada. Dada, Dada, Dada.[62]

This text is full of allusions and communicative paradoxes that create an unstable, irritating, and dynamic communication with the audience that undermines the original function of the manifesto to "manifest" a program or idea. In this regard, it is telling that Huelsenbeck starts out by invoking the concluding sentence of the *Communist Manifesto* ("Working man of all countries, unite!"[63]/"Noble and respected citizens of Zurich, students, craftsmen, workers, vagabonds, aimless people of all countries, unite."). He alludes not only to the tradition of the political manifesto but also to the specter that undermines the possibilities of clear programmatic messages. Accordingly, Huelsenbeck does not present a clear understanding of the goals and characteristics of Dada as Marx and Engels's manifesto did for communism, but continues only to present the empty shell of an ideological concept. It creates a specter that from now on could haunt the newspaper channels of the early twentieth century.

Huelsenbeck continues to mock the assertive tone of political proclamations and promises to change the world of art and poetry, as well as to end the war. These great political and aesthetic promises, however, are immediately disappointing, because the Dadaist wants to change all these things through nothing. He promises great achievements and possibilities of "Dada," but he continuously emphasizes in his proclamation that "Dada" means nothing.

The central definition of the term "Dada" as "nothing" may appear to the reader or contemporaneous spectator as a cheap trick (one wants to constitute something through nothing). This word play is a kind of burlesque slapstick version of Odysseus's cunning against the Cyclops. By calling himself "nobody," Odysseus makes it impossible for the Cyclops to explain who injured his eye. Odysseus is successful in finding a descriptive form for himself that does not have the power to refer back to him. Similarly, with an ironic twist, Huelsenbeck proposes "Dada" as a remedy for improving poetry, painting, and for ending the war, but the empty term "Dada" is only filled with the ultimate hollow concept—namely, "nothing." Spectators from this audience, when their friends ask them what Huelsenbeck has suggested for ending the war, or for refining art, find themselves in a similar situation as the Cyclops. They can only say "Dada." The friends will ask: "Yes, but what is 'Dada'?" They can only answer: "Nothing."

Precisely this helplessness resonated in press reports about Dada. When journalists attempted to describe Dada, they often merely replicated the semantic instability that was constructed through the Dada manifesto. A visitor reporting about the Dada soirée on July 14, 1916, expresses his inability to describe the event by acknowledging that when he attempts to stammer about Dada, he does so only in a way as one approaches a great mystery.[64] A report in the *Zürcher Morgen-Zeitung* from July 29, 1918, leaves journalistic prose behind, explicitly "adopts Dada language,"[65] and continues in a metaphoric and fragmented language.[66] This adaptation of Dadaistic language comes to its full development in an article in the *Züricher Post* from July 26, 1918, about a performance of Tristan Tzara that was completely written in a fragmented form that is reminiscent of the telegraph style of Marinetti's *parole in libertà*.[67]

The irritation of the audience that resonates in these newspaper reports plays with communicative preconditions. Huelsenbeck's brief speech begins by warning the audience that what he is going to present may hit them like a bullet.[68] This produces a tension, and the audience expects something radically new and world-changing. However, what Huelsenbeck presents is literally nothing. Huelsenbeck invites the audience to witness the proclamation of a new artistic movement; he, therefore, proposes something that implies an understanding. Yet, what Huelsenbeck offers cannot be understood.

Through these strategies, Huelsenbeck introduces a structure that resembles the economy of the parasite. According to Serres, the parasite does not enter into an exchange, but rather takes without giving.[69] It distorts and irritates exchange of equal values and thereby generates a new communicative situation. The host tries to exclude the parasitic intruder, who disturbs an ongoing communication. The Dadaistic proclamations operate in an analogous way to parasites. They do not contribute a specific idea or program to a public conversation, but hook into communicative expectations and disturb them. They do not add anything substantial to a dialogue; they are irritations that trigger a perplexity at what Dada might be. These reactions of the audience can be interpreted as attempts to reduce noise—the incomprehensibility of the Dada message. The collective guessing tries to transform it into a noise-free, understandable content, and the outrage attempts to shut down the noise. But both attempts fail. Dada cannot be translated into a communicable content that is a noise-free message, precisely because it is not a message but rather an intended disturbance of communication.

This parasitical relationship is not merely destructive. Although it does not exchange goods, it produces a form of communication. This communication is not limited to the actual moment of the performance; the reports about the Dada events continue to communicate this vague understanding that remains open to speculations and only triggers further communication. The press coverage can be seen as an attempt to compensate for the asynchronous economy of the parasite. The attempt of the public discourse—be it the press or the audience—to decode "Dada" indicates a longing for a meaning, but since the Dadaistic messages just mimic the unpredictable noise in the channel, no message can be definitely be extracted, and an endless speculation in the press begins.

Huelsenbeck's proclamation sets off an irritation by intercepting the established exchange between stage and audience. This noise is not merely destructive, but also generates the topic "Dada" and provokes the audience's reactions to reduce Dada to an artistic movement alongside Futurism, Cubism, or Expressionism. Only a reduction to a specific program would configure a Dadaistic enterprise that provides an understandable content. The Dadaists try to avoid precisely this transformation of Dada into a static entity, because it would lose its initial dynamic and could be subsumed under a certain, maybe Expressionistic, form of art—it would no longer function as an irritation. "Dada" is created to subvert and distort the contemporaneous system of isms, and not to become one of them. It is supposed to operate as noise in the cultural economy, and thus to become an object of endless speculations.

Spreading the Parasite

Huelsenbeck's manifesto, as one of the first articulations of Dada, created the parasitic structure of this term and brought it into the media discourse. The Dada manifestos reiterated this strategy and amplified it in order to contaminate the public sphere even more with this parasitic construct. Hugo Ball's opening manifesto, presented at the first Dada soirée in Zurich, July 14, 1916, shows that clearly:

> Dada is a new form of art. This is obvious from the fact that until now nobody knew anything about it and tomorrow all of Zurich will talk about it. Dada stems from the dictionary. It is awfully simple. In French, it means hobbyhorse. In German: Addio, leave me alone, goodbye, see you later! In Romanian: "Yes, indeed, you are right, that's how it is. Of course, of course. We'll do that." And so on.
>
> An international word. Only a word, and the word as movement. It is simply awful. If one makes a form of art out of it, this has to mean that one wants to remove complications. Dada psychology, Dada literature, Dada bourgeoisie, and you, dearest poets, you who have always rhymed with words, but never the word itself. Dada world war and no end, Dada revolution and no beginning. Dada my friends and also-poets. Esteemed evangelists. Dada Tzara, Dada Huelsenbeck, Dada m'dada, Dada mhm' dada, Dada Hue, Dada Tza.
>
> How does one achieve eternal blessedness? By saying Dada. How does one become famous? By saying Dada. With noble gesture and with decency. Until insanity, until unconsciousness. How can one dismiss everything eel-like and journal-like, everything nice and preppy, everything overmoralized, animalized, affected. By saying Dada. Dada is the soul of the world, Dada is the show-stopper. Dada is the best lilymilksoap in the world. Dada Herr Rubiner, Dada Herr Korrodi, Dada Herr Anastasius Lilienstein.
>
> This means, plain and simple: Swiss hospitality cannot be regarded highly enough, and in all things aesthetic everything depends on the norm.[70]

Ball's claim that "Dada" is an "international" word is central to his manifesto. At first, the emphasis on the international character of Dada can be understood as a general political statement suggesting that for Dada nationality is meaningless. Second, Dada is international because it is not restricted to any national language.[71] Ball's internationalism, therefore, has not only a political but also a linguistic dimension. Dada is restricted neither to one language nor to one single meaning. This linguistic ambivalence of the expression "Dada" enables this term to draw in more and more meanings. Ball plays with the dynamic structure of the word and writes: "Only a word, and the word as movement." This claim is ambivalent: on the one hand, it refers to "Dada" as the name of an artistic "movement." On the other hand, it could refer to the later claim by Dada to cover the entire earth with Dada as an international movement.[72] More importantly, it states that this word remains dynamic in its linguistic quality and therefore implements the parasitic logic that was already central to Huelsenbeck's manifesto.

The term "Dada" cannot simply be filled with one set of meanings. For Ball and Huelsenbeck what "Dada" can incorporate is not determined, but dynamically growing—in a permanent "movement." Just as for Huelsenbeck, so also for Ball, "Dada" does not simply signify the opposite of what is being said. Rather, "Dada" indicates a dynamic polysemantic structure. To make this point more explicit, Ball addresses "Dada" as a newly founded art form, but also states that this identification entails an intolerable reduction of Dada's complexity or "complications." Dada generates, as a parasite, noise through implementing complexity that distracts the reception of Dada texts, performances, or art. By "implementing complexity" I mean a strategy that avoids coming up with one single meaning or definition of Dada. Complexity is generated by the attempt to keep the notion of Dada open and dynamic. To demonstrate that Dada possesses such an irreducible structure, Ball shows how it is possible to generate an infinite number of compounds through the prefix "Dada." The examples "Dada Psychology, Dada Literature, Dada Bourgeoisie" show that this prefix can be used for everything, and thus any reduction of complexity and identification is impossible. The parasite "Dada" can affix itself to any word in any language and turn that word into a host.

Certainly, this structure is not restricted to "Dada" alone, but includes all parts of the language that have no fixed meaning. Any linguistic object that is not rigidly coupled to a semantic system can be connected to any element of that language, precisely because it is not determined. "Dada" is one of these numerous empty variables (such as "gaga," "debo," and the like) that can be integrated into the linguistic game without giving any further predication.[73] This structure again correlates to the parasitic economy through which Dada takes sounds and letters from the language without giving any defined meaning in return.

The Dada manifestos construct an empty linguistic parasite that does not have any specific meaning, but distorts established communicative patterns instead. The audience cannot react to the Dada performance as they would respond to a "normal" stage act. Out of this noise emerges a desperate desire to ponder what Dada could be. Yet the intervention of Dada into the process of understanding does not lead to finding a definite meaning. Instead it fuels a new dialogue about the empty term "Dada." A newspaper report on the soirée of July 16, 1916, shows that

Huelsenbeck and Ball were quite successful in injecting their parasitic concept into public discourse:

> What is "Dada," this incomparably lapidary word, taken from children's babble? It is a symbol for everything. For hate and for love, for good and for evil, for arrogance, profundity, nonsense, monotony, madness, lunacy, and stupidity.... In accordance with the universal versatility of the great Dada, the program of the Dadaists exhibited a truly Dada-like richness.[74]

This newspaper article completely absorbs the parasitic logic as staged by the Dadaists. First, it refers to the indeterminacy of Dada as a prelinguistic element. Second, the journalist presents "Dada" as an empty variable that can be filled with anything. The author of the article further adopts the rhetoric of Dada manifestos and gives a self-referential definition of "Dada": the universal character of "Dada" would be supported by a truly "Dadaistic" richness. This sentence does not say anything about Dada or the Dadaistic program; it rather injects the Dadaistic mockery of programmatic writing into the public discourse of the newspaper. It thereby implements the distorting logic of the parasite into the newspaper, which now can spread into the public realm. The article clearly testifies to such a contamination: it does not convey news; it just presents circular information that does not configure a determined content of the Dadaistic program.

This is one example of how Dada used contemporaneous mass media. Because of financial restrictions, the Dadaists were not able to engage in the media circus as Marinetti did. This, however, does not mean that they did not use the functioning of newspapers and journals for their ventures. They recognized the press as an important part of their propaganda machine, which they used in their parasitic exchange. The statement by the Dadaist Klabund from 1919 makes this clear: "The Press speculates without end over Dada. This can only be in keeping with our aims."[75] It was not important whether or not the press presented Dada in a positive light. It was important that Dada had an impact on the mass media and therefore on public communication in general.

PARASITES IN BERLIN

In 1917 Huelsenbeck migrated from Zurich to Berlin, where he met Hausmann, who was immediately fascinated by this strange concept of Dada. The spark of Dada soon caused a wildfire that not only captivated numerous artists such as Johannes Baader, Hannah Höch, and Wieland Herzfelde and his brother John Heartfield, but also attracted a great crowd. While the Dada evenings in Zurich were comparatively intimate gatherings, Dada events greatly expanded in Berlin, and the newspaper reports were full of astonishment that the Dadaists performed mostly in front of full houses. An anonymously published flyer even warned about the Dadaist evening in Karlsbad on March 5, 1920; it stated that these performances were a mere rip-off ("Geldmacherei") and identified the Dadaists as greedy parasites that abused the public hunger for sensations without presenting anything of value.[76] Although it is doubtful that the Dadaists were primarily driven by financial incentive, the observation of the author of this "warning" that the Dadaists were not productive and just fed on the work of others is not completely wrong. Not only the famous collages used materials produced by other media spheres, but also the manifestos tapped into the discourses of the time and abused their products to create a very unstable message that did not provide any meaningful information. This, however, sparked the interest and productivity of the metropolitan press. Major newspapers such as *Berliner Tageblatt*, *Berliner Börsen-Courier*, or the *Vossische Zeitung* soon reported on this new movement.

When it comes to the relationship to the press, the most eminent figure in Berlin Dada was certainly Johannes Baader, the self-proclaimed "Oberdada." Baader was a mastermind of media manipulation. He preceded Jean Baudrillard's famous assertion that the Gulf War never happened[77] with the claim that the First World War was solely a product of the newspapers.[78] He also frequently published his own obituary in Berlin papers,[79] and showed thereby that he did not shy away from anything in order to have his name in the press.

Baader, however, started his career as an eccentric persona far before Dada. He was an educated architect, and one of his most ambitious and, of course, never-realized projects was the building of a World Temple that would have been 1500 meters high and was supposed to house all religions and belief systems in harmony.[80] His friendship with Hausmann had begun already in 1905, and both were interested in all kinds of strange and occult practices. Actually, Hausmann's interest in cosmological theories, which I discuss in more detail in the last chapter, can be traced back to Baader. Baader followed a megalomaniacal religious agenda and stylized himself into the "president of the globe [Erdball]"[81] and even as a reincarnation of Jesus Christ; his self-proclamation as "Oberdada" is thus comparatively down to earth. However, he strategically abused the Dada movement for his own performances and scandalous interventions. One of his first actions connected to the Dada movement was that he claimed all Nobel Prizes in the name of Dada.[82] He also organized in 1918 a happening in the Berliner Dom proclaiming "What is Jesus to you? You could care less!"⁸³ Most famously he disturbed the National Assembly in Weimar on June 6, 1919, by distributing copies of the flyer "Dadaists against Weimar."⁸⁴ This form of self-stylizing caused criticism within the Dada group, and he himself can be described as a parasite within the Dada movement. In a letter to Tzara he addresses this point:

> Comrades in dada! My declarations do not all bear the dada façade, but they do have the dadaistic effect and are so calculated. For this reason I ask France not to get upset with the "Oberdada." The "Oberdada" is but a dadaistic bomb for the purpose of exploding every National Assembly and every regime in power, most of all, however, the German regime.⁸⁵

Baader's performances certainly profited from his affiliation with the group, but he was also without doubt a main factor that drew the journalistic interest on Dada Berlin. As Karl Riha points out, Baader was recognized by most Dadaists as a unique persona, who with great authenticity represented the Dada spirit.⁸⁶ However, what "Dada" actually meant was not very clearly articulated by the Oberdada. Also, the other Dada proclamations remained for the Berlin media as mysterious as for the journalists in Zurich. Berlin Dada continued the subversive tactics of the Zurich period to integrate "Dada" as an unstable semantic parasite into the public discourse.

The "Dadaistisches Manifest," from 1918, is an especially vicious example of how Dada Berlin implemented the parasite. In contrast to the already discussed Zurich manifestos, this text appears to present rather straightforward claims on the goals and artistic methods of Dada. It almost mimics the structure of the Futurist Manifesto by stating a concise program. As the text reads, "the signers of this manifesto have, under the battle cry 'Dada!!!!' gathered together to put forward a new art, from which they expect the realization of new ideals."⁸⁷ The targets of the Dadaistic attacks in this manifesto were openly defined as Expressionism, Italian Futurism, and the Weimar bourgeoisie. Laying out the field of conflict, the manifesto opens with an aesthetics of topicality:

> Art in its execution and direction is dependent on the time in which it lives and artists are creatures of their epoch. Their highest art will be that which in its conscious content presents the thousandfold problems of the day, the art which has been visibly shattered by the explosion of last week, which is forever trying to collect its limb after yesterday's crash. The best and most extraordinary artists will be those who every hour snatch the tatters of their bodies out of the frenzied cataract of life, who, with bleeding hands and hearts, hold fast to the intelligence of their time.⁸⁸

According to this text, the optimal aesthetic paradigm represents an art that closely relates to the eruptions and antagonisms of the present moment. This art permanently engages in daily debates and thus coincides with the functioning of the press to continuously present news. Expressionism, according to the manifesto, failed in such an endeavor, and this is already the point where the rhetoric differs significantly from the Zurich texts. The manifesto does not open up an ironic interaction with the audience. Instead of mocking their audience, the Dadaists present themselves reminiscent of the way in which the Futurists used language in their manifestos. The world is not presented as playful confusion, but rather as a battlefield. The language of the manifesto is explicit: explosions are understood as central to aesthetic production and connote war as the father of all things.[89] The artist is torn apart and reassembles himself again, or in the violent language of the manifesto "reißt sich zusammen," which, literally translated, means "to rip oneself together."

Nonetheless, this scene—which stages a combat—refers not to the Futurist battlefield, but rather to the Dadaistic metropolis and all its forms of mass communication: "Hatred of the press, hatred of advertising, hatred of sensations are typical of people who prefer their armchair to the noise of the street."[90] This metropolis, Berlin, is further identified as the founding place of Dada.[91] Such a strong claim—and the fact that members of Dada Zurich and Dada Paris signed this manifesto—makes a face-value reading of the manifesto implausible. This impression is reinforced by the paradoxical closing sentence, which ironically undermines the positive/deterministic tone of the manifesto: "To be against this manifesto is to be a Dadaist."[92] This first manifesto of Berlin Dada apparently differs from other Dadaistic efforts, because it seemingly provides a relatively consistent description of the movement and its artistic practices. It is, however, hard to understand how this heterogeneous group could have agreed on such clear definitions. This gives a clue that the strong rhetoric is merely a performative trick. To sign such a pamphlet would be very contradictory to every Dadaist, but as the final sentence indicates, the fact that one does not agree with the manifesto identifies one as a Dadaist. Thus, if the group of people who really signed the manifesto are Dadaists, they do not agree to the content of the manifesto.[93] As a consequence, the meaning of "Dada" is left undefined and open, echoing the "nothing" of the Zurich manifestos.

This ironic constellation constitutes a paradoxical situation, which enables the signatories to agree with certain aspects of the manifesto and yet, at the same time, to distance themselves from the content. This paradox is in accordance with the Dada project of generating a program that cannot be ascribed to a single person or identified with a specific content.

It becomes impossible to decide whether someone really belongs to the Dadaistic movement or not.

As both reports from the time and scholarly research emphasize, this manifesto provoked an outrage in the audience and triggered the interest of the press, and the last sentence is considered to be the major irritant.[94] The sentence is so powerful, because it openly states the parasitic economy that was fundamental to the Zurich manifestos. Up to this point, provocations had been clearly codified by formulating strategies and exposing enemies. Now, the place from where these attacks were launched was no longer recognizable. Identification with this Dadaistic manifesto unveiled the persons who were actually not Dadaists. The sentence further removed any possibility of not becoming a Dadaist. Dada emerged as a position that nobody could escape. Everyone was Dada—either by calling themselves Dada or by attacking Dada. The list of signatories also alluded to the abusive tactics of Dada. It is hardly imaginable that all these persons had read and agreed to the program, and Hausmann acknowledged that it was even a common practice in Dada to just put the desired names as signatories on a manifesto.[95]

Berlin Dada and Its Critics

In the "Dadaistisches Manifest," Huelsenbeck does not codify Berlin Dada, but rather sums up the vocabularies of the contemporaneous social discourses. Similar to Serres's parasite, he only takes up the exchange of ideas without adding any unique definable program to the circulating ideas. Huelsenbeck does not constitute a place for Dada, but implements Dada within the discursive language of art and politics. Dada does not appear as an additional art movement, but as indefinable noise in the context of the vivid art scene of the Berlin metropolis. This was the general trajectory of the manifestos. Their specific feature was that they did not provide a clearly understandable message, but that they irritated the press so that they could start their speculations.

A very insightful contemporaneous press report, "The Trained Audience,"[96] clearly identifies the Dada attempt to remain unstable as a trick to keep the cultural critics engaged. Franz Schulz, the author of this article, who would become a famous screenplay writer, put the relationship between Dada and the feuilleton in the following picture:

> Involuntarily, there comes to mind the picture of the two boys climbing a staircase, each of them wanting to get a step ahead of the other. Involuntarily, this picture comes to mind if one follows the competition of the Dadaists and

the critics. For both groups, it's about being on top, about not letting the other be in charge.⁹⁷

According to Schulz, the relationship between Dada and the press was a dynamic one, in which the one party reacted on the assertion of the other. A claim by Dada was answered by a journalistic attempt to identify a trait of Dada or to critique an utterance or performance. Schulz emphasized that the journalists were in a trap ("Zwickmühle"). Because Dada was so unpredictable, if critics would have rejected Dada as mere nonsense, they would have been in danger to appear as very stupid, if Dada should finally have emerged as the new all-encompassing wisdom, which could not be completely ruled out. Thus, according to Schulz, critics kept a distanced but interested relationship to Dada and made mostly very general statements debating the young or immature nature of the movement, and so forth.⁹⁸ Raoul Hausmann's manifesto "The German Philistine Is Angry" underlines this relationship to the press, by reflecting on how Dada was perceived by cultural critics.

> No, don't attack us, gentlemen—we are already our own enemies, and we know how to hit ourselves better than you. You must see that your positions do not matter to us at all, we have other limbs at arm's length. You can plug your intellectual business all you can, you can beat hard on your belly so that a god takes pity on the sound—we have already chucked away this old drum long ago. We bear, squeak, curse, laugh at the irony:
>
> Dada! For we are—ANTIDADAISTS!⁹⁹

Dadaists have realized that Dadaism—attacked by cultural critics—is already outdated. As a consequence, Dadaists become Antidadaists. The Dadaistic self-understanding already recognizes Dada as something that is or has to be overcome. Dadaism reflects on itself and thereby criticizes itself. Here, Hausmann internalizes the "competition," as identified by Schulz, between critics and Dadaists within the Dada movement itself. Hausmann recognized this Dadaistic self-understanding as a heterounderstanding in a much more appropriate response to the Dadaistic movement than the outside criticism by the Expressionists.

Although this claim can be understood as a mocking reaction to criticism, there is more to it than that. The understanding of Dada as the enemy enabled Hausmann to differentiate a further category, namely "Antidadaism." That is to say, the Dadaists reevaluated their position in such a way that they distanced themselves from their prior ventures and said that they were no longer Dadaists. With this gambit, they recognized Dada as something different from themselves and therefore escaped any attack launched on Dada. This strategy was not designed to establish a more differentiated picture of Dada as an artistic movement that entered in a phase where it criticized its prior ventures. Rather, Antidadaism functioned as the beginning of an endless stream of transformations.

Antidadaism emerges when a Dadaistic program seems to be established. Only through distancing from itself—one might call it self-alienation—is Dada able to maintain a dynamic structure that still is able to disturb public communication. If the Dadaists were not to become Antidadaists, they would remain in a position that is determined by public reception. Hausmann openly proclaimed that this withdrawing from the position that was ascribed to Dada was an intended effect: "There you have it! Save your maltreated bones and stitch your tattered puss, you did everything in vain! That you cannot pinion us against the wall, that is what makes us solemn."[100] As Schulz predicted, Hausmann tried to create a structure through which it became impossible to restrict Dada to one specific position. This did not only secure the flexibility of Dada, but also presented the central provocation offered by Dada: the newly emerging Antidadaism did not imply a positive program that, for example, opposed Dadaism. Instead, it was a practice of intervening in or disturbing communicative interaction. As a parasitic noise, the position of Antidadaism undermined a clear exchange of ideas of what Dada was. The Antidadaistic activities consisted of questioning and eliminating codified aesthetic programs that did not provide anything positive. More precisely, they also attacked all members of the movement who would have engaged in such codified practices. What replaced the codification of aesthetic rules was not a positive program, but rather a fluctuating concept of nonsense, a semantic noise that prohibited the fixation of a Dadaistic nucleus.

This is precisely what Schulz saw as the fundamental mechanics of Dada. However, Schulz in "The Trained Audience" also recognized that this relationship to the press was not a harmonious or even funny cat-and-mouse game, but a constant abuse of the press for advertisement purposes. Schulz clearly points out that the Dadaists depended on this coverage, because they needed to sell tickets for their Dada evenings.[101] Even if this economic reason might not completely explain the intentions of Dada manifestos, it certainly shows that the Dadaists most literally used the press as a host. Hanne Bergius critically remarks that the exaggerated provocations weakened after a short period of time and collapsed into a message accepted and even desired by the press.[102] Bergius's assessment is correct: Dada could not contain its "anti-"nimbus; it rather became part of the mass media. However, I would like to emphasize that the Dada project consisted in precisely such an integration in mass media channels as a parasite. The Dadaists were not so much interested in rejecting bourgeois norms and aesthetics as they were in trying to get the contemporary press interested in the movement. As I outlined, contemporaneous reports identified this practice often as a simple abuse of media coverage for financial gain, but I would like to suggest that this rhetoric is a subversive tactic to occupy media discourses and to irritate them through parasitic, asynchronous exchange. Contaminating and abusing the channel was the intention of Berlin Dada and not the destruction of the press. It also needs to be emphasized that the contemporaneous press was very willing to report about the Dada events and, thus, also profited in an intricate way from the parasitic interventions.

COMMUNICATING THE PARASITE

The avant-garde movements of Futurism and Dadaism subverted the sociohistorical and aesthetic construction of the manifesto as it was established in the nineteenth century. In his book about Dada manifestos, the literary historian Alfons Backes-Haase points out for late-nineteenth-century art movements that the manifesto served as a communicative interface for reuniting the public with an art that was based on an increasingly abstract aesthetic system. It constructed the communicative bridge for bringing art and spectator together.[103] Already the Futurist Manifesto undermined this function and served not only to explain methods and goals of aesthetic production, but also to manipulate public communication and to insert a new mythology in the discourse. Dada manifestos subverted the role of manifestos as aesthetic messengers even more.

Futurist manifestos constructed a rich picture of a world to come, in which man merged with machine. Futurist art had a central function in accelerating this development, but the manifesto cannot be reduced to a theoretical treatment for such aesthetic or rather industrial practices. Programmatic texts rather implemented themselves as parasites with the help of mass media networks into the public discourse in order to transform communication. Step by step, these texts injected technology as mythology into the society for building up a consistent Futurist universe that had the power to establish a Futurist ideology of technology. The Futurists thereby abused an established repository of a sociocultural imaginary for their purposes and occupied the technological channels of mass media dissemination as greedy parasites that longed for an almost viral infection of all cultural spheres with the new ideology of Futurism.

Dada manifestos operated with quite different strategies. Dada did not try to develop a positive program or consistent imaginary as Futurism did. Dada did not give fixed definitions, but rather constructed a complex calculus that continuously undermined attempts to specify a concrete place or program of Dada. Because of this structure, Dada manifestos cannot be read as argumentative or discursive texts. Rather, the Dada manifestos deconstruct the determining power, the discursive and political function of the genre "manifesto" through their own performativity. The manifestos appeared as noise that triggered outrage or discussion without adding an identifiable message or program to the public discourse. This strategy enabled Dada to shift positions constantly and thus to remain dynamic. These tactics mimicked and exploited the functioning of mass media. The rapid expiration date of any established understanding—as it is exercised in Hausmann's manifesto—corresponds to the speed of the newspaper, which in a daily rhythm corrupts an established understanding of the world through its news.[104] As Hanne Bergius argues, this exploitation not only lays bare the illusionary character of mass media,[105] but also fuels the press machine with the hardly comprehendible and digestible concept of "Dada." In fact, the press absorbed the polyvalent tactics of Dada and generated an endless number of reports and speculations about Dada—in October 1919 Tristan Tzara was already able to count 8,590 articles dedicated to Dada.[106] However, Raimund Meyer's assertion that "the press mutated to a Dada artifact"[107] overstretches Dada's impact. Dada did not take over the press, but assimilated its procedures to the processes of the media industries, without losing a subversive and irritating character.

The difference between Futurism and Dada lies in the degree of self-reference and irony that they incorporate into their projects. What they have in common is their construction of media events through their manifestos. What Timothy Benson says about the Dada manifesto also holds true for Futurism: "[T]he text shifted from a content-laden cultural carrier to an event or incident in a transitory configuration."[108] Dada and Futurist proclamations were not simply static texts, but events, constructed and disseminated through the mass media. While on the one hand Futurism attempted to control the construction of Futurist imagination through the manifestos, Dada strategically spread out confusion of what Dada is and what it defines. However, both share a parasitical subversion that simultaneously uses, provokes, and shapes mass media discourses.

CHAPTER 2

POETIC MEDIA EFFECTS

AT THE TURN OF THE TWENTIETH CENTURY, modernism began to lose faith in language as a tool for representing the world. Modernist authors saw that linguistic means failed to express thoughts or to communicate emotions to other human beings. Language was perceived as an old and odd system without expressive power, or as an organism corrupted by modern modes of address such as journalism and commercial advertisement that only produced flat clichés of sentiment and experience. Hugo Ball criticized words as empty shells,[1] Hugo von Hofmannsthal referred to words as rotten mushrooms in the famous fictitious letter of Lord Chandos,[2] and Filippo Tommaso Marinetti claimed that the syntactical structure of language was too slow for the Futurist world.[3] All these complaints contribute to the same diagnosis: language itself is sick and has to be reconstructed according to a modern conception of the subject, the world, or media.

Keeping this therapeutic agenda in mind, the poetic production of Dada and Futurism is quite astonishing. Instead of providing a language that is clearly understandable, the poetry of these avant-garde movements exposes its reader to nonsense and noise, fragmented and distorted language. Even more astonishing, both groups created poems consisting only of vowels and consonants or random words containing hardly any meaning. They employed advanced typographic design for irritating their audiences and assembled random material in disturbing visual collages. To sum up, both movements segmented the stream of discursive communication and thereby approached noise. Their rebuilding of language appears rather as a destruction of linguistic means than as an attempt to create a more efficient or "better" form of communication.

As I will discuss in this chapter, the avant-garde did not attempt to reconstruct a language that appealed to a hermeneutically founded understanding, but to a form of communication that resonated with the transmission channels on modern battlefields, and the information entropy created by modern media technology. This new language did not arise from mystical vision, as the early Dadaist Hugo Ball noted in his diary,[4] but emerged as a parasite from new media technologies that now were able to register and process semiotic material without reference to its meaning. The poets of the avant-garde were not inspired by a muse, but abused the noises produced by media technologies such as the telegraph or the typewriter for their purposes.

This chapter reflects on the media technological foundation of Futurist and Dadaist poetry and argues that apparent similarities between Futurist and Dada poetics represent two different responses to media technological developments. Futurist poetry—principally Marinetti's *parole in libertà*—exposes the reader to a scattered stream of words without any syntactical structure. This "telegram style" can be regarded as highly disturbing. However, Marinetti does not simply provoke his audience with meaningless linguistic detritus; rather, he wants to expose his readers to a forceful poetical language that can be received even amid the noise of battle or mass traffic. Marinetti's poetics does not so much exhibit disturbance as it creates a language that remains resistant to noise. That is, Marinetti's stream of words is not so much a noisy representation of the battlefield as a model for a language that can be transmitted in noisy environments as well as through the static of early wireless networks.

The Dada project can be seen as a precisely contrary operation. It is not the creation of a language resistant to noise that is important, but the generation of noise through poetry. Especially, the poetry of Raoul Hausmann and Richard Huelsenbeck does not operate on the level of meaning, but rather disturbs the act of reading or listening.

However, what Dada and Futurism have in common is that both abused modern systems of language processing, from the telegraph to modern typography, in order to construct their new linguistic forms of expression. Language was further conceptualized as an immediate access to the body, and both movements aimed at a language that was understandable in a simple physiological reaction and not in a complex hermeneutical reflection. The poetry of both movements did not speak to the mind, but was intended to implement communicative interaction on a physiological level.

Poetics of Matter

Futurism became canonized primarily as an art movement, and as its legacy the paintings and sculptures of Boccioni, Carrà, and Balla stand out. As an emblematic element of Italian modernism, Boccioni's sculpture

"Unique Forms of Continuity in Space" even found its way on the Italian 20-cent euro coin. However, Futurism was the creation of a poet. When Marinetti published his Futurist Manifesto in 1909, he did so as a writer who was already quite established in the literary metropolis of Paris as well as in Italian circles.

Marinetti began his career as a poet very early, when he still was a student in Alexandria, Egypt. His admiration for Zola got him in trouble, and he even was expelled from his Jesuit school.[5] Although Marinetti successfully pursued, back in Europe, his university education as a lawyer, his true passion remained poetry and he kept an impressive publication record. Most significantly, he coedited the journal *Poesia*, in which he opened a debate about the *vers libre*,[6] that is, the importance of a modern poetic language that is no longer bound to a static system of rhyme and rhythm. Even if Marinetti rejected the *vers libre* in his Futurist time, this work can be seen as a first step toward the liberated words in his Futurist poetics. However, Marinetti was not only a lyrical poet; his pre-Futurist work includes several theatrical plays. The most significant plays in regard to his later Futurist aesthetics are *Roi Bombance*, which drew its content and figures from baroque forms of the grotesque, thereby anticipating the hyperboles of Futurist texts,[7] and the play *Popées electriques*, which portrayed the American engineer John Wilson, who designed robots that started to haunt his love life and that of his wife; this play prefigured the Futurist agenda of subjugating love and intimacy under a technological regime.[8]

The first text, however, that acknowledged Futurism explicitly was the novel *Mafarka the Futurist* from 1909. From its content, motives, and language, it certainly differs from the reduced poetic language that Marinetti envisions in his Futurist manifestos of poetry. Mafarka is a strange *Übermensch* in a premodern African society, and the narrative is full of obscene, decadent, and even fairytale-like scenes. What it shared, however, with the Futurist Manifesto was that Marinetti did not conceptualize this text as a literary work, but as a scandalous piece of advertisement. The book was quickly censored and banned from the market, but the ban, of course, only increased its publicity and established Marinetti's reputation as a rebellious author who challenged traditional aesthetic and bourgeois norms.[9]

It is also interesting to see that the publication of a Futurist poetics was something that happened only three years after the Founding Manifesto. Although the first Futurist manifestos such as the Founding Manifesto and "Let's Murder the Moonshine"[10] have an explicit aesthetic character that is rooted in a tradition of symbolist tropes and the grotesque, they do not establish their own poetics. Also, the manifestos of Futurist painters predate Marinetti's theory of a Futurist language, which he centrally developed in the "Technical Manifesto of Futurist Literature"[11] from 1912 and in the manifesto "Destruction of Syntax"[12] from 1913.

In both manifestos Marinetti presents the framework for a Futurist poetics that separates itself from other forms of modernist, symbolist, or decadent writing with which Marinetti experimented in his pre-Futurist time. Here, he most importantly distances himself from the *vers libre* and acknowledges that this lyrical form of expression is still bound to the prison of syntax. Certainly, Marinetti describes in this text how the Futurist language becomes minimalistic, only consisting of nouns, verbs in the infinitive, mathematical formulas, and so on, and suspending syntax as an organizational structure. More importantly, however, he attempts to introduce a materialistic notion of literature that is no longer chained to human understanding and cognition. Precisely this dehumanization liberates Marinetti's *parole in libertà*. It is not merely the segmented and free-floating character of words in Futurist poetry. This transformation of language is only the method; the goal is to construct a poetic language that exists in its sheer materiality. As Marinetti puts it:

> Syntax was a kind of abstract cipher that poets used to inform the crowd about the color, musicality, plasticity, and architecture of the universe. Syntax was a kind of interpreter or monotonous cicerone. This intermediary must be suppressed, in order that literature may enter directly into the universe and become one body with it.[13]

Accordingly, the author of this poetry is no longer perceived as a cognitive entity, but as a mechanism that involuntarily or, as Marinetti mostly calls it, "intuitively" writes down words. The words emerge automatically from the hand, liberated from the control of the brain, as Marinetti famously formulated in the supplement to the "Technical Manifesto on Futurist Literature":

> The hand that writes appears to detach itself from the body and extends itself very freely from the brain, which likewise is detached from the body and becomes aerial, looking from above with a terrifying clarity at the sentences that unexpectedly come out of the pen.[14]

This might sound like surrealist forms of automatic writing, but it is not intended to unveil the unconscious. It is rather thought out as a notation of the real, as transcription of universal and cosmological structures, and as a process that the human mind cannot achieve consciously, because it is confined in its structures of thinking. For Marinetti, the complexity of the world cannot be understood by rational means but must be felt intuitively, because intuition links the sheer materiality of the world with the human senses. ("Through intuition we will conquer the seemingly unconquerable hostility that separates out human flesh from the metal of motors."[15]) The model for this sensitivity is not a highly sensitive human being, but technological equipment like the gramophone that scans matter without any conscious judgment. This intersection between mechanical data processing and human perception is something that Marinetti explicitly develops in his manifestos on tactility and that I discuss in the last chapter.

Applied to Futurist language this means that poetry should not be a device for understanding and representing human subjectivity. Marinetti's claim that the "I," the subjective perspective, has to be removed from poetic language indicates precisely that. What Marinetti wants to put in place of a subjective poetry is a materialistic one: "To substitute for human psychology, now exhausted, the lyric obsession with matter."[16] Poetry becomes an exploration of matter. Intuition and divinatory processes become technological procedures of reading/scanning. Poetry is not geared toward a recognition of human sentiments, but toward an intuition into the nonhuman material and technological structures of the world. Certainly, at the foundation of this poetics stands the development of modern media technology.

> Instead we should express the infinite smallness that surrounds us, the imperceptible, the invisible, the agitation of atoms, the Brownian movements, all the passionate hypotheses and all the domains explored by the high-powered microscope. To explain: I want to introduce the infinite molecular life into poetry not as a scientific document but as an intuitive element. It should mix, in the work of art, with the infinitely great spectacles and dramas, because this fusion constitutes the integral synthesis of life.[17]

This passage stems from the Manifesto "Destruction of Syntax," which significantly starts out with a reflection on how modern technologies have affected human beings. This introductory part called "Futurist Sensibility" is mostly concerned with the acceleration of life in the early twentieth century; the passage above, however, makes clear that Marinetti also recognized the force of new optical media and the ability to dissect reality through media technology as essential for the contemporaneous society. The task of man is to develop an intuitive sensibility that is on par with the analytic power of modern media technology, and also as mindless as these technologies. For Marinetti, man should not be aided by, but should become media technology. Futurist poetics are an integral part of this project through its attempt to create a mindless form of language that finds its models in the technologies of cinema and the telegraph.

High-Speed Poetics

> Moreover, I combat Mallarmé's static ideal with this typographical revolution that allows me to impress on the words (already free, dynamic, and torpedo-like) every velocity of the stars, the clouds, aeroplanes, trains, waves, explosives, globules of seafoam, molecules, and atoms.[18]

In this quotation Marinetti distances himself from his predecessor in typographical experiments, Mallarmé, and demonstrates that Futurist poetry does not have anything to do with a language on a human scale, but approaches the speed of technological media as well as of cosmic and atmospheric phenomena. Speed becomes once again the central narrative of Futurist imagination; it is the essential characteristic that distinguishes Futurist poetry from other modernist forms of language production, at least in Marinetti's mind. This has a central consequence for the function of language and constitutes the foundation for a Futurist understanding of communication. Language no longer serves as a mere representative tool, but as a logistic system that organizes, processes, and transports data. In fact, all Futurist modifications of language are not so much aimed at improving its representative function as its efficiency through accelerating and compressing the information of linguistic material. Marinetti privileges in his poetics informatics over representation—that is, he focuses on the logistic structure of language—and theorizes how linguistic material can be efficiently processed without reflecting on its meaning. Concerning Marinetti's "wireless imagination," Timothy Campbell asserts likewise that for Marinetti "only the speed of the transmission will determine its merits as lyrical production,"[19] and Johanna Drucker also clearly recognizes that the transformation of language undertaken by Futurists is not so much interested in the implementation of thematic topics such as airplanes and cars that correspond to the new gadgets of modern life, but is rather concerned with modes of communication.[20] Marinetti attempts to enable a high-speed recognition of complex data through his *parole in libertà*; this is not merely a realism that mirrors the speed of an accelerated modernity, but the Futurist dehumanization of language that constitutes a strategic abuse of modern media technology in order to construct a form of communication void of any subjectivity.

Thus, Marinetti's poetics entails a communication theoretical project: to process the maximum amount of information with a minimum of linguistic material. This efficiency is not only the aim of Futurist poems but also the principal strategy of modern advertisement, journalism, and military communications. In Futurism, poetic language becomes even more reduced or optimized to a highly efficient and mechanical form that attempts to approach processing rates of technical media, more precisely of telegraphy and film. The high efficiency of mechanical and electric data processing indicates further a technological environment in which human minds cannot keep up with the amount of information processed in modern communication networks. Therefore, Futurists do not ask human beings to carry modern poetics on their own. Instead, they turn to machines in order to look for new means of expressivity. This is exactly the parasitical shift that Marinetti undertakes in his first manifesto about Futurist literature from 1912. His text starts out from a scene, in which he tells the story of how he enjoyed a flight over the industrial site of Milan. In his words, this moment gave birth to the Futurist poetics of *parole in libertà*.[21]

As Jeffrey Schnapp points out in his essay "Propeller Talk," *parole in libertà* emerge from an intimate communication with the engine.[22] Marinetti describes the plane in his first poetological manifesto as the inspiring muse: "And the propeller added."[23] Now, what does a propeller have to say about poetics? One point of Marinetti's agenda calls for technological hegemony in poetic language. As he puts it, "We want to make literature out of the life of a motor, a new instinctive animal."[24] The machine replaces the human subject as a source of lyrical expression. In addition, Marinetti asserts that the syntax of human language undermines the ability to accelerate the processing of linguistic material. "A pressing need to liberate words, to drag them out of their prison in the Latin period! Like all imbeciles, this period naturally has a canny head, a stomach, two legs, and two flat feet, but it will never have two wings."[25] The syntactic structure—which brings with it several forms of redundancy and indecision—is recognized as a merely human framework, a slow linguistic structure that will never reach the velocity of flight.

For Marinetti, the human is only a parasite that can profit from technologies, and quintessentially, he himself is in the opening scene of the manifesto nothing else than a parasite of the airplane. In Futurist poetics, the human being is no longer perceived as an agent but as a parasite stripped of its subjective agency, and matter takes its place.[26] Precisely this materialistic turn highlights the speed and technology of language processing that stands at the center of Marinetti's poetics, and places the human subject as a parasite at the periphery of communicative exchange.

As Marinetti's account of poetics emphasizes, in Futurism lyric language is not understood as an intimate speaking that connects the subjectivity of two beings, but rather as a highly efficient mode of data processing. Therefore, Marinetti does not imagine a simple sender-receiver system as the foundation of poetry, but a self-referential network of linguistic materialism, in which man can only tap into as a parasite. As Marinetti points out:

> Be careful not to force human feelings onto matter. Instead, divine its different governing impulses, its forces of compression, dilation, cohesion, and disaggregation, its crowds of massed molecules and whirling electrons. We are not interested in offering dramas of humanized matter. The solidity of a strip of steel interests us for itself; that is the incomprehensible and nonhuman alliance of its molecules or its electrons that oppose, for instance, the penetration of a howitzer. The warmth of a piece of iron or wood is in our opinion more impassioned than the smile or tears of a woman.[27]

Marinetti's poetics constitutes a radical dehumanization and materialism. Thus, every aspect of language that adds an individual character is suspect for Futurist poetics, because it might cause interruptions and could slow down the data transfer. Stylistic brilliance and syntactic complexity are banned as contaminations from Futurists poetics, which proposes in its place a language that is stripped down to its bare bones:

1. One must destroy syntax and scatter one's nouns at random, ...
2. One should use infinitives ...
3. One must abolish the adjective ...
4. One must abolish the adverb ...[28]

The prescriptions that Marinetti calls for eliminate morphological modifications such as inflections of the words from lyric language. The single word appears as a fixed linguistic element that can be quickly processed. Friedrich Kittler remarked that Marinetti's strategies for eliminating redundancies, such as crossing out personal pronouns and adjectives, correspond to established standards in telegraphy offices as well as military commands.[29] The entire catalogue of the Futurist language, as it is developed in "Technical Manifesto of Futurist Literature" and "Destruction of Syntax," is dominated by the use of nouns and verbs in the infinitive as well as the replacement of words by mathematical symbols. This choice of linguistic elements points directly toward an acceleration of the data stream generated by Futurism. As Marinetti outlines his agenda, "I proposed instead a highly rapid lyricism."[30]

This acceleration, however, is not only a simplification but a compression of data. This becomes clear when Marinetti favors the use of onomatopoeias—not so much as a means for exact representation, but rather as a way of processing a great amount of information in just a few words.[31] In his work *Zang Tumb Tumb*, Marinetti uses exactly this constellation of letters to refer to the sound of field guns. In the earlier "Battle: Weight + Odour,"[32] he adopts word-sound constructions like "tumbtumb" simulating a bombing, "pic pac pun pan" indicating ricochets, and "tatatata" sounding out a machine gun. The reason for the extensive use of onomatopoetic expressions is that they are not conventionally determined. They refer directly to material pre-verbal sounds. The onomatopoeias that Marinetti uses are not established as lexical items—as is the case with the verb "to purr," for example. They are not bound into the system of language; their reference is not linguistically determined; they have no established conceptual meaning; they are icons[33] that represent complex impressions like noises.[34] Thus, Marinetti ascribes a strong representative quality to onomatopoeias. For Marinetti this feature is important not only because it enables the reproduction of noncoded phenomena such as noise through written language, but also because it condenses a multitude of sensory effects in one word. Onomatopoeias constitute linguistic expressions of non-lexically coded sensations and compress these sensations in just one term.[35] This compressed language can no longer be extracted through hermeneutical reasoning, but has to be processed with minimal conscious intervention, such as when a telegraph operator transcribes Morse code or the brain brings together the flickering images of the film in a continual sequence.

CINEMATIC "PAROLE IN LIBERTÀ"

The Futurist conceptualization of this form of data compression has its origin in media technology. The technique of juxtaposing single short elements in a continuous stream is, for example, reminiscent of film.[36] More precisely, as Paul Virilio and Friedrich Kittler remark, Marinetti combines the features of film and flight surveillance.[37]

As I have mentioned above, the "Technical Manifesto of Futurist Literature" starts out with a flight scene, and Jeffrey Schnapp points out that Marinetti began to compose his manifesto two years before its publication at the flight show at Brescia.[38] In fact, Virilio's remark that flight generated a new synthetic form of perception[39] is also articulated in Futurist poetics. Marinetti states that "[j]ust as aerial speed has multiplied our knowledge of the world, the perception of analogy becomes ever more natural for man."[40] This connection between perception and flight is preserved in the speedy passing sequence of frames in film, which is still apparent in the uninterrupted sequence of *parole in libertà*. As Marinetti emphasizes,

"Poetry should be an uninterrupted sequence of new images, or it is mere anemia and greensickness."[41]

Reading Futurist poetry mimics the perception in flight, thus, the "words in freedom" must become short, and one has very little time to perceive them. The stationary objects perceived from a plane and the individual frames on film vanish faster than one can perceive the particular objects on the earth or the single photographic images in film. These elements are no longer isolated items—they merge together through the speed of the mechanical movement. Similarly, poetry is also supposed to exhibit a stream of continuously changing impressions and to compress these elements into one sensation. The poetical operation peculiar to these media technologies of abbreviation—emphasized in the "Technical Manifesto"—is "analogy."

However, Marinetti breaks with an established form of the analogy that is articulated in the structure "as A is to B, so C is to D." Marinetti states that "[a]nalogy is nothing more than the deep love that assembles distant, seemingly diverse and hostile things."[42] Analogy is for Marinetti not a logical operation, but a form of data compression that binds together—through a merely mechanical and technologically created velocity—heterogeneous material. The speed in which one element is followed by another in modern media systems forces the human perception to recognize objects and impressions distant from one another as intrinsically intertwined. Moreover, because speed as such is at the center of his concerns, Marinetti is particularly obsessed with abbreviating analogies themselves. More often than not in the "Technical Manifesto," when Marinetti says "analogy" he means "metaphor" in the sense that the analogy should be condensed in just one term. As he puts it: "To render the successive motions of an object, one must render the chain of analogies that it evokes, each condensed and concentrated into one essential word."[43] What is at stake is thus not a comprehensible logical form of communication, but a highly condensed language that cannot be unpacked through hermeneutic intervention, but must be experienced in an "intuitive" way. The decoding of these analogies is a detecting rather than an understanding of language, and it is tempting to suggest that Marinetti's analogies allude to the mechanical processing of "analog" media. This, however, does not hold, because the notion of "analog media" only emerged after the Second World War.[44]

Nonetheless, even if these analogies circumvent rational understanding, Marinetti's analog style entails an effect of estrangement or complexity that he wants to adopt in order to train the reader. "The broader their affinities, the longer will images keep their power to amaze," says Marinetti, a conviction that powers his rejection of the conventional wisdom: "One must—people say—spare the reader's capacity of wonder. Nonsense!"[45]

Thus, words in freedom are supposed to become highly compressed data packages that contain a stream of highly complex information. This is at least an objective Marinetti wants to reach. In fact, Marinetti's actual poems did not fulfill this agenda. The more or less lexical language of *parole in libertà* consists of rather simple words and onomatopoeias that designate a mostly identifiable meaning.

> Noon ¾ flutes groans dogdays bangbang alarm Gargaresch crash crackling march Clanking backpacks rifles hoofs hobnails cannons manes wheels caissons jews fritters bread singsongs cobblers whiffs glistening rheum stench cinnamon mildew flux reflux pepper brawls vermine whirlwind orange-flowers filigree misery dice chess cards jasmine + nutmeg + rose arabesque.[46]

These are the first lines of Marinetti's text "Battle Weight + Odour," published in the supplement to the "Technical Manifesto on Literature." The text presents the sensations of a military desert camp and displays these elements in a manner that alludes to prose rather than to experimental poetry. It is also possible, as Perloff claims, to understand the serialization of words as reminiscent of lists or catalogues.[47] Marinetti does not, however, employ any organizational hierarchy such as the alphabetic or numerical order for determining the sequence of words, as would be typical for a list. The words are on display as naked linguistic material and the lack of any meta-structure that controls the composition of the words—except the spatiotemporal coordination on the page that establishes a bare order of reading—supports Marinetti's intended acceleration of the reading process.

In fact, Marinetti's poetry as a mere stream of words without any morphological superstructure creates a strongly reduced form of narrative prose. From a narratological point of view, Marinetti's texts constitute a significant particularity. Since he disables the temporal structure of the verbs, his texts are bound to a presence that renders narrative categories such as the time of the narrative and the narrated time unimportant. The infinitive transcends tense, and the reader operates in a kind of eternal present. Temporal modification can only be indicated by naming the date or the daytime ("noon"). In this regard, *parole in libertà* abuses the medium of film. In film, additional information such as the insertion of a date or phrases like "5 years ago" indicates temporal changes, not the medium of film itself.

The montage of single shots and single words is based on juxtaposition and can be described in the terminology of film montage.[48] Most famously, Sergei Eisenstein outlines the distinction between two forms of montage—the "epic" and the "dramatic"—in his text "The Dramaturgy of Film Form."[49]

> According to this definition... montage is the means of unrolling an idea through single shots (the 'epic' principle).
>
> But in my view montage is not an idea composed of successive shots stuck together but an idea that DERIVES from the collision between two shots that are independent of one another (the 'dramatic' principle).[50]

The "dramatic" concept—a collision of shots from different locations, or objects, and so on—resounds in Marinetti's theory of an "analog" juxtaposition of two greatly heterogeneous terms. Nonetheless, even if on a conceptual level Marinetti is close to agitprop, most of his sequences of liberated words would be—in Eisenstein's terminology—a merely "epical" construction of the scene, which means a simple successive series of elements that construct a coherent picture. A "dramatic" conflict that brings heterogeneous material together is only to be found in a few parts of Marinetti's poems. For example,

> Avant-Garde: 20 meters battalions-ants cavalry-spiders streets-fords general-island couriers-grasshopper sands-revolutions howitzers-tribunes clouds-grills guns-martyrs shrapnel-aureoles multiplication addition division howitzer-subtraction grenade-cancellation to gush to cast landslide blocks avalanche.[51]

In this passage, words do not appear simply as a stream of linguistic material, for some elements are closely connected to others—as indicated by the hyphens. "Battalions-ants cavalry-spiders streets-fords general-island" are examples for such an analog juxtaposition of heterogeneous terms. Here, Marinetti connects two different pictures in one association. The semantic power of these combined terms is, however, not very exciting. In most cases there is not a collision, but rather a semantic congruency that binds both words together. For example, "battalions" and "ants" are two words that cause each other no irritation whatsoever.

It is, however, also not at the heart of Futurist poetics to create complex dialectical excitement. Marinetti certainly toyed with ideas that were similar to Eisenstein's aesthetics of conflict, and an interest in struggle is also essential to Futurism, as Marinetti repeatedly claims throughout his manifestos. The deep structure of Futurist poetry, however, is not geared toward a complex dialectical understanding, but toward a continuous sensual overload with data, and this is exactly what Marinetti's poems provide. Marinetti's lengthy poetic texts such as the novel *Zang*

Tumb Tumb, which is written in free-word style, are not meant to be studied in a slow, reflective reading, but to be ingested in a continuous, uninterrupted process so that they do not address the reflective understanding but the immediate intuition of the reader. Marinetti's poems mirror the uninterrupted sequence of pictures of the film that the human sensorium assembles on a sheer physiological level into a continuous movement.

SHOCK THERAPY: FUTURIST TELEGRAPHY

Marinetti attempts to create a new form of expression that corresponds to the immediacy and efficiency of communication technologies. He tries to leave the human being behind and rethinks language as a self-referential system that abuses humans only as a network consisting of multiple senders and receivers. The cinema was a technological model that showed how a nonhermeneutical and asyntactical construction of language might be possible; the technology of the telegraph serves Marinetti to further explicate his poetics. Most centrally, in the poetological text "Destruction of Syntax" Marinetti describes how somebody who just left "a zone of intense life" like the battlefield, revolution, or traffic would express his impressions:

> He will begin by brutally destroying the syntax of his speech. He wastes no time in building sentences. Punctuation and the right adjectives will mean nothing to him. He will despise subtleties and nuances of language. Breathlessly he will assault your nerves with visual, auditory, olfactory sensations, just as they come to him. The rush of steam-emotion will burst the sentence's steampipe, the valves of punctuation, and the adjectival clamp. Fistfuls of essential words in no conventional order. Sole preoccupation of the narrator, to render every vibration of his being.[52]

What Marinetti describes as the excited state of mind, and therefore as the origin of modern poetics, is a well-known pathological phenomenon in his time. In his *History of the Train Journey*, Wolfgang Schivelbusch points out the new experience endured by passengers of the nineteenth century in a train wreck, which was similar to the experience of soldiers after bombardment. Such passengers experienced psychic trauma, even in the absence of physical injury.[53] Marinetti connects these pathological disturbances to the mode of language use, arguing that a traumatized person would not be able to communicate in whole sentences, because shock undermines syntactic competence and destroys the learned schemata of communication. Expressions are no longer governed by the rules of the language but by the distress of the nervous system: the functions of the body replace the functions of the mind.

Marinetti uses this neurological model to compare human trauma to the malfunction of machines under extreme conditions by describing the linguistic structure expressed by trauma victims as an old steam engine that is not strong enough to handle the pressure of war or traffic. The "steampipe" of the engine explodes; regulation of energy is no longer possible. The machine explosion stands for the pathological human state. This metaphorical shift indicates that Marinetti's poetics is based on a hardware problem: the material devices are no longer able to process information. The vibrations produced by the steam engine or by the battlefield are much too strong for the technology through which they must pass. What is needed instead is a different, a more modern channel to transmit and to process the "vibrations" of the subject.[54] The medium that transmits information at high speed is the telegraph, and indeed the telegraph becomes according to Marinetti the proper device for articulating the experience of the soldier. As he states, the soldier "will reveal the analogical foundation of life, telegraphically, with the same economical speed that the telegraph imposes on reporters and war correspondents in their swift reportings [racconti superficiali]."[55] Here, Marinetti understands the economy of telegraph communication as a model for his poetry, and the telegraphic impulses represent the stress in the nervous system of the soldier. Just as electrical power is the precondition for the telegram, so his nervous physical conditions are the material precondition of his narration.[56] Marinetti did not develop this comparison of telecommunication and the nervous system. Psychophysical scientists from the nineteenth century also described receptive nerve cells as technological communication systems. For example, Hermann von Helmholtz compared nerves to the telegraph and William James described them as "telephones into which the material world speaks."[57] In the nineteenth century, electricity was the concept that brought the nervous system and new communication networks into proximity.

The nervous state of the soldier indicates a strategy for distributing information that is typical for Futurist poetics. As Marinetti puts it, the soldier wants to propel his impressions into the nerves of the audience. The aim is not simply to produce noise, but to establish a connection between his nervous system and that of his counterpart. Every listener should receive a maximum amount of energy, should be in the same nervous state of mind. The soldier wants to render the circuits of his and the audience's nervous system parallel. Gestures and noises that the soldier produces have a forceful sensory quality, and the audience has no choice but to suffer the stimulation inflicted by the Futurist performance. The narrator affects the audience's entire system of experience. This effect is based on the structure of the nervous network, in which the soldier wants to embed his listeners. He extends his shocked sensory network to the receiver's sensibility; ultimately, inhabiting it as a parasite and hijacking the neural circuits of the other with the soldier's disturbing irritation, this model will—as I discuss in the last chapter—return in Marinetti's radio aesthetic.

The parasitical nature of this communicative situation becomes clear by recognizing that the war report of the soldier does not yield clearly comprehensible information about the war zone. Rather, it testifies to the speed and mode of communication in modern warfare; it reproduces the parasite that occupied his nervous system. Accordingly, Futurist poetry mimics the telegram style not for the sake of representing a picture of the modern world—the telegraph—but in order to force a high-impact experience on the audience. Thus, the most striking feature of Marinetti's poetics is not the representation of battle noises, but rather an acceleration of the processing rate of language. In the quotation given above, Marinetti privileges the processing speed of the telegraph ("economical speed") over the content transmitted by the media ("racconti superficiali"). In the "Technical Manifesto of Futurist Literature," he states that language is incarcerated in and slowed down by syntax. Accordingly, Marinetti calls for a liberated language that matches the speed of aeronautics and telecommunication.

It is important to keep in mind that Marinetti's new economy of language optimizes communication in two respects. At first, *parole in libertà* are supposed to have a high impact on the recipient, and they should be perceived even in the presence of loud background noise. The force of the soldier's utterance testifies to that. Futurist poetry is a modified form of language—Marinetti reduces syntactic and morphological structures of the language—for optimizing the data stream of expressions. This reconfiguration of language not merely simplifies but rather compresses, through the use of onomatopoeias and analogies, complex sensations. It also erodes the understanding that the subject is in charge of language production. The poetic language of the traumatized soldier is no longer a controlled handling of language, but an explosive, uncontrollable fit. It is not the mind of the soldier that is speaking, but the telegraphic communication network of his nervous system that is producing the utterances. Futurist language inhabits communicative networks in a parasitical way and emerges as clear, simple, forceful, but uncontrollable eruption that spreads out by affecting its audience on a physiological level. This shock will be ideally amplified and further transmitted by the listeners of Futurist poetry to the society as a whole. In this way, Futurist poetry is designed to subvert and undermine all social interaction through its parasitical intervention. However, the signals emitted by Futurist poetry do not constitute an irritating static that contaminates communication channels, but highly compressed data packages that are supposed to rule the circuits of discourse.

COMMUNICATION AS THE PRESENCE OF NOISE: DADA POETRY

From the very beginning, sound poems and word constellations were an integral part of Dada performances. In a diary entry from March 11, 1916, Hugo Ball refers to a performance in which Richard Huelsenbeck read a poem that was later published in his book *Fantastic Prayers*.[58] In this entry Ball emphasizes the performative aspects of Huelsenbeck's reading and highlights the gestures that accompanied Huelsenbeck's words: "When he [Huelsenbeck] enters, he keeps his cane of Spanish reed in his hand and occasionally swishes it around. That excites the audience. They think he is arrogant, and he certainly looks it."[59] This remark reveals a problem particular to any inquiry into the nature of Dada poetry. Although the poems were published as printed texts, several Dada texts imply a "stage value" that cannot be appropriately translated into printed or written language—the aggravation of Huelsenbeck's gesture, for example.[60] This problem is particularly apparent in the early works of the Dadaists in Zurich; later on, Raoul Hausmann in particular—but also Huelsenbeck—aims at a poetic language that incorporates, through deictic or synesthetic strategies, such performative or multimedia effects into the medium of the written/printed text itself. However, the performativity of language that cannot be captured in writing is of special importance to Hugo Ball, and he acknowledges that the absence of a performative dimension is symptomatic of the poetry of the previous two decades.

> Nowhere are the weaknesses of a poem revealed as much as in a public reading. One thing is certain: art is joyful only as long as it has richness of life. Reciting aloud has become the touchstone of the quality of a poem for me, and I have learned (from the stage) to what extent today's literature is worked out as a problem at the desk and is made for the spectacles of the collector instead of for the ears of living human beings.[61]

The importance of an immediate linguistic effect on the audience is already indicated in this passage. Poetry is in Ball's view an acoustic medium that addresses the ears of the audience. Furthermore, poetry should not be a calculus composed at the desk, but the poem should be constructed for performance. The medium of poetry—Ball emphasizes this point frequently—is spoken language, the voice and not the written word. Although such a concentration on the acoustic channel cannot be ascribed to Dada poetry in general, the emphasis on performance and reading aloud incorporates the main goal of Dada art: to furnish an experience that intrinsically incorporates all the senses of the audience.

Such a strategy is already known from the Futurist performances—and Marinetti's poetry and Russolo's bruitism were well known in the Dada group.

> With the sentence having given way to the word, the circle around Marinetti began resolutely with "parole in libertà." They took the word out of the sentence frame (the world image) that had been thoughtlessly and automatically assigned to it, nourished the emaciated big-city vocables with light and air, and gave them back their warmth, emotion, and their original untroubled freedom. We others went a step further. We tried to give the isolated vocables the fullness of an oath, the glow of a star. And curiously enough, the magically inspired vocables conceived and gave birth to a new sentence that was not limited and confined by any conventional meaning. Touching lightly on a hundred ideas at the same time without naming them, this sentence made it possible to hear the innately playful, but hidden, irrational character of the listener; it wakened and strengthened the lowest strata of memory.[62]

Ball understands his project as an extension of the Futurist agenda. His understanding of Futurist poetics as a liberation of language fits with his own freeing of language from the slavery of conventional use. Ball's project, however, goes in a different direction than the Futurist isolation of words. The Dada poet attempts to charge isolated linguistic material with a new quality that triggers the imagination of the listeners and reactivates almost forgotten memories. As the literary scholar Eckhard Philipp points out, this attitude toward language does not so much correspond to Marinetti's poetics, but rather is inspired by Wassily Kandinsky's work *Concerning the Spiritual in Art*.[63] In Kandinsky's theory, the segmentation is not aimed at an acceleration of language as in Futurism, but rather points to a deeper, hidden sensation contained in the segmented linguistic material.

> The apt use of a word... repetition of this word, twice, three times or even more frequently, according to the need of the poem, will not only tend to intensify the inner harmony but also bring to light unsuspected spiritual properties of the word itself. Further than that, frequent repetition of a word... deprives the word of its original external meaning.[64]

Kandinsky focuses exclusively on the phonetic structure of language and is not interested in the sediments of lexical meaning—a strategy that also surfaces in Ball's poetry when he avoids the use of lexically determined expressions. For Kandinsky, poetic quality does not lie in the system of language. It is not perceived as a network for generating meaning, but rather as a sound system in which single units have a specific tone and character.

This is the origin of Dada poetics, and it is aimed at a new language that points to something like a natural or mystical certainty. In what follows, however, I will show, after a further discussion of Ball's poetry, that Dada poetics soon developed into a quite different direction; that is, it did not intend to establish a new "deeper" reference but eroded meaning. More concretely, I will discuss how the disturbance of the audience intended by the cabaret performance in Zurich becomes a feature of the texts, so that the Dada poems function as a calculus of language or linguistic material that produces its own disturbance. The parasite is nothing that invades language, but emerges in the process of reading; the parasite becomes a feature of the coded text itself.

While Futurism constructed a highly condensed language that was supposed to circulate in communication channels without any ambiguity, Dada poetry undermines any certainty. As I will argue, Dada language is subversive in the sense that it erodes any possibility of being understood. While Futurism aims at an immediate pre-hermeneutic understanding, Dada stages confusion through semiotic complexity. This becomes especially apparent when Huelsenbeck reworks the Zurich poetics in Berlin and Hausmann translates this logic into an aesthetic of medial and physiological entropy.

BALL, NIETZSCHE, AND DIONYSUS

Even if Ball can be seen as the founder of Dadaist poetics, he greatly diverges from a media aesthetic that was foundational for Futurism as well as for Berlin Dada. Ball stays distant to the Futurist obsession with an efficient and economic design of language transmission, because his own project does not focus on the efficiencies of language, but rather on addressing a language that triggers the unconscious being of the listener. While Marinetti affects the nervous system of the audience with his poetry, Ball targets the primal instincts of humankind. Therefore, the mode of transmission, the proper medium for Ball's poetry, is not the variety theater or the telegraph, but a mystical ceremony, a sacral act, a church service. Ball refers exactly to these liturgical structures in his famous report about his readings as a "magic bishop" in the Cabaret Voltaire.

> I had now completed "Labadas Gesang an die Wolken" [Labada's Song to the Clouds] at the music stand on the right and the "Elefantenkarawane" [Elephant Caravan] on the left and turned back to the middle one, flapping my wings energetically. The heavy vowel sequences and the plodding rhythm of the elephants had given me one last crescendo. But how was I to get to the end? Then I noticed that my voice had no choice but to take on the ancient cadence of priestly lamentation, that style of liturgical singing that wails in all the Catholic churches of East and West.[65]

Ball's appearances become rituals that celebrate a mystical contact with language. He intends to free the human subject from the foul language of journalism and redirects language to its ritualistic magic.[66] He acknowledges a process of filtering language that constructs a pure language, but this pure process refers back to a Dionysian experience in which the subject gets lost in a mystic sight.

> Noises (an rrrr drawn out for minutes, or crashes, or sirens, etc.) are superior to the human voice in energy.... The noises represent the background—the inarticulate, the disastrous, the decisive. The poem tries to elucidate the fact that man is swallowed up in the mechanistic process. In a typically compressed way it shows the conflict of the vox humana [human voice] with a world that threatens, ensnares, and destroys it, a world whose rhythm and noise are ineluctable.[67]

According to Ball, his sound poetry stages the fundamental tragedy of human life. The poem appears to be in contrast to the noises of the environment, but it is not the case that the poem could free human subjectivity from background noise. Rather, Ball's poetic language introduces his sound poem as a tool that displays the intrinsic battle between human subjectivity and its de-individualizing environment. The poem enables a glimpse into the Dionysian depths of human existence. Ball draws this figure of thought—that human existence is threatened by a force that covers up differences and individuality—from Nietzsche. Ball began to study Nietzsche's philosophy early and worked on a dissertation titled *Nietzsche in Basel*, but he never completed it.[68]

Nietzsche introduces the distinction between the Dionysian and Apollonian in his first major work, *Birth of Tragedy*, in which the Apollonian stands for a strict and ordered form of art, while the Dionysian signifies a chaotic, unconscious form of experience in which differences are dissolved, fundamental epistemological distinctions such as background and foreground are annihilated, and subjectivity disappears: the Dionysian stands for the sheer reality, while the Apollonian provides an epistemologically structured access to the world. Nietzsche identifies the mere recognition of the Dionysian nature with terror.

> In the same work Schopenhauer has depicted for us the tremendous terror which seizes man when he is suddenly dumbfounded by the cognitive form of phenomena because the principle of sufficient reason, in some one of its manifestations, seems to suffer an exception. If we add to this terror the blissful ecstasy that wells from the innermost depths of man, indeed of nature, at this collapse of the *principium individuationis*, we steal a glimpse into the nature of the Dionysian, which is brought home to us most intimately by the analogy of intoxication.[69]

Humankind is terrified when it loses its epistemological access to the world. Nietzsche acknowledges, however, that in ecstasy we feel a pleasure by glimpsing into such an epistemological abyss. For Nietzsche this ecstatic gaze constitutes a tentative involvement with the Dionysian principle. It is only a "glimpse into the nature of the Dionysian" and does not completely unveil the unstructured nature of the Dionysian. For Nietzsche the dialogue of the Sophoclean drama is such a medium, one that enables a glimpse into the chaotic phenomenality of nature, but also protects subjectivity from being completely lost in the chaos of the Dionysian. As Nietzsche intimates, Sophoclean language is beautiful and well organized on the surface, but in fact it refers to a dark Dionysian mythology. The clearly characterized hero in the Greek drama—which Nietzsche compares to an image projection ("Lichtbilderscheinung")—implies such a protective gaze.

> When after a forceful attempt to gaze on the sun we turn away blinded, we see dark-colored spots before our eyes, as a cure, as it were. Conversely, the bright image projections of the Sophoclean hero—in short, the Apollonion aspect of the mask—are necessary effects of a glance into the inside and terrors of nature; as it were, luminous spots to cure our eyes damaged by gruesome night.[70]

In this passage Nietzsche compares the optical phenomenon of the afterimage to the language and masks of ancient Greek drama. Nietzsche recognizes the light spots on the retina as devices that protect the eyes. In the same way as this physiological protection, the hero reveals and simultaneously conceals an insight into the raw essence of nature and tragedy. Nietzsche briefly mentions in the quoted passage that this also applies to the use of masks, and in fact Ball alludes to this Nietzschean idea in a diary entry, when he is discussing Marcel Janco's use of masks in the Cabaret Voltaire:

> Janco has made a number of masks for the new soiree, and they are more than just clever. They are reminiscent of the Japanese or ancient Greek theater, yet they are wholly modern.... Not only did the mask immediately call for a costume; it also demanded a quite definite, passionate gesture, bordering on madness.... What fascinates us all about the masks is that they represent not human characters and passions, but characters and passions that are larger than life. The horror of our time, the paralyzing background of events, is made visible.[71]

In a way that is similar to Nietzsche (who also alludes to the protective function of masks), Ball refers to the Greek and ritualistic context of mask use and recognizes masks as tools that give insight into the horrors of time and into the background of life. On the one hand, the masks demand from the actor a certain gesture that borders on madness. In Nietzschean terms, it exposes them to a Dionysian experience. On the other hand, the masks demonstrate passion and characters that are "larger than life" and can be understood in analogy to the determinacy and clarity of the hero in the Sophoclean drama. The playing with masks mediates a Dionysian experience. This mediation now makes it possible to approach the "paralyzing background of life," because it is constantly backed up by a structuring medium.

Ball's sound poetry operates on the same level as Sophocles's language or Janco's masks. Ball states that the poem shows that human existence is swallowed up by a noisy and industrialized world. Now, the sound poems, articulated by a human being, do not simply duplicate the noisy background, but indicate for Ball the residues of human individuality that are still not devoured by mechanistic processes that contaminate language in modernity.

Ball's attitude toward language stands in contrast to modern forms of mechanically reproduced information. He addresses the noises of sirens—one might include the noises of phonographic media—as a power that is capable of overwriting human articulation.[72] He identifies journalism as spoiled language[73] and condemns the silent mode of reading as inappropriate for poetry. The noise emitted by modern media technology constitutes for him a threat and not, as for Marinetti, a field of inspiration. Ball's poetry, however, contrasts clearly not only with the Futurist technology of poetic language, but also with Berlin Dada—especially with the poetics of Huelsenbeck and Hausmann. Ball's linguistic mysticism still wants to reconstruct a kind of Ur-language, while the poetry of Berlin Dada aims not to construct, but to disturb in order to abuse the structure of speech produced by mass media. Ball tried to undermine the aleatoric rules of the discourse network of 1900 and attempted to exclude disturbance with its parasitic implications from his poetry. However, Huelsenbeck soon turned this poetics into a parasitical project that abused the possibilities of modern typography, and one of his first attempts was the printed representation of Ball's famous poem "Karawane."

Huelsenbeck's Poetics of Error

The poetic procedures that Ball describes in his diary are closely linked to the actual moment of performance. Ball emphasized that his poetry is not designed as written literature but as an oral gesture, which targets what Kandinsky called the "inner" sound of language. From this perspective, it is surprising that Ball's poems—especially his most famous poem "Karawane"—were published in Dada anthologies as texts.

There is an explanation for that, at least for "Karawane": As it was published in the 1920 *Dada Almanach*, this text is much more Huelsenbeck's creation than Ball's. At that time, Ball actually had left the Dada movement, and the poem constitutes a good point of departure for understanding the media aesthetics of Dada poetry. I suggest reading this poem as a first attempt at Dadaist poetry, that is, a parasitic abuse of the semantic and semiotic structures of language—one that inspired the work of Huelsenbeck and Hausmann—rather than as the exercise in language mysticism for which Ball's poetics stands.

In fact, the poem does not simply expose the reader to a completely random collection of sounds and words, but organizes the lyric material so that a meaningful interpretation of the poem is not problematic. Most importantly, the title "Karawane" (the only clearly recognizable word of the poem), which denotes an oriental caravan scene, defines a frame of reference for the following letter constellations. Such oriental themes were quite typical for Dada and the reference to oriental or African culture functioned to legitimize the use of an estranging language.[74] "Karawane," however, does not simply imitate the sounds of a tribal language; it also depicts an entire scenario in an African landscape.

The title of the poem, "Karawane," functions as a referential frame that forms an expectation in the reader. The cue to an oriental scene is immediately satisfied by the first word of the poem, "jolifanto," which brings to mind "elephant." The expressions "russula" ("Rüssel" means "trunk" in German) "tumba," and "ü üü ü" support such an interpretation. The other sound constellations evoke pictures of falling cargo ("falli bambla"),

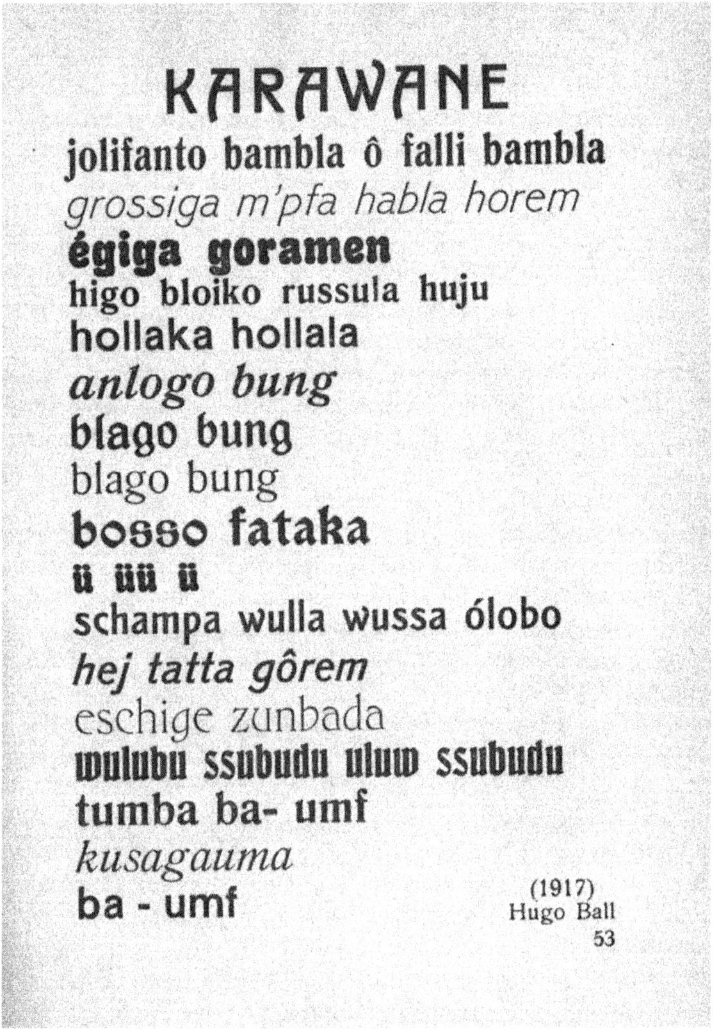

KARAWANE

jolifanto bambla ô falli bambla
grossiga m'pfa habla horem
égiga goramen
higo bloiko russula huju
hollaka hollala
anlogo bung
blago bung
blago bung
bosso fataka
ü üü ü
schampa wulla wussa ólobo
hej tatta gôrem
eschige zunbada
wulubu ssubudu uluw ssubudu
tumba ba- umf
kusagauma
ba - umf

(1917)
Hugo Ball
53

Figure 2.1   The poem "Karawane" from Richard Huelsenbeck, *Dada Almanach* (1920)

workers and travelers shouting at each other ("hollala"), or the mighty steps of the elephants ("ba-umf"). "Habla" could be associated with the Spanish verb for speaking. "Bosso" could refer to sounds of an African language or signify "boss." Whatever the associations might be, there is no point at which this picture of an African landscape is systematically interrupted, for any part of the poem can be integrated into the associations. The only inconsistency is constructed by the typesetting (see figure 2.1), which changes from line to line but does not perform any connotative function.

The poem is completely stage-able in an aural performance. It does not contain any nonphonetic expression, the hyphen in "ba-umf," for example, indicates a pause or that "a-u" should not be pronounced as a diphthong. There are no punctuation marks such as ";:'." that have an exclusively syntactic function and no phonetic representation.[75]

Ball's text presents a surprisingly consistent picture that generates a somewhat understandable text by means of connotative and onomatopoetic strategies.[76] The only disturbing element is the continually changing typography. The wild mixture of different fonts does not underline, but also does not disturb the reading process. It just hangs onto the words of the poem and irritates the reader's expectation. This little, in this case almost merely decorative, playfulness will be transformed into a strategic irritation of the reader. Huelsenbeck's poems from the Zurich time already show an increasingly scattered and subversive handling of language. They exploit the associative, self-referential, and phonetic qualities of language for the purpose of undermining the expectations of the audience. Disturbance creeps into these poems as a parasite that constantly irritates reading processes on an almost subcutaneous level, a strategy that he expanded in his comprehensive collection of poems *Fantastic Prayers*.

Huelsenbeck tells the story that, when he proudly presented *Fantastic Prayers* to his mother, she burst into tears and declared the poems complete nonsense.[77] This reaction mirrors in some ways the general reception of this first published collection of Dada poems. Huelsenbeck was quite disappointed with the reactions to his poems and confessed that his poetry did not have a great impact either on its audience or on other writers.[78] Eckhard Philipp remarks that this disappointment reflects on the reception of the printed version rather than the effect the poems had when performed. Philipp further contests—similar to my comments on Ball's poetry—that Huelsenbeck's poems cannot be interpreted as texts that were supposed to be read silently, and that the only appropriate way to approach these texts would be to reconstruct the manner of their performance. As evidence for his claim, Philipp refers to passages in which the printed text of Huelsenbeck's poems imitates the response of the audience.[79] I agree with the observation that Huelsenbeck incorporates elements that imitate the performance in the text, but I draw a different conclusion. The performative elements in the text indicate to me that Huelsenbeck tries to construct poems that have a "stage-effect," even when read silently. The first poem of *Fantastic Prayers* makes this intention evident:

> Ebene
> Schweinsblase Kesselpauke Zinnober cru cru cru
> Theosophia pneumatica
> die große Geistkunst = poème bruitiste aufgeführt
> zum erstenmal durch Richard Huelsenbeck DaDA
> oder oder birribum birribum saust der Ochs im Kreis herum oder
> Bohraufträge für leichte Wurfminen-Rohlinge 7,6 cm Chauceur
>   Beteiligung Soda calc. 98/100%
>   Vorstehhund dam birridamo hola di funga qualla di mango
> Damai da dai umbala damo
> Brrs pffi commencer Abrr Kpppi commence Anfang Anfang...[80]

These are the first lines of the poem "Ebene." In contrast to the other poems of *Fantastic Prayers*, the title is not indicated by a bold typeface. The title is rather implied in the first line of the poem. The lines appear as a random collage of word material that refers for example to military industries or the "philosophical background" of Dada ("Theosophia pneumatica").[81] In a more careful reading, one can see that the first lines define the setting and constitute a self-referential gesture. "Ebene" can be interpreted as the stage of the performance, the pig bladder is part of the drum (it is the drum-head), and "Zinnober" could indicate the color of the curtain. Now, what is about to happen is a "theosophia pneumatica," that is "die große Geisteskunst = poeme bruitiste" that is staged by Huelsenbeck, right here, right there ("DaDA"). The word "dada" is now used as a deictic gesture and indicates the place of performance ("da" means in German "there"). Philipp would probably argue that it indicates the historical setting of the Cabaret Voltaire. I contend, however, that "dada" points to the actual text in front of the reader.

After the first lines, the textual presentation of the stage ends and the performance starts "commence Anfang Anfang."[82] Now, a different poetic strategy becomes dominant: the central aesthetic operation of the poem is an alternation between expressions that connote some meaning and word constellations that appear as mere nonsense. For example,

> Arbeit
> Arbeit
> brä brä brä brä brä brä brä brä brä
> sokobauno sokobauno sokobauno
> Schikaneder Schikaneder Schikaneder[83]

The first two lines consist of two lexical German words ("Arbeit"/"work"), while the third line is not a meaningful word, but could be read as an onomatopoetic reference to work or to a child's screaming (or some such).

The fourth line appears as a word, but it is no word of the German language. "Schikaneder" seems to be a similar case, and its reading as an actual reference to the author of the libretto of *The Magic Flute*, Emanuel Schikaneder, does not really give this line more sense. What is important to notice is that this poem plays with the connotative quality of language in a way that is quite different from Ball's "Karawane." While the title "Karawane" allows the reader to integrate the word material in a unified experience, the poem "Ebene" operates with a calculus in which a connotative field (such as work) is evoked, only to be disturbed thereafter. This disturbance reaches the point where the reader cannot decide whether an element carries meaning or not. Meaning becomes a vicious parasite; every word could be interpreted either as a disturbance or a meaningful element. Noise and message can no longer be differentiated from one another. The following line represents another example of this phenomenon:

Balu blau immer blau Blumenpoet vergilbt das Geweih[84]

It is impossible to decide whether "balu" is a typographic error or not. It is not clear if it is supposed to mean "blau" (blue) or to coin the word "balu." At this point, intended and corrupted language cannot be distinguished from each other. But the consistency, which the poem preserves, is that all the parts of the poem stay within the limits of performability—that is, the poem can be performed orally without leaving out any of its elements.

Huelsenbeck's text does not provide an understandable message. It strategically disturbs the reader's expectations. The reader is forced to make decisions on whether an element is or is not meaningful. The poem, however, does not give an ultimate answer to the correctness of the decision of the reader and leaves him or her in a limbo of undecidability instead. The logic of the parasite fully enters into Dada poetry. Meaning itself becomes a parasite that cannot be located in the poem. The poem becomes a complex calculus of the presence and absence of meaning, a development Berlin Dada expands in its typographic design.

"DER DADA 1"

While early Dada poetry had its place on the stage of the cabaret or in public manifestations, in Berlin (with its increasing variety of printed publications) Dada poetry more and more became a textual phenomenon. Dada artists were active in modernist and expressionist journals such as *Der Gegner* or *Die Aktion*. Probably the most eminent publication was the journal *Der Dada*, edited for the most part by Hausmann and

Figure 2.2 Front page of *Der Dada 1* (1919)

Baader. The first issue of *Der Dada* leads with a title page that demonstrates the semiotic complexity of Dada poetry and typographic design (see figure 2.2).

Visually, the title page is relatively simple. In contrast to later issues of *Der Dada*, the front page is not used solely for the presentation of a complex photomontage, but rather gathers together different typographic elements and only some pictorial ones. It is difficult to decide whether the title page functions only as a cover—like a magazine title page—or already provides the articles (in the manner of the front page of a newspaper). Baader and Hausmann juxtapose the title of the magazine, the price, a visual poem, a brief article, and a short announcement. Each of these elements has an individual character. Yet they form a collage that imitates the visual appearance of a newspaper. The poem "dadadegie" in the center of the page gives a more precise indication of the complex nature of these constructions (see figure 2.2). This poem repeats the structure of the entire page, in that it combines heterogeneous semiotic material, iconic pictures, numbers, Latin and Hebrew letters, as well as discursive and formulaic writing. On a semantic and semiotic level, this collage generates different paths of reading the entire layout.

In his book *Raoul Hausmann. Dadasoph*, Michael Erlhoff interprets elements of the poem. The title "dadadegie" alludes to an elegy, which corresponds in its mourning character to the interjection "Ach" that stands in the center of the poem. The calculus of 13 divided by 7 is correct, "3,14159" is the number pi to five decimal places, the row of numbers constitutes just the shuffled period from 1 to 11, and the stamp of the "Zuchtverein"/"breeding association" in the upper left corner corresponds to the cow in the lower right corner of the page. As Michael Erlhoff acknowledges, the semiotic material provides several possibilities for an associative interpretation, but no interpretation will achieve a coherent result that is wholly satisfying.[85]

One is not able to construct a definite interpretation out of the textual collage; confronted by the page, the reader sighs ("Ach"). Erlhoff sees the reason for this in the pictorial character of the text.[86] The poem is a hybrid constituted by pictorial and textual elements. This mixture exposes the reader to a disordered arrangement of elements that cannot simply be read, because the whole lacks a determined textual orientation. The poem can also not simply be regarded as a picture, because the elements have both a pictorial function and a range of other semiotic functions, too. The various numbers disseminated all over the page invite a search for numerical patterns that goes beyond any merely pictorial function of the signs. Through this juxtaposition of various semiotic systems, the text challenges established modes of reading and generates through its intertwining of pictorial and textual elements a variegated semiotic surface that simultaneously presents the medial qualities of numerical, pictorial, and alphabetic systems.

In her essay "Writing, Notational Iconicity, Calculus: On Writing as a Cultural Technique,"[87] the German philosopher Sybille Krämer points out that writing is mostly understood as a representation of continuous speech, and the use of writing as a cultural technique makes us forget that "texts, like images, depict a two-dimensional, visible order in space."[88] Furthermore, Krämer acknowledges that every kind of writing—and not only formal symbolic systems—has an operational function through which symbols can be manipulated. The most important feature for operational writing is the space of writing. The space in linear writing indicates semiotic structures that do not correspond to phonetic qualities. In calculus, the two-dimensional space is not simply the writing ground, but also a matrix through which every element takes on a special function or value in relationship to the other elements on the page. Likewise, the Occidental form of writing with its determined orientation (to be read left to right, top to bottom), lines, and pages has operational features that make it possible not only to read coherently, but also to scan the text for single passages by using the matrix of lines.

Hausmann and Baader's poem "dadadegie" presents to the reader different operational forms of writing blended one into another. It juxtaposes incongruent sign systems such as Latin and Hebrew letters,[89] stamps, and a calculus. Erlhoff is quite right to observe that this construction is so irritating precisely because it does not operate primarily on a pictorial level. He contends that a photomontage as an iconic medium is still able to integrate great antagonism into one frame. The arrangement of different pictures from advertisements and newspapers may appear completely chaotic, but in fact it produces a coherent pictorial impression. The combination of different forms of writing leaves the reader helpless, because all the elements cannot be integrated into one uniform process of decoding. It remains difficult to decide whether to perceive the elements as pictures or as symbols. As Michel Serres acknowledges, the parasite is not placed in a specific location, but occupies the relationships of a system.[90] Accordingly, the disturbing effect of this poem is generated through a strategic perturbation of the relationship of the single semiotic elements to one another.

The importance of the poem lies not in its content, not in its connotations or denotations, but rather in the meta-semiotic quality of the constellation. The signs refer neither to a meaning nor to other signs. Instead, they refer to their own mode of operation. They indicate the structure of the writing ground. The task of the reader is not to decode a meaning, but rather to experience and travel through the page. The signs on the page do not have the capacity to involve the reader in contemplative reading, but constantly irritate the reader in a parasitic manner. Thus, Walter Benjamin's remark in the artwork essay that Dada poetry opposes contemplation is certainly right in reference to "dadadegie."[91] What the reader actually experiences is the material pre-condition of writing, the operational matrix of the page. This game starts immediately. In the first place, the reader has to orient the page correctly—not an easy job given the competing axes that confront the reader. Then, the biggest-sized characters of the page ("Ach" and the row of "3") support the reading direction of the Latin alphabet, but this impression becomes distorted by the vertical row of letters on the right side and by the two-dimensional quality of the calculus. In this way, the signs distort the reading process and draw attention to their semiotic and not to their semantic qualities.

The function of the signs in "dadadegie" does not lie in their representational quality, but in their capacity to disturb the reading process. This operation applies not only to the poem "dadadegie," but also to the title page as a whole. Certainly, the text in the lower left corner can be read as an actual text, but the "wrong" orientation of the poem "dadadegie" generates a distortion that forces the reader to reconsider the entire layout of the page. Irritation accompanies the reading process as a greedy parasite that feeds on the reader's desire to discover meaning.

Hausmann's Body Poetics

In the year 1918, Raoul Hausmann designed two "poster poems," "fmsbw" and "OFFEA," together with the typesetter Robert Barteset.[92] Whereas the (probably) first poem "fmsbw" can easily be quoted with a standard set of typographic signs ("fmsbwtözäupggiv-..?mü"[93]), the (probably) second poem incorporates a graphical element, namely a pointing finger that is not a simple letter or punctuation mark (see figure 2.3). However, what both poems have in common is that they consist of a random selection of letters from a letter box. Hausmann conveys the excitement of this experiment with the visual qualities of letters in his autobiography. "After all, letter poems are there to be seen, but also to be looked at—so why not make posters out of them?... That, Dunnerschlag, had been unheard of."[94] Behind this excitement stood probably an insight into the intermedial structure of writing: signs are able to produce meaning, but also have an aesthetic side, and the "poster poems" have precisely this capacity to demonstrate the aesthetic dimension of the signs. The reference that is contained in symbolic sign systems is distorted by the random selection of the individual letters, as Rudolf Kuenzli points out in his essay on Dada semiotics:[95] "If they [the poems] have a semiotic function, then these poster poems seem to have a metasemiotic one: the series of arbitrarily chosen letters points to the arbitrariness of any letter sequence."[96] The poems are literally nonsense, because they do not carry meaning; they merely display a random series of letters. Yet this is not completely true. The arbitrariness does not mean that the poems do not establish a certain structure. In fact, both poems carry information about the experimental

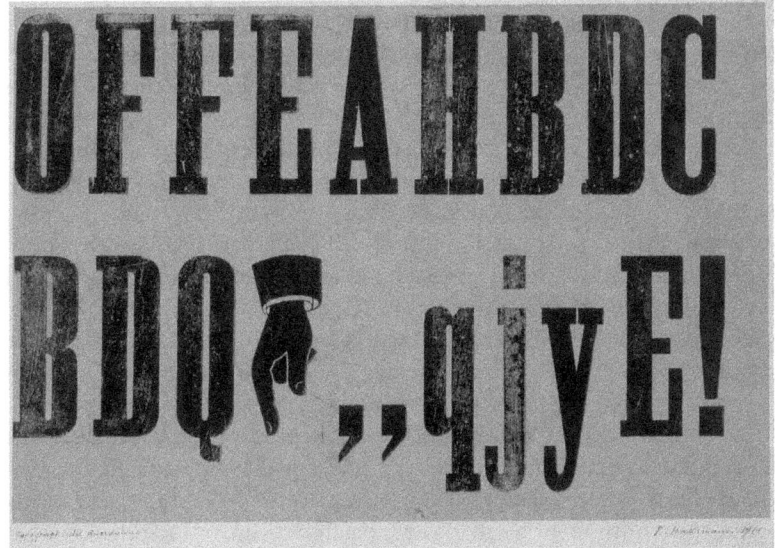

Figure 2.3 "OFFEA" by Raoul Hausmann (1918), Berlinische Galerie

setting in which they were created. They refer to the information source that Hausmann used in order to generate the letter constellations. This becomes clearer when one compares the two poems. Hausmann gives no information about "fmsbwtözäu" in his autobiographical report; nonetheless it is probably correct to assume that "fmsbwtözäu" was the first poem, because the set of used signs seems to be more limited than in the second poem. The first poem uses only the lower case, and seems to be a simpler trial run. The typographical set of the second poster appears to be more extended, because the poem contains lower and upper cases and other typographical features such as the pointing hand.

What the poem indicates is not some determined meaning, but the structure of the typographic medium when it is operated in a purely mechanical fashion without cognitive intervention. It is important to note that this strategy produces not only a merely random period of letters, but also a statistical representation of the information source. This means that the letter sequence is dependent on the frequency of the signs in the letter box. There is a high probability that letters, which are in the box in a greater number, are selected more often. Accordingly, because "F," "B," and "m" appear in the poem more often than—for example—the letter "y," we know that they are comparably frequent letters in the letter box.[97]

This exploration of the statistical structure of language is an important development in Hausmann's poetics that points toward an investigation of the medial function of language. Such a mechanical construction, however, does not correspond to an understanding of language as a tool that is supposed to convey meaning, but rather alludes to media engineering and cryptography.[98]

Given that the enemy could easily intercept radio signals and telegraph lines, electronic communication networks created a new demand for security in war. In this way, the central question of cryptography arose: how is it possible to increase the probability that an interceptor cannot decode a transmitted message? In this regard, the cryptographer's natural enemy was the statistical deep structure of language. In every language, certain letters or components are used more frequently than others. The frequency of a letter is therefore a sign contributing to the decoding of an encoded message.[99] Hausmann exploits this character of language and media in general. His "poster poems" represent the deep structure of the information source that he was using.[100] Marshall McLuhan's dictum that "the medium is the message" takes on its most literal meaning here: the poems show nothing other than the medial structure of their information source.

This interpretation is complicated by the fact that Hausmann emphasizes the multimedia quality of the poster poems: "Big, visible letters, thus letter poems, even more than that, I immediately said to myself: optophonetic! Different sizes for different emphases! Consonants and vowels, this croaks and yodels very well! Of course, these letter-poster-poems had to be sung! DA! DADA!"[101] Hausmann realizes that these poems animate a performance and that the aesthetic quality of the letters corresponds to a certain mode of acoustic utterance. The Dadaist recognizes a synesthetic—or, in his terminology, *optophonetic*—effect in these texts. To me, however, this claim seems like wishful thinking. In fact, the optophonetic feature—that is, the simultaneous presence of a visual and an acoustic impression—cannot be ascribed to the poems as their essential quality: the poems expose a medium of the written language—the letter case—containing signs that cannot be pronounced (such as the pointing finger) and that, therefore, have no immediate acoustic representation. With the claim that the poems would be able to provoke an acoustic sensation, Hausmann alludes to his separate and rather grander project of developing an optophonetic art (which I discuss more thoroughly in Chapter 5). The "poster poems," however, have an important quality. They explore the configuration of language on a very technical level, something that Hausmann extends in his poetics toward the exploration of human articulation in general.

In contrast to the "poster poems," the poem "Kp'erioum" is clearly a sound poem in which the arrangement of letters, indeed the entire

POETIC MEDIA EFFECTS 77

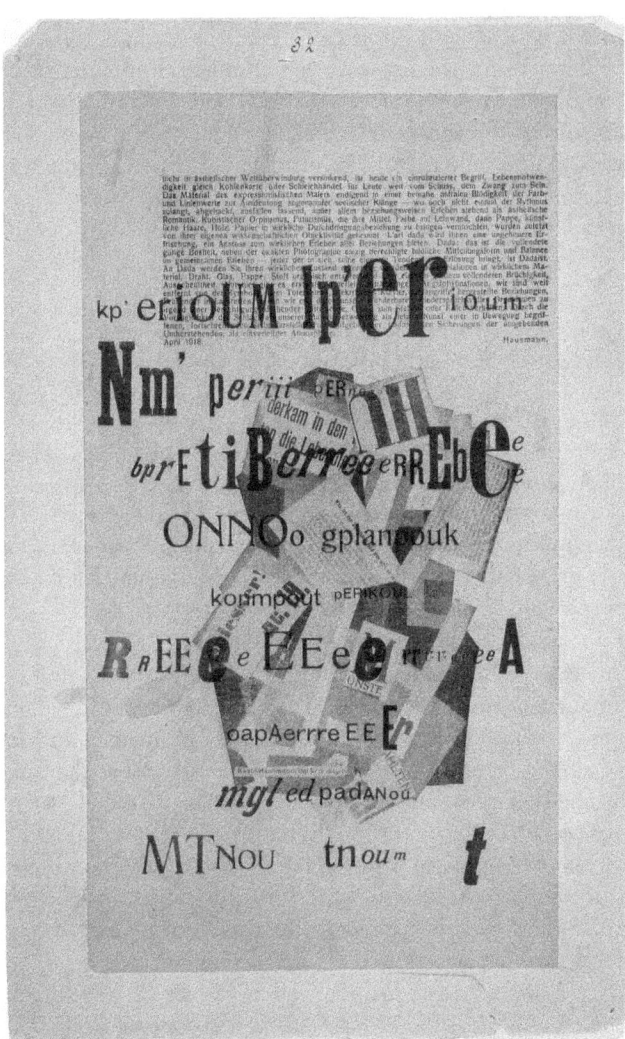

Figure 2.4 "K'perioum" by Raoul Hausmann (1920), Berlinische Galerie

typesetting, serves as a notation for the phonetic quality of each sign (see figure 2.4). In contrast to "dadadegie" the signs do not disturb the process of reading or refer, keeping "fmsbwtözäu" in mind, to the experimental setting in which they were produced. Instead, the text functions as a notation, the sizes of the letters correlate to a phonetic value—the bigger the letter, the louder its articulation. At first sight, this character of the poem as a phonetic transcription suggests that the text is written primarily for an oral performance, but Erlhoff emphasizes in his interpretation of the poem that Hausmann tried to convey volume and potential pronunciations through the optical structure of the texts. Erlhoff argues that the reader was supposed to hear the poems when he or she saw them.[102]

While Erlhoff emphasizes the primacy of written notation, Peter Demetz claims in his essay "Varieties of Phonetic Poetry"[103] that this notational factor is not of great importance to Hausmann's optophonetic poems:

> We do not have many scores because Hausmann rarely intended to transform his sounds into graphemes; in striking contrast to Schwitters, who works on his sound texts with great care and uses many signs usually found in musical scores, Hausmann never bothered systematically to preserve his recitations in print. Perhaps I should say that while seemingly belonging to the early sound poets of our century, he was not really one of them; to him, I suspect, it was not the sound and the sound strings that mattered but only the way in which the sounds were produced by the human apparatus of articulation. Ultimately it was not the phonetic element which was of concern to him, but the exercise of the articulatory motor impulse in a physiological sense.[104]

For Demetz, the actual text is simply not the central concern of Hausmann's poetics. Demetz does not understand Hausmann's optophonetics as art but as a vibratory exercise, an exploration of the body. The poem exposes the reader to an exercise rather than to a readable text. The text becomes an irritating parasite that challenges human vocal cords. As Demetz argues, the function of the poem does not lie in a signification, but rather in physical training: the letter combinations do not carry meaning—indeed, they are very difficult to articulate. I agree with Demetz that the actual form of the spoken or performed poem was not of much importance, but that the physiological effect it evokes is decisive.[105] In this context, Demetz refers to one of Hausmann's most problematic manifestos, the "Manifesto of the Law of Sound" ("Manifest von der Gesetzmäßigkeit des Lautes").[106] With its title, this manifesto suggests a poetological content. But the text appears as a nonsense that does not have anything to do with poems or literature. The only thematic thread in this manifesto is smoking, and Demetz interprets this manifesto as a meditation on breathing and articulation: "to him [Hausmann] smoking is a productive emblem of how breathing is disciplined in a recurrent rhythm."[107] Smoking serves here as metaphor for a disciplined and rhythmic way of breathing.[108]

Furthermore, Demetz recognizes in Hausmann's poetry a "physiotherapeutic" rather than poetic effect. As Demetz notes, "Hausmann pushes his experiments beyond the confines of literature to anthropology or physiotherapy."[109] Indeed, Demetz's guess that Hausmann adapts some kind of yogic breathing is quite plausible. In a typescript from 1924 ("Turel stellte an den Anfang seines Vortrages 'Geometrie des Lebens' "),[110] Hausmann refers to *The Science of Breath and the Philosophy of the Tattvas*,[111] a book that deals with a cosmic theory of yogic breathing.

Going beyond Demetz's analysis, I would like to emphasize that this corporeal feature of Hausmann's poetics—through which poems become a physiological training—corresponds to the semiotic experiments in *Dada* 1 and to "fmsbw" in the sense that the texts are not used to convey a specific meaning, but to expose the medial pre-conditions of poetic production. "dadadegie" indicates the function of different semiotic systems, the "poster poems" expose structures of print, and—according to Demetz—"k'perioum" points to the vibratory system. What all these texts have in common is that they refer to medial qualities through disturbing their own medium. They all perturb the act of reading, silent or aloud. The fact that the version of "kp'erioum" planned for the never-published collection of Dadaistic texts *Dadaco* was printed on top of a text and a collage underlines this intent of irritation and disturbance (see figure 2.4). By disturbing receptive and productive processes in such way, Hausmann confronts the readers with the internal features of speech and writing that they would not consciously perceive if they were not be perturbed. Here, noise sensitizes the audience to the semiotic complexity of the mass-medial world that surrounds them. It further can be read as a didactic lesson in the logic of the parasite. The poems produce in a physiolinguistic feedback loop the experience that in complex communication parasites emerge. These parasites, however, are not external intruders, but created by the process of articulation itself.

Poetry and Media Parasites

Dada and Futurist language is parasitical in the sense that it abused media technologies from modern typography to cinema and the telegraph and used the human subject merely as a host to send and relay his or her poetic messages/physical impulses. The text that demonstrates this exploitative logic that is not concerned with representation but with a feedback of media itself is Tristan Tzara's "To make a Dadaist Poem":

> To make a Dadaist Poem
> Take a newspaper.
> Take some scissors
> Choose from this paper an article of the
>   Length you want to make your poem.

> Cut out the article.
> Next carefully cut out each of the words
>   That makes up this article and put
>   Them all in a bag.
> Shake gently.
> Next take out each cutting one after the other.
> Copy omnisciently in the order in which they
>   left the bag.
> The poem will resemble you.
> And there you are—an infinitely original
>   Author of charming sensibility,
> Even though unappreciated by the vulgar herd.[112]

Tzara explicitly mocks poetic expression that is grounded in a subjective sensitivity. He claims that Dada poetry created through mere random selections will represent the author's subjectivity. In fact, such a poem does not exhibit anything like a subjective expression, or a specific message. It is a sheer feedback loop extracted from and injected back into mass communication. This example displays clearly the double strategy of Dada poetics. The Dadaists intended to generate a form of poetic expression, and they strategically abused a new nonsemantic understanding of language that became accessible through modern media-technological channels, which no longer processed meaning. The distortion, interruption, and randomization of communicative patterns foreground the materiality of communication. Dada poetry participates as a parasite in the discourse networks of its time and becomes a sheer media effect.

In a way that is comparable to Tzara's experiment, Marinetti's poetics aims to liberate words from their static prison of syntax. Both understand the words of language as elements that can be freely manipulated and reassembled. Marinetti, in contrast, does not intend to reflect critically on the communication systems of modernity, and rather wants to assimilate lyrical language to the processing rate of modern media technology. He does not embrace the parasitic logic of complexity in the same ways as Dada. While Dada invites the parasite, Marinetti aims at a linguistic code that bans parasitic intrusion from communication, but abuses the human and technological communication networks as its host, thereby conflating human and technical modes of communication.

CHAPTER 3

PARASITIC MEDIA

THE AVANT-GARDE FLOURISHED IN A TIME when the distribution of mass-produced visual material exploded. This development began with the invention of photography in the nineteenth century by the French inventor Nicéphore Niépce and the French artist and physicist Louis-Jacques-Mandé Daguerre. It was continued through the chronophotographic instruments of the French physiologist Étienne-Jules Marey and the British American photographer Eadweard Muybridge for recording movements, and found its mass media distribution through the cinema and modern illustrated journals. As the media theorist Friedrich Kittler pointed out, photography enabled this new, modern culture of visuality, because it was the first medium to store visual data and to make it transmissible.[1] Visual material, as Walter Benjamin highlighted in his artwork essay, could now not only be stored but also taken from its context and reproduced independent of its origin.[2] Paul Virilio emphasized that this mobility of the image coincided with a military mobilization of optical media and that the increasing presence of cameras produced and extended the surveillance of the battlefield as well as the society as a whole.[3]

The avant-garde profited from both sides of such a mobilization of images. They used the ability of the photograph to decontexualize information, and they employed the possibility of juxtaposing visual material as a form of representing and surveying the society. Marinetti's typographic poems, such as "Synthesis of the War,"[4] are nothing more than topographic diagrams visualizing the process of warfare, and the Dada collage displays a simultaneous representation of the society from a panoptic point of view.

Especially in regard to photography, Futurism as well as Dada feasted again as parasites on the new products of technological media. Further, the abuse of visual media, where the avant-garde drew from photography, science, warfare, and cinema, created a new, technologically constructed perspective on reality. The insight to link collage to media technologies, however, is not new. In the artwork essay, Benjamin already brings collage and the medium of film in close proximity. He recognizes in the Dada collage a low-tech version and even predecessor to the medium of film.[5] This statement, however, is odd, because film started reassembling raw material significantly earlier than Dada. The French trickster Georges Méliès was among the first to explore the creative potential of the moving images in his variety theater that the brothers Lumière, the famous inventors of the cinema, mostly used for the documentary purpose of screening people leaving the factory or a train arriving at a station. However, although Benjamin's description is highly problematic in regard to historiography, it clearly points out the similarities between film and collage. These media use indexical material that is external to their mediality; they are parasitic media. They depend on the reality that they reproduce as a host. If an outside object did not exist, photographic media would not be able to display anything. When we follow Kittler's claim that film belongs to the realm of the imaginary,[6] we can see even clearer the parasitic character of these media. With its ability to feed from the discourses of reality, film transforms them and creates a new illusionary construction where connections between previously unconnected elements emerge—without this parasitic abuse of traces of the real, no illusion could be created through film.

This parasitic nature of the photographic image was not only celebrated by the avant-garde. It is true that the Dadaists greatly embraced this parasitic character of the photograph in their montages, but Futurism rejected the photographic medium at first, and only absorbed it in the canon of Futurist arts after the brothers Anton Giulio and Arturo Bragaglia combined the tracing of motions that was developed in the ergonomic sciences of the nineteenth century with the instantaneous representation of photography.[7] In fact, Umberto Boccioni as the leader of the Futurist painters intended to establish an aesthetic that distanced itself from photography, because it was not concerned with a static representation, but aimed at a dynamic involvement of the spectator into the energy of an image. The Futurists tried to paint their famous "lines of force," which were not sheer representations of the speed and force of the modern world, but proposed to transcend the frame of the picture and to affect the spectators. They not only represented movement but also wanted to make the spectator move. The brothers Bragaglia were able to reconcile Futurism with photography because they made precisely this logic central to their art.

The early Dada experiments with film show that also this movement had its problems with the parasitic nature of photographic media. Painters such as Hans Richter and Viking Eggeling created the absolute film as a self-referential medium that tried to cut itself off from the representation of traces of the real. However, especially Richter's films departed from this approach in the late twenties and ended up embracing a Dada aesthetic of montage, in which a new world was constructed through reassembling fragmented traces of reality. Berlin Dada was especially explicit in creating such a form of visuality that fed as parasites from the images of mass media. I will discuss this parasitic abuse of the new mass media circuits of photojournalism by focusing on Hannah Höch's collage *Dada Rundschau* and the work of John Heartfield. I will demonstrate that Höch creates a new panoptic view on society that generates in a self-referential gesture not a representation of the reality of modernity but a simulacrum of mass media discourses, and show how Heartfield creates a visual subversion in a mimicry that abuses established visual codes.

THE FUTURIST REJECTION OF PHOTOGRAPHY

As Giovanni Lista outlined in his book *Futurism and Photography*[8] and Gernaldo Regnani argued in his essay "Futurism and Photography,"[9] Futurists used photographs from the very beginning as means of propaganda. There are numerous pictures that represent Marinetti and his fellow Futurists in heroic poses. However, Lista points out that the Futurists already viewed these images critically; Marinetti and his friends did not greatly appreciate the potential of photography to display every aspect of human life, including intimate moments that might show weaknesses and sentimentalities. Thus, they hardly used snapshots, but hung on to a rather simplistic art of the portrait, in which they could show themselves in a way they liked to be viewed—that is, as reckless outcasts in elegant suits or military uniforms. As Lista shows, photography became an important medium for Futurist propaganda mostly because of its technical reproducibility, and the Futurists made use of photographs as motives for postcards that could easily be distributed; however, they were very reluctant to turn it into a medium of original Futurist expression.[10]

Futurists were apparently aware of the fact that the photographs of stylized heroic postures were hardly at the core of their ideas for new forms of expression, and it took quite some time until Marinetti sanctioned the inclusion of photography in the canon of Futurist art. Marinetti published such a manifesto, which the photographer Tato coauthored, in 1930.[11] This manifesto finally acknowledged the works of the brothers Bragaglia, devised a program of photography as a nonrepresentative art, and ended with an almost enigmatic formulation: "All of these studies aim at extending the possibilities of the science of photography into pure art and at automatically assisting its development in the fields of physics, chemistry, and war."[12] This brief assessment summarizes the promise that Marinetti saw in this medium.

The statement shows clearly that Marinetti recognized that photography was not solely developed as a medium of artistic production, but also contributed to scientific inquiry. This is especially true for the photographic registration of movements. After Niépce and Daguerre established the foundation for photographic reproduction, this medium got into physiological laboratories, where Marey and Muybridge constructed devices for recording movements in freeze frames (see figure 3.1).[13] The goal of this chronophotography was thus to slow down the dynamic of life and to condense it in a form that was accessible to scientific inquiry. This agenda was certainly not acceptable for Futurism. In the "Technical Manifesto of Literature," Marinetti decries photography as a faulty mode of representation. ("Up to now writers have been restricted to immediate analogies. For instance, they have compared an animal to a man or to another animal, which is almost the same as a kind of photography."[14]) For the Futurist discourse, photography was not a marvel of the machine age, but a simplifying reproduction of the world that had much more in common with passatistic forms of art than the dynamic forms of expression that Futurism called for. As Sarah Carey outlined in her essay

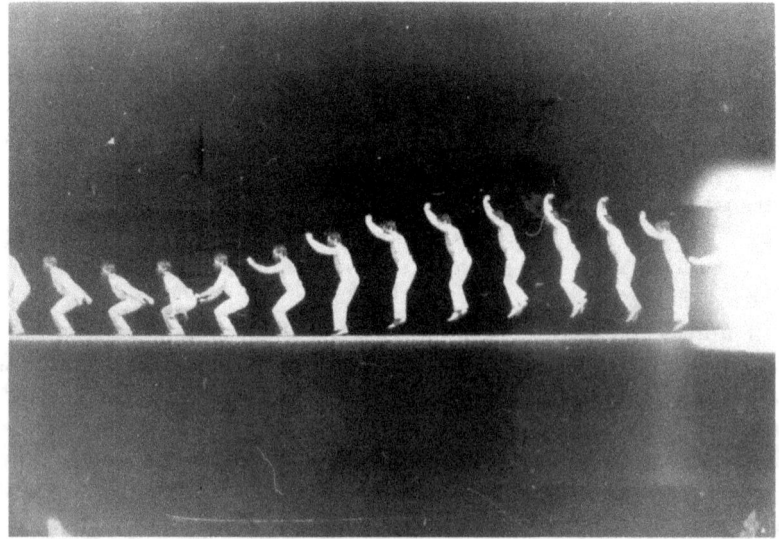

Figure 3.1 "Jump" Chronophotograph (1888), College de France

"Futurism's Photography,"[15] photography was perceived as a *rigor mortis* that stopped the flow of every *élan vital*.

This rejection of the technical medium of photography clearly demonstrates that the Futurist attitude toward technology was far away from a simple affirmation. The photographic image, a well-established technology in the early twentieth century, was rejected as a medium of Futurist expression. Especially the Futurist painters disliked the mechanical gaze of the machine, because they recognized in it a completely static representation of the world. However, they did not reject an apparative gaze per se. As outlined in the "Technical Manifesto of Futurist Painting," Futurists greatly appreciated technologies such X-rays that unveiled a completely different phenomenology: "Why should we forget in our creations the doubled power of our sight, capable of giving results analogous to those of the X-rays?"[16] Further, in this text the Futurists carried on the arrogance against all things human: "Our renovated consciousness does not permit us to look upon man as the center of universal life. The suffering of a man is of the same interest as the suffering of an electric lamp."[17] Thus, the turn against photography does not indicate a rejection of technology and a reentry of human sentiments, but criticizes a limit that the Futurists saw in this technology. They were not opposed to new imaging technologies, but these technologies should surpass the phenomenality of the human sphere and create a new scientific image of the world.

The Futurist doctrines of technology did also not coincide with the sober functionality of physiological and psychological test apparatuses that segmented reality into an ordered system; Futurists recognized technology as a medium that would open up a dynamic and unpredictable world. Although central to Futurist aesthetics, Muybridge's and Marey's chronophotographic freeze frames represent the exact opposite of what Futurist painters imagined as the visuality of the new century. The Futurist painters developed a visual language that stood somewhere between the representations of auratic lines and mathematical curves. Their dynamism tried to visualize a reality that was not accessible to human experience and they created images through the accelerated and accelerating technologies of the time.

Futurist painting tried to compress or collapse aspects of several new and newer forms of technological representation that were drawn from X-rays and electromagnetism, and recharged these technological images with an esoteric or rather ethereal understanding of force as life force. As Linda Henderson has shown, in Boccioni's art, esoteric and scientific understandings of vibration and ether intersect,[18] and Futurist forms of visual representation can be in general understood as constructing an explosive amalgam of scientific practices and a transcendental agenda.

The concluding statement of Marinetti's manifesto on photography that I have quoted above takes up this connection between photography and science and points to a more complex dialectics. The transformation of photography to art not only expands its own realm, but feeds back into science, thereby advancing technological modes of scientific inquiry. This might have been partially wishful thinking from the Futurist side; however, Marey's and Muybridge's works, too, were no simple representations of reality, but highly manipulated technological images. The chronophotographic pictures did not represent objects in their natural contexts, but were highly constructed: soldiers had to march only for them, birds were flying through the laboratory, and the subjects were dressed in white suits so that a great contrast between fore- and background would be visible.[19] In this sense, these images were similar to the Futurist photographs, because they did not intend to display a personality, but the movement became, in an analytic gesture, almost detached from the moving body. Boccioni's "lines of force," which were the central elements of Futurist paintings, emerged similarly as a highly artificial form representing a world that is not accessible to the unaided human eye.

LINES OF FORCE

It is quite surprising that Boccioni, the greatest opponent to photography in the Futurist circle, was one of the first in the Futurist context to experiment with this medium. In fact, his photographic explorations predate Futurism. The photograph "I-We," from the first decade of the twentieth century, displays himself simultaneously from several perspectives as multiple persons standing in a circle. This image was probably arranged through a mirror system that projected these different perspectives on a photographic plate.[20] It does not represent reality, but creates through a parasitic reduplication an imaginary realm in which Boccioni clones himself not unlike several films by Georges Méliès that deal with inexplicable reduplications of objects and persons. This image demonstrates clearly that Boccioni did not focus on a naïve representation of reality, but intended to dig deeper and to display through imagery a reality that is not open to immediate technological forms of representation—for example, the psychological complexity of a person. He connects in this sense to a tradition of early silent film with its most famous example, *The Student of Prague*, in which the cinematic technology is used in order to transcend the visible reality by visualizing the story of a doppelganger.[21] However, Boccioni was not so much interested in constructing romantic counterworlds as in expressing a reality that is not accessible either to human perception or to modern media technology, but is nonetheless at the core of the rapidly changing world of the early twentieth century.

The question of an authentic representation of movements and dynamics is a central concern for art at least from Lessing's *Laocoon* on,[22] and Paul Virilio opens his book *Vision Machine*[23] by highlighting precisely this debate. He summarizes a discussion between the painter Auguste Rodin and the sculptor Paul Gsell about the true representation of movements in painting and photography. While Gsell is fascinated by the exact and therefore realistic representations of "frozen" movements in chronophotography, Rodin defends painting: " 'No,' Rodin replies, 'It is art that tells the truth and photography that lies, for in reality time does not stand still, and if the artist manages to give the impression that a gesture is being executed over several seconds, their work is certainly much less conventional than the scientific image in which time is abruptly suspended.' "[24] For Rodin, painting is close to an experiential world and therefore closer to reality; this resonates to a certain degree with Boccioni's doctrines of Futurist painting, in which the experience of a dynamic moment should be emulated.

Bocconi was the leading painter in the Futurist circle and assumed for the pictorial and plastic arts a position of leadership that even challenged Marinetti's hegemony. One of the first manifestos that carried his name was the "Manifesto of the Futurist Painters"[25] from 1910. Here, the painters did not so much articulate their own visual language as they rejected contemporaneous art that, according to Marinetti's doctrines, was rooted in an adoration of old masters, for the Futurist painters the art of their time was inspired by historic pieces and again made for an exhibition in the museum and would not keep any promise of innovation. The strategies for Futurist innovation were articulated much more precisely in the "Technical Manifesto" of Futurist painting, published only three months later. The "technique" of Futurist painting is here summed up as an interactive "dynamism."

> The gesture which we would reproduce on canvas shall no longer be a fixed moment in universal dynamism. It shall simply be the dynamic sensation itself.
>
> Indeed, all things move, all things run, all things are rapidly changing. A profile is never motionless before our eyes, but it constantly appears and disappears. On account of the persistency of an image upon the retina, moving objects constantly multiply themselves; their form changes like rapid vibrations in their mad career. Thus a running horse has not four legs, but twenty, and their movements are triangular.[26]

Like Rodin's statement, this manifesto advocates for an appropriate representation of reality as constantly in flux. This is not a surprise; for Futurism, the reality is in a permanent process of acceleration and movement. The representation of this movement is at the heart of the Futurist aesthetics and not the analytic dissection of movements that Marey and Muybridge had achieved. However, Futurists stay in the laboratory of life sciences. As Linda Henderson has pointed out, the Futurist reality is marked by vibrations, that is, curves that express the true dynamics of life.[27] Boccioni connects here to the physiological studies of the nineteenth century that represented vital processes such as pulse, fatigue, and blood pressure through graphical curves.[28]

Like these scientific investigations, Futurist painting attempts to render the "dynamic sensation, that is to say, the particular rhythm of each object, its inclination, its movement, or, more exactly, its interior force."[29] However, these vibrations are not solely representations of forces, but "force-lines" that transpire to the spectator.

> With the desire to intensify the aesthetic emotions by blending, so to speak, the painted canvas with the soul of the spectator, we have declared that the latter must in future be placed in the centre of the picture.
>
> He shall not be present at, but participate in the action. If we paint the phases of a riot, the crowd bustling with uplifted fists and the noisy onslaughts of cavalry are translated upon the canvas in sheaves of lines corresponding with all the conflicting forces, following the general law of the picture.
>
> These force-lines must encircle and involve the spectator so that he will in a manner be forced to struggle himself with the persons in the picture.
>
> All objects, in accordance with what the painter Boccioni happily terms physical transcendentalism, tend to the infinite by their force-lines, the continuity of which is measured by our intuition.
>
> It is these force-lines that we must draw in order to lead back the work of art to true painting. We interpret nature by rendering these objects upon the canvas as the beginnings of the prolongations of the rhythms impressed upon our sensibility by these very objects.[30]

In this point, Futurist painting transcends literally the representative realm of physiological laboratories. Representing is conceived not only as a display of complex processes, but as an affective force that involves the spectator. Benjamin's statement that Dada poetry hits the reader like a bullet[31] finds here its Futurist articulation, and in an intricate reentry, ballistics might have been at the foundation of all these Futurist aesthetics.

Christian Asendorf asserts that it is probable that the Futurists were at least partly familiar with ballistic photographs by the Austrian physicist Ernst Mach that show the air waves surrounding a projectile in motion.[32] In 1887 Mach and Peter Salcher developed a procedure to photograph projectiles in supersonic speed, which created images displaying complex patterns caused by the different air pressures surrounding the projectile.[33] These representations are in between Marey's chronophotography and Futurists's lines of force, because these air vortices do not only indicate the behavior of the projectile in a given moment, but are essential to the ballistic dynamic of the projectile, that is, its motion.

Even if this relationship to Mach's research and Boccioni's visual agenda cannot completely be proven, as Asendorf asserts,[34] Futurist painting is without doubt located in close proximity to movement studies that erupted in the nineteenth century. However, Boccioni's camp is particularly close to ergonomic scholars such as the Italian physiologist Angelo Mosso, who did not attempt to segment singular movements, but traced the "lines of force" that stood behind physical work.[35] A synthetic approach and not an analytic interest drove the Futurists, and the brothers Bragaglia attempted to transform photography into a tool for a synthetic representation of the world.

Photodynamism

The brothers Bragaglia attempted to include photography in the canon of Futurist art. They were quite aware of the rejection of photography through Boccioni and articulated an art of photodynamism that turned the detested *rigor mortis* into the universal dynamism that Futurism called for. Their photographs were constructed through overexposure so that the movements of the captured subject were represented through continuous traces visualizing the path of action (see figure 3.2). These practices constitute a counterstrategy to chronophotography, and the Bragaglias were more than aware of that. In fact, the 1911 text "Futurist Photodynamism"[36] represents a discussion of how cinematographic practices of the nineteenth century differ from their work.

Certainly, Futurist photography was significantly concerned with the question of how it differed from traditional photographic techniques. However, even the Bragaglias attested that they relied on the same technology as Niépce, Daguerre, Marey, and Muybridge: "If it can be associated at all with photography, cinematography and chronophotography, this is only by virtue of the fact that, like them, it has its origins in the wide field of photographic science, the technical means forming common ground."[37] Nonetheless, the way in which this technology is applied is

Figure 3.2 "Suonatore di violoncello" (1913–14) by A. and A. G. Bragaglia

new. This clearly points out the parasitic nature of the art of the brothers Bragaglia; they abused the existing technology of photography in order to transcend the current discourse and to generate something that did not contribute to the science of photography, but rather disturbed it. The Bragaglias confirmed that these pictures could only appear in comparison to other contemporaneous photographs as fuzzy and imprecise:

> So it follows that when you tell us that the images contained in our Photodynamic works are unsure and difficult to distinguish, you are merely noting a pure characteristic of Photodynamism. For Photodynamism, it is desirable and correct to record the images in a distorted state, since images themselves are inevitably transformed in movement.[38]

For the *fotodinamista*, these blurry effects are not an irritation, but a representation of the world that is more appropriate, but not accessible to immediate perception. This distortion of reality implied, ironically, that photodynamism had a better access to reality, because reality is not representable as a static construct, but has to be displayed as a dynamic simulation. Photography is not intended to create an imaginary, but was used to provide a record of reality that also took the constant changes of the world into account. Thus, photodynamism did not constitute a clear-cut separation from photography and science, but continued the photographic agenda of a more objective representation of the world. For one, the Bragaglias see in the traces of movement literally "trajectories,"[39] and the resonances between Boccioni's aesthetic and Mach's ballistic experiments continue here. Secondly, and more importantly, photodynamism continues with an interest in the graphical curve as a means of scientific representation. The aim of the Bragaglias was to represent movement in a continuous way like the technology of the kymograph (an instrument to register data in analog graphical curves).

> Besides which, cinematography never analyses movement. It shatters it in the frames of the film strip, quite unlike the action of Photodynamism, which analyses movement precisely in its details. And cinematography never synthesizes movement, either. It merely reconstructs fragments of reality, already coldly broken up, in the same way as the hand of chronometer deals with time even though this flows in a continuous and constant movement.[40]

In comparison to photodynamism, photography, chronophotography, and cinematography are digital media that segment reality in clearly distinguishable units. Photodynamism attempts to point out that reality is not composed of single moments, but is a continuous flow. It is the analogous curve, the wave, or the frequency that interests the Bragaglias, and they share this interest with the Futurist composer Luigi Russolo. As I will discuss in Chapter 4, Russolo was dissatisfied with a tonal system that was based on individual notes, and he introduced a form of notation that relied on continuous lines. He wanted to expand the field of music to "microtonal" dimensions, something that clearly resonates in photodynamism.

> To put it crudely, chronophotography could be compared with a clock on the face of which only the quarter-hours are marked, cinematography to one which the minutes too are indicated, and Photodynamism to a third in which are marked not only the seconds, but also the intermovemental fractions existing in the passages between seconds. This becomes an almost infinitesimal calculation of movement.[41]

Again, it is not the juxtaposition of images that interest the Bragaglias, but an uninterrupted representation of temporal processes. Their photodynamism did not record single moments but attempted a real-time processing that provided a more accurate representation of reality. Photodynamism was an intrinsic parasitic project. Not only because it used a parasitic medium, but also because it disturbed and irritated established photographic practices. It also continued an exploration of scientific ideas and was not an irrational rejection of the scientific discourses with which photography was deeply connected.

Futurism, however, was aware of the parasitic dangers of photography. In Futurism, painting and photography were not supposed to create a simple representative trace of reality, but to unlock a new phenomenality, in which a new understanding of the world and the structure of forces and objects became possible. Dada developed a more relaxed relationship to the parasitic undertones of photography, although absolute film, which was largely developed by artists close to Dada, attempted to undercut the representative nature of the medium as well.

DADA AND FILM

When thinking of Dada, complex, ironic, and satirical collages come to mind that abuse pictorial material cut out of newspapers and advertisements. In his artwork essay Walter Benjamin recognized this visual language as closely linked to the juxtaposed images of film[42]; however, the early Dada experiments with film did not simply coincide with the art of collage as it peaked in Berlin Dada. The early forms of Dada visuality as they were developed in Zurich were much closer to abstract painting than to photographic satire and echoed the Futurist anxiety against the photographic image. The French German painter and poet Hans Arp is in this sense an important example. In the Zurich era of Dada, he developed a visual language that did not embrace a distorted representation of the everyday, but consisted of biomorphic shapes. His famous wood reliefs display layers of rounded forms that evoke the morphology of organic entities such as cells, membranes, or amoeba. However, these works had no clear correlation in nature; they were not representative, but established a new phenomenological realm by creating hybrids between nature and man-made objects. As Arp acknowledged in a text titled "Art Is Fruit," it was not his intention to create a representation of nature: "I love nature, but not its substitutes. Naturalist illusionist art is a substitute for nature."[43] Accordingly, his images and sculptures did not embrace the illusionistic qualities of media technology, but established a new visual language that transcended mimetic representation.

In a similar vein, the early engagement with the photographic image in Dada circles did not go for a parasitic representation of reality, but rather attempted to achieve a media technological subversion of the photographic image itself. The most famous example is in this regard the so-called Absolute Film. In the early twentieth century, several painters turned toward the medium of film in order to expand the visual experiments that they had done in abstraction. Most famously, Walter Ruttmann, Hans Richter, and Vikking Eggeling left the canvas behind and embraced celluloid as a new medium of artistic expression. These artists came from abstract painting and did not explore the possibilities of medial entropy like the Dadaists, but attempted to unleash the self-referential power of the artistic material itself. It was not geared toward a tactic disturbance, but aimed at a new visual sensibility that left representation behind.

The history of abstract film, however, pre-dates these experiments. The Futurists Arnaldo Ginna and Bruno Corra are known as the first creators of nonrepresentational films. In 1910, they began painting directly on the celluloid to create colorful shapes and they had in mind a synesthetic aesthetic that they documented in texts such as "Abstract Cinema-Chromatic Music."[44] These films are lost, but according to their comments, it is evident that they were in line with Boccioni and the brothers Bragaglia in their attempt to use film not simply as a reproductive medium but as a mechanism to open up a new phenomenological space. However, they were not so much interested in constructing a dynamism than in exploring a "music" of colors, and they understood their films as a transcendence of painting toward music.[45]

In 1921 Hans Richter and Walter Ruttmann continued the work on a self-referential form of film. They produced the first movies that would become known as "absolute film." *Lichtspiel Opus 1* by Ruttmann and *Rhythm 21* by Richter do not use images with a photographic resemblance, but juxtapose abstract shapes that have no direct resemblance to outside objects. Richter and Ruttmann created these forms by painting with oil color on glass plates or using wax or plasticine to form shapes, and they photographed these shapes with a film camera.[46] Thus, they used the photographic image, but attempted to subvert the indexical nature of the medium by producing a strange object that had no resemblance with objects in everyday discourse. Although Richter's and Ruttmann's films differ, because Richter mainly used clear, geometric forms and Ruttmann adopted softer organic shapes, they share the basic aesthetic in that they emancipate film from being a representational tool. As in abstract painting, film depicts a self-contained world that does not need an outside reference. It is a rebellion of artistic forms and means that attempt to emancipate art from the petit bourgeois demand to represent reality.

However, this rebellion was not satisfying for Dada. Dada recognized in the struggle of shapes an outcry of the objects, but also saw that abandoning the parasitic nature of film and photography also emptied out the subversive power of the medium. This is suggested not only by the photo collage in Berlin Dada that uses clearly referential images, but also by Richter's later films. Most famously, his short movie *Ghosts before*

Breakfast supports such an interpretation; this film shows a rebellion of objects against the human being and the laws of physics. Hats fly around, a bow tie gains its own dynamic and tyrannizes its owner, a head detaches and attaches again, a fire hose acts according to its own will, and many more things happen—nothing behaves as it should. In fact, Richter uses photographic images of everyday objects in a similar way to the abstract shapes in *Rhythm 21*, by moving everyday objects like the abstract shapes according to a compositional logic and not on the basis of the laws of physics. However, this transposition has a decisive impact. Here, abstract shapes no longer create their own consistent world, but familiar objects produce an uncanny feeling of alienation. The absolute film turns into a horror movie, and Richter's later work appears to be much closer to the distorted, magic worlds of the trickster Méliès than to the compositional canvases of Kandinsky. In fact, the famous moon from Méliès' *Trip to the Moon* reappears in Richter's *Two Pence Magic*. In the later essay "The Film as an Original Art Form,"[47] Richter supports this assessment by asserting that a clash between documentary and absolute film produces precisely such a cinematic irrationality:

> The *external object* was used, as in the documentary film, as raw material, but, instead of employing it for a *rational* theme of social, economic, or scientific nature, it has broken away from its habitual environment and was used as material to express irrational visions. Films like *Ballet Mechanique, Entr'acte, Emak Bakia, Ghosts Before Breakfast, Andalusian Dog, Diagonal Symphony, Anemic Cinema, Blood of a Poet, Dreams that Money Can Buy*, and many others were not repeatable in any other medium and are essentially cinematic.[48]

For Richter, these films are essentially self-referential. Film shows what is only possible in film. However, the difference between the purely abstract and the later films is that, for example, *Ghosts before Breakfast* dissects the rules of habitual knowledge and reassembles the world in a new disturbing vision. This shift toward "magic," as Richter also calls it in the essay,[49] brings us into the center of the visual language of Berlin Dada. Collage is here not used as a way to juxtapose shapes and to construct a new unseen abstract visual world, but the photographic image is used in order to distort an established understanding of the world. The medium of photography itself becomes parasitic and creates a subversive irritation.

Parasitic Visuality in Berlin

When Dada came to Berlin, it collided with a mass media world that did not exist to the same degree in Zurich. The mass society of the metropolis was soaked in advertisements, and a relatively new medium, the illustrated magazine, communicated the news of the day and high society to its audience. The Dadaists ripped these newspapers apart conceptually as well as literally and assembled them again in their montages. In this use of material taken from mass media lies a significant difference to the Futurist experiments. While the Futurists manipulated photography, in a parasitic abuse, as an instrument of scientific investigation, Dada reused photographs disseminated through mass media. Dada fed on a cheaply available commodity that constituted an everyday discourse.

Not surprisingly, the Dada artist who intensely contributed to the development of the collage or montage technique, Hannah Höch, worked for the Ullstein Verlag, the most important publisher of the Weimar period who also published the *Berliner Illustrirte Zeitung*. Höch was employed at a smaller magazine, *Die Dame*, that focused on pattern designs (*Schnittmuster*). It is also evident that Hausmann obsessively read illustrated journals in order to stay up to date with the newest scientific discoveries.[50] The involvement of Dada with this new form of visual journalism was intense and truly parasitic. The art of photomontage, which is certainly one of the most famous products of Berlin Dada, took from this form of publishing and reassembled a new disturbing and entropic imagery from these materials. The Dadaists recognized this and even asserted their parasitic behavior in the catalogue to the 1920 Dada exhibition in Berlin:

> Whenever vast quantities of time, love, and effort get wasted on the painting of a body, a flower, a hat, the casting of a shadow, etc., the Dadaists say that what we need to do is take a pair of scissors and cut out from these paintings, these photographic representations.[51]

This statement intentionally erodes the position of the artist as a creative force and displays the Dadaist as a parasite that destabilizes the already established connections that one can find, for example, on the cover of an illustrated journal. They are no longer interested in creating unique forms of art, but happily abuse already produced material. The creative activity begins with a destruction of images and continues with reassembling this material, with the technical procedure of montage, as Hausmann asserted:

> I also needed a name for this technique, and in agreement with George Grosz, John Heartfield, Johannes Baader, and Hannah Höch, we decided to call these works photomontages. This term translates our aversion at playing the artist, and, thinking of ourselves as engineers (hence our preference for workmen's overalls) we meant to construct, to assemble our works.[52]

The Dadaists embraced a machine aesthetic and the material, the photograph, was also the product of a machine. Hausmann refers to these works as photomontages, because he recognizes in the assembling of the pictures an intrinsically technical process that takes mechanically produced items and puts them together. However, the term "photomontage" is problematic for describing the works of Berlin Dada, because it can be argued that a photomontage should only consist of the arrangement of photographic materials through negatives, which would lead to the construction of an integrated whole picture that is produced by the exposure of combined photographic images—John Heartfield would become a master of this technique.[53] The technique that Hausmann mentions is rather collage, derived from the French verb *coller*, "to glue," and in fact Höch referred sometimes to her work as "Klebebilder"/"glued images."[54] However, Hausmann wanted to emphasize the technical character of this procedure, "montieren/assemble," whereby also heterogeneous material such as photographs, writing, and other images can be assembled together. The Dadaists participated in this technological discourse not as actual engineers but as parasites abusing this technological terminology for their artistic purposes. Hausmann's collages or montages *Tatlin at Home* and *Self-Portrait* and the sculpture *Spirit of Our Time* underline this attitude by visualizing the modern subject as a parasite embedded in a media technological charged environment. On the basis of these explicit attempts to bring Dada in a close relationship to mechanical forms of production, I suggest that the term "photomontage" is, within the Dada discourse, also justified for images that do not exclusively consist of photographs, but combine photographic elements with other media such as writing or painting.

However, the Berlin Dada collage did not embrace the machine age without also being critical of it. The Dadaist machines did not display the lines of force that Futurist paintings represented. The Dada cyborgs, as Matthew Biro calls them,[55] did not emerge as indestructible bodies as portrayed by Marinetti, but showed fragile hybrid structures that appeared as broken and reassembled. It is central to many montages of Berlin Dada that they did not hide their inherently fragmented structure as heterogeneous parts that were merely glued together. Reassembling the shiny and complete world of photojournalism after a parasitic intervention was precisely the subversive power that the Dada collage entailed. Hanne Bergius points out: "Marginalized by the media, the artists tried to unhinge these illustrations by strategic acts of subversion, using the media's own statements and picture material."[56] Bergius describes here the parasitic feedback that did not destroy but irritated and altered the behavior of the host. Also, Brigid Doherty remarked that the appearance of brokenness or distortion creates a literally physiological shock aesthetic, mimicking the trauma of war.[57] However, Bergius points out that there was a limit to the destructive will of Dada:

> With the Berlin Dadaists, the media reality itself was to have its say in both word and picture. It was characteristic of Dada Berlin that the quotation remained identifiable and legible. The reality of demonstrable facts, even if decomposed, deformed, and disfigured remained their point of reference. The new and alienating context in which the citations were inserted was not to extinguish its memory but on the contrary to present glimpses of its old meaning behind the new contexts. The citational and montage aspects of text and images was pulled into a network of allusions inciting reflection, challenging, and activating judgments, setting the world in motion and penetrating into political spaces of action.[58]

This is precisely what I have described as a parasitic subversion. The aim of Dada montage is not destruction, but a tactical omnipresent irritation that shakes up established communicative conventions and reassembles loose parts in a new constellation. The degree of rupture and integration, of displacement and entropy constitutes the array that various Dada artists occupied and is reiterated in the legends about the invention of photomontage.

Within Berlin Dada there are two different accounts about the invention of photomontage, one by Hausmann and Höch, and one by Grosz and Heartfield. Hausmann tells the story that he and Höch got to the idea of montage when they were on a vacation trip at the Baltic Sea in 1918. There they found in almost every house the pictures of a soldier in front of barracks, and the head was replaced with a photographic portrait, so that this mass-produced image became more individual.[59] George Grosz describes the invention of montage as follows:

> In 1916, when Johnny Heartfield and I invented photomontage in my studio at the south end of the town at five o'clock one May morning, we had no idea of the immense possibilities, or of the thorny but successful career, that awaited the new invention. On a piece of cardboard we pasted a mishmash of advertisements for hernia belts, student song books and dog food, labels from schnaps and wine bottles, and photographs from picture papers, cut up at will in such a way as to say, in pictures, what would have been banned by the censors if we had said it in words. In this way we made postcards supposed to have been sent home from the Front, or from home to the Front. This led some of our friends, Tretyakov among them, to create the legend that photomontage was an invention of the 'anonymous masses'. What did happen was that Heartfield

was moved to develop what started as an inflammatory political joke into a conscious artistic technique.[60]

Both of these stories have in common that photomontage was not developed as a unique artistic activity, but came out of practices to deal with the realities and representations of the First World War. The attempt to give war a more human face (in the story of Hausmann and Höch) and the attempt to disguise information (in the case of Heartfield and Grosz) were abused in the artistic practice of Dada toward opposing aims. In the hands of the Dadaists, the photomontage tried to provide an undisguised and explicit representation of a world that was glossed over by the soothing images generated through mass media. Höch's and Heartfield's accounts, however, differ in how they handle the integrity of a gestalt and how they exploit the visual entropy that becomes possible through montage. While Höch describes a simple displacement as the origin of montage, Heartfield points to a visual noise that mimics cryptographic strategies and in fact was intended to hide a subversive message. The aesthetic of montage is located in this spectrum. Interestingly, it is Höch who embraced, at least in her early collages, the entropy that Grosz described, and Heartfield should become a master of displacement as Höch and Hausmann had seen it on their vacation trip.

Höch: Media Reflections

Hannah Höch was one of the few women within the Dada movement, and she contributed significantly to its visual language. She began in 1918 to assemble her "Klebebilder," and her early works were in tune with the Dada idea to represent a chaotic reality of life. However, this aesthetic of entropy, most significantly articulated in the famous collage *Cut with the Kitchen Knife Dada through the Last Weimar Beer Belly Cultural Epoch of Germany*, was only the beginning of Höch's engagement with this technique. She created an art of collage in which she constructed heterogeneous figures in a careful and surprising arrangement; especially her series *From an Ethnographic Museum* demonstrates a form of collage that transcended Dada aesthetics, and was extended in her scrapbook that she composed in the early thirties to a sensitive art of visual composition. However, in my discussion I would like to focus on her work in the Dada period.

Höch was one of the Dadaists most closely connected to the circuits of mass media. She worked for the journal *Die Dame*, and Ullstein's *Berliner Illustrirte Zeitung* (*BIZ*) was her main source for visual material. In her youth, Höch had received a profound training in arts and crafts with a focus on drawing. Her initial access to visuality was thus not derived from an engagement with high art, but with its applied dimensions. Her work at *Die Dame* was in line with that. There she created pattern designs (*Schnittmuster*) for knitting, crocheting, and embroidering.[61] Thus, for her the notion of cutting and assembling objects from prefabricated shapes was not only an artistic technique but also her job. However, her collages do not display the seamless structure that one would expect from a well-designed dress. Quite to the contrary, her images do not cover up the seams, do not hide the fact that they are composed, but openly display the fact that reality is made up from a great amount of heterogeneous elements—the visible cut was a central element in her aesthetics.

The famous and widely discussed *Kitchen Knife* collage demonstrates this agenda.[62] This image is not only Höch's most famous piece, but also became an iconic image for how Dada saw the world. This relatively large collage represents a panoptic view on the Weimar society, in which "the great Dadaists" are confronted with the "Anti-Dada movement," in a world that is filled with dancers, politicians, scientists, cogwheels, and roller bearings. The entropy of the image consists of not only a great magnitude of visual material but also a layering that exposes the single elements as such. It is not that the objects and persons are disconnected; they are rather connected, as pointed out by Maud Lavin, in an allegorical fashion, creating a complex net of signification.[63] Nonetheless, they overlap each other, constantly endangering the figurative integrity of each element. Although Höch's collage demonstrates a great panorama, it remains principally cut out of pieces; the elements are glued together, but they are not reintegrated.[64] The apparently random distribution of mechanical objects throughout the image underlines this fragmented aesthetic. These objects are not integrated cogs in a machine, but parts that suggest that they belong to something, but it is unclear where they actually fit. On the basis of this incongruence, the eye will not end wandering across the image and therefore it constructs a dynamic synopsis of Weimar culture. Höch constructed in a similar way a panoptic gaze that included a more explicit reflection on mass media in her montage *Dada Rundschau* from 1919 (see figure 3.3).

Already the title suggests an engagement with mass media. "Rundschau" has the literal meaning of "panoptic view," but the more common use of the term is in the names of daily newspapers such as *Frankfurter Rundschau*. Accordingly, Höch's image mimics the function of the newspaper as identified by Marinetti as "a synthesis of the day"[65] in a visual arrangement. The combination of writing and images also reminds of the visual appearance of modern tabloids, where the front page is dominated by headlines and images. This impression is not unjustified, because

Figure 3.3   "Dada-Rundschau" (1919) by Hannah Höch, Berlinische Galerie

the scenes and events that Höch represents indicate current news. The most prominent images are the photographs of the chancellor Friedrich Ebert and war minister Gustav Noske in swimsuits, which already caused a media scandal when they appeared in the *BIZ* on August 24, 1919. Höch took up this scandal in her montage, reusing the implications already created by mass media, namely that the two most powerful politicians of the period were in a fragile and intimate situation, thereby indicating the vulnerable state of the new democracy. This mocking of authoritarian figures continues through the soldiers in the lower left corner who are identified in the subtitle as singers or speakers for hire. This demotion of power is counteracted by the women in the upper right corner who represent the newly established political presence of women in the Weimar Republic. In 1918, women had gained the right to vote and could run for office from January 1919 on. The line "Deutsche Frauen in die Nationalversammlung"/"German Women in the National Assembly" rehearses this emancipatory event, and the proclamation in the lower left corner, "Freiheit. Schrankenlose für H.H."/"Freedom. Unrestricted for H.H.," apparently points to the liberation of Höch herself and thus echoes the political emancipatory change on a personal level. In her book *Cut with a Kitchen Knife*, Maud Lavin recognizes a gendered aspect as the main focus of *Dada Rundschau* and argues that Höch created "an utopian allegory of freedom of movement, internationalism, and modernity out of this specific political victory for woman."[66] I would be careful with such an optimistic reading of this image. This montage contains traces that unveil the still persistent male domination. Men are not only displayed as ridiculed as in the case of Ebert and Noske. The figure in the center of the top that Lavin identifies as Woodrow Wilson's head on a young female athlete's body saluting the toga-wearing women of the national assembly[67] appears to me more like a form of male flight surveillance observing the newly empowered women, which is underlined by the voyeuristic male gaze represented through the eyes in the upper right corner. Further, the glued-in words "Lesen und an Männer und Frauen weitergeben!"/"Read and give to Men and Women" do not only mention men and women equally as the receivers of this message and thus carry an emancipatory connotation, but more importantly identify this image as propaganda and thus as part of mass media.

Dada Rundschau is not an autonomous work of art that proclaims and asserts women's emancipation, but a conglomerate of mass-media-produced information that is juxtaposed in order to generate a panoptic view, a "Rundschau." It does not display an allegory of political events, but a synopsis of the mass media communication of these events. It does not touch a reality outside of mass media, but points, in a self-reflexive gesture through pictures from the newspapers, back to the newspapers themselves. The title *Dada Rundschau*, translated as "There, there newspaper" ("da" in German means "there"), makes this reading even more apparent. The crucial difference between newspaper reports about women in the national assembly and Höch's depiction of these events does not so much lie in the representation of a feminized utopia as in the fact that Höch's collage displays this political event as something that is created and conveyed through mass media.

Höch's Dada collages do not simply unfold a panoptic view on the society but reduplicate in a fragmented synthesis the gaze that mass media had fixated on this reality. Höch does not unveil a new view on reality but intervenes in the reality-generating machines of mass media. It constitutes a parasitic intrusion that irritates the relationship between mass media and reality.

Heartfield: Mimicry

Even after Dada, Heartfield and Höch continued to create photomontages. While Höch developed the collage almost into a private form of expression that incorporated an aesthetic of difference by constructing hybrid figures that synthesize, for example, in the image series *From an Ethnographic Museum*, Western and other cultural discourses, Heartfield designed a primarily political form of photomontage that unveiled the injustices of the Third Reich and the developments leading up to it. Another difference is that Höch's collages displayed, in a self-referential gesture, mass media, but were not themselves part of it, and Heartfield's photomontages were mostly designed as magazine covers, most importantly for the *Arbeiter Illustrierte Zeitung* (*AIZ*). This difference also has a significant impact on the phenomenality of the cut in their work.

Höch exposes in her collages the split, the edge between the elements of the image. This is also perceivable in the spatial dimension in her pictures. Her *Klebebilder* are not flat, but consist of identifiable layers. Heartfield, in contrast, worked with combining photo negatives and integrated all elements of a picture in a homogenous, flat image that could easily be reproduced in a newspaper. Dawn Ades even points out that Heartfield's images can at first sight hardly be distinguished from actual photojournalism and asserts that "the immediate impression is almost that of an extraordinarily lucky piece of reporting."[68]

This integrative rhetoric is, however, no less subversive than Höch's art. It constitutes, as Douglas Kahn has outlined in his book on Heartfield,[69] a subversive tactic of mimicry. This tactic does not exhibit, as in Höch's work, the heterogeneous character of the news of mass media, but assimilates apparent contrasts in a consistent image, thereby imitating the smooth surface of the cover of an illustrated journal. It is the mockery of the frictionless reporting of mass media that is at the core of Heartfield's aesthetic—a mimicry of mass media, as Kahn asserts:

> Mimkry can be discussed in the abstract in its relation to a hoax of total simulation. In such a hoax, the imitator (or mime) is poured into and grafted upon the mold and behavior of the original. Any protrusive discrepancies are

tucked and filed down to seamlessness (seme-lessness). All evidence of sources, labor and other histories, and moments of the object or act are submerged well within the reified norms of the original.

In stopping short of a hoax, mimikry brings corresponding and contradictory aspects of both the original and mime to the fore, in the manner of modernist self-reflexivity. Unlike the bulk of artistic modernism, however, mimikry reflects back not only upon its own act but brings the social existence of the original, with which it is inseparable, into scrutiny. The complex resultant movements between original and mime (disguise, confusion, ambivalence, discovery, revelation, among others) constitute the true elements orchestrated within the tactic of mimikry.[70]

Certainly, Heartfield's famous montages from the Nazi period clearly demonstrate such a tactic in which photomontage integrates heterogeneous elements into a shocking simultaneity. However, Kahn argues that mimicry was already present in the very beginning of the practice of photomontage. As he points out, the story about Grosz and Heartfield assembling subversive postcards is already mimicry in a very literal sense, because the subversive political messages are disguised by the fact that the montages have a resemblance to standard postcards.[71] The practice of mimicry is a hiding, and it enables a subversive intrusion, as Kahn points out: "In circumstances of strict censorship, such as WWI and the Nazi period, mimikry was used simply to gain access to a public, at times, apparently any public."[72] It is a subversive form of publicity, and it abuses in a practical way established media convention to inject through a subversive manipulation its message in the discourse.

One of the first published photomontages that Heartfield had created was the figure of his brother Wieland Herzfelde interspersed with a ball as his belly (see figure 3.4). This montage appeared for the first time on the cover of the Dada magazine *Jedermann sein eigener Fussball* and was reused, slightly modified, on the back/advertisement page of *Der Dada 3*. This very simple and almost innocent montage prefigures the subversive aesthetic that became prevalent in the Nazi period. At first—and this separates it from Höch's work in the Dada period—it does not display a chaotic panorama and does not present a multitude of assembled figures, but consists just of a slightly manipulated figure. The man does not appear as a distorted, assembled figure; he is an integrated body. The ball is not an alien element, and even the tie is arranged in a way that it supports the impression of this figure being one. It mimics the image of a bourgeois subject, but integrates a nonsensical Dadaistic gesture. The collision between the ball and the body is only provocative in its seamless integration and not in its

Figure 3.4   "Der Dadaist Wieland Herzfelde" by John Heartfield from *Der Dada 3* (1920)

conflict. However, while on the front page of "Jedermann sein eigner Fussball"/"Everybody his own Soccer Ball," this figure functions as an ironic and iconic figure underlining the title, the iteration of this illustration on the back of *Der Dada* 3 gives it an even more subversive function. Here, the mimicry is no longer directed toward the bourgeois society, but what is mimicked is the Dadaist discourse. The function of this illustration is to sell books from the Malik Verlag. Therefore, Dada mimics itself to convey a purely commercial message. This is not supposed to be an anticapitalist critique of Dada; it is only justified that they advertised their publications. However, Heartfield's collage demonstrates the way in which Dadaists reused images in a complex subversive manipulation and did not even stop abusing their own mass media discourse. The visual aesthetics of Dada consisted not in a discursive critique of existing conditions, but in a parasitical and self-reflexive exploitation of material circulating through mass media channels.

STATIC FILM

The main goal of Dada as well as Futurism was to subvert the representative function of the photographic medium and to turn it into a form of agitation that would force the spectator to act. Hausmann sums this up in a 1931 lecture:

> People often assume that photomontage is only practicable in two forms: political propaganda and commercial publicity. The first photomonteurs, the Dadaists, started from the point of view, to them incontestable, that war-time painting, post-futurist expressionism, had failed because of its non-objectivity and its absence of convictions, and that not only painting, but all the arts and their techniques needed a fundamental and revolutionary change, in order to remain in touch with the life of their epoch. The members of the Club Dada were naturally not interested in elaborating new aesthetic rules... But the idea of photomontage was as revolutionary as its content, its form as subversive as the application of the photograph and printed texts which, together, are transformed into a static film. Having invented the static, simultaneous and purely phonetic poem, the Dadaists applied the same principles to pictorial representation. They were the first to use photography as material to create, with the aid of structures that were very different, often anomalous and with antagonistic significance, a new entity which tore from the chaos of war and revolution an entirely new image: and they were aware that their method possessed a propaganda power which their contemporaries had not the courage to exploit.[73]

Certainly, Hausmann's speech is more polemical than historically correct. The Dadaists were not the first to assemble preexisting elements or even to manipulate photographs,[74] but they recognized, with Hausmann in their center, that photomontage had a unique power, because it drew energy from the media discourses that it tried to subvert. It literally implemented a feedback loop by reusing prefabricated images of the society of the Weimar Republic. Hausmann's very strong claim that "the members of the Club Dada were naturally not interested in elaborating new aesthetic rules" can be understood along these lines. Their goal was not to create a new code of artistic expression, but to recode the material already present. This was, however, not a revolution but an irritation of the pictorial media practice in the Weimar Republic. As in the Heartfield example that I have discussed above, Dada is not opposed to advertisement and commercialization. Rather, it is hard to decide to which sphere the image belongs. As Kahn calls it, Dada engages in mimicry, meaning that Dadaists participated in a parasitic abuse of images in order to irritate visual communication.

The irritating effect is, according to Hausmann, a subversion of a medium, namely the transformation of circulating visual material into a "static film." With this formulation Hausmann alludes to the static or simultaneous poems of Dada Zurich; this reference remains a bit enigmatic, since he refers to the merely phonetic and thus hardly visual aspect of these poems. The "static film" that Hausmann recognizes in the collages of Berlin Dada did not use meaningless syllables, but imagery; the picture fragments still represented something, but radically recoded the manipulated images. These photomontages were images in stasis, because they did not juxtapose images in a temporal sequence, but threw them together in one moment, thereby irritating and transcending their original context and meaning.

Hausmann apparently contradicts the Futurist agenda with his term "static film." Boccioni rejected photography and film precisely because he saw in them only a representation of the world in stasis. For him, art should break up this media technological *rigor mortis* and create impressions that not only showed movement but "moved." His goal was to transcend the realm of representation and to bring the dynamism to the spectator. The brothers Bragaglia intended to carry Boccioni's "universal dynamism" over to photography, but their attempts coincide with Hausmann's aesthetic in the sense that the "static" picture was supposed to display a dynamic activating impact. Hausmann's "static film" is not a simple photograph, but tears photographs apart in order to show the world's complex dynamic. Likewise, Bragaglias' images are static films in the sense that they display movement as a whole and not the single phases of a movement. They synthesize and they do not analyze. Certainly, Marey's and Muybridge's chronophotography can also be described as static films. They transform a movement into static units; however, the central clue of Hausmann's term is that it is inherently antagonistic. Chronophotography lacks this tension, because it tries to separate the simultaneous impact that is, for example, generated by a gesture into single units that then lose their power of signification. In contrast, Dada and Futurism tried to display static images that expressed an inherent dynamic.

The "static films" of Futurism and Dada have in common that they subvert the generic function of the photographic medium to create simple indexical images. They bring the fluidity of life in a "dynamic stasis" that exposes a reality not accessible to immediate perception. To unlock such a new phenomenological sphere was the goal of the parasitic intervention of Futurism and Dada in the medium of photography, and both movements have in common that they attempted to transcend this medium through a feedback loop. Clearly, the Dadaists reused photographs produced by the photographic industry, but also the brothers Bragaglia fed through overexposure a photograph into a photograph. This becomes apparent in comparison to chronophotography; while Marey and Muybridge juxtaposed single frames, photodynamism practically took these single frames and fed them back into each other. These feedback loops connect the photographic experiments to the theatricality of the avant-garde, where the artists provoked the audience to create an echo of their own "poetic" screams, thereby feeding the audience's reaction back into the entire performance. This technique of feedback is not only a performative trick and a visual strategy, but will also become fundamental for the media technological engagement of the avant-garde with noise and sound.

CHAPTER 4

PARASITIC NOISE

THE ABILITY TO DISTURB ENEMY COMMUNICATION WITH NOISE became a central capacity of the military throughout the twentieth century. Certainly, intelligence on the battlefield, as the Prussian general Carl von Clausewitz pointed out in the early nineteenth century, was always impacted by noise or, in his terminology, by "friction."[1] However, with the development of electromagnetic transmission and electronic amplification, noise warfare achieved a completely new importance. Jamming transmitters were used in the Second World War to garble enemy signals,[2] electromagnetic impulses emitted by nuclear explosions threatened to disable Cold War communication networks,[3] and the Israeli army in 2005 created literal "sound bombs" through the loud boom of supersonic jet planes.[4] These examples show that it is important to be "louder" and more powerful than the enemy, because noise crashes the ability to communicate, to operate, and to react. Such noise is no longer a parasite irritating a communication network, but an event completely overwriting the system.

The avant-garde movements of Futurism and Dada dreamed about such noise bombs, but they were only to a very limited degree able to create them. The reason for that was partly based on the simple fact that they had no access to technologies that would create such a volume. However, this makes the attempts of the avant-garde bruitists even more interesting, because they had to find strategies that did not simply knock out dominant media, but amplified the parasitic noise that was already contained in them. In electrical engineering, "parasitic noise" signifies an unintended element that accompanies a signal, but nonetheless emerges in a communication circuit.[5] Michel Serres bases his understanding of the parasite on this notion and recognizes it as a condition of all communication.[6] Indeed, parasitic noise is not limited to electric data transmission, but existed also before and beside electronic communication circuits. Early phonographic technologies were eminently cursed by these parasitic noises. Such perturbations were extremely hard to eliminate and were not simply external forces, but produced through the materiality of the medium itself. Minimal errors in the record or the needle, side noises caused by the driving mechanism, and many other things set off all kinds of unintended noises. One of the major German journals on the development of phonographic media, *Die phonographische Zeitschrift*, was full of suggestions for improving technologies of recording and reproduction in order to limit the amount of noise.[7] These developments coincided with the noise performances of the avant-garde. As I argue, Futurism and Dada experimentations with noise emerged out of a "phonographic" understanding of acoustic events that no longer distinguished clearly between sound and noise.[8]

Especially the Futurist noise composer Luigi Russolo tried to foreground the parasitic background noise that the engineers of the time attempted to eliminate.[9] He created an art of noises (*l'arte dei rumori*) based on technological devices that exploited the acoustic properties of the gramophone and the sonic qualities of many different materials. From 1913 on, he performed noise symphonies with noise intoners, so-called *intonarumori*, which greatly fascinated Marinetti, who enthusiastically funded Russolo's exploration of this new sonic world. However, Russolo did not shock his audience with the loud imitation of disturbing industrial noises—his listeners were already used to a new and technological realm of sound and noise. Industrial machines, cars, trains, but also phonographic media with their ability to store, to reproduce, and to commercialize all kinds of sonic events, had already significantly changed practices of listening.[10] As Russolo outlined in his manifesto "The Art of Noises,"[11] he wanted to expand and not simply affirm this experience by producing not merely louder, but more complex sonic sensations. He conceptualized an abstract model of noises of the modern world and created devices, the *intonarumori*, that extended the complexity of industrial noises and fed it back to contemporaneous listeners.

Russolo saw in the timbre of the materials that he used for his noise intoners the possibility to generate new sonic complexities and to train human ears to these sensations. This structural feedback of more complex or "amplified" noises connects to Russolo's idea of overwriting a given reality. He recognized noise as a significant part of the modern environment and imagined instruments to cancel it out with his own acoustic material. Further, Russolo understood his art of noises as a structural simulation of the battlefield and tried to create a truly Futurist noisescape. The Futurist noise machines failed, however, in this regard, because they lacked significant amplification, and actually turned back, as I will discuss, into parasitic noise that was overwritten by the reaction of the audience.

The Dada movement emerged around the same time as Russolo's art of noises became known throughout Europe. In fact, the Dada celebration of noise and bruitist poetry can be understood as a more or less direct reaction to Russolo's ideas. However, Dadaists did not just copy the art of noises, but rather created in a misappropriation of Futurist concepts their own version of noise art. This becomes apparent by the fact that the Dada noise experiments did not much depend on media technology. Instead of reassembling noise machines, the bruitist experimentations in Zurich embraced the wild and animalistic aspects of noise and created a vitalistic version of it that had hardly anything to do with a Futurist noisescape. Ironically, this neglect of noise technologies made the Dadaist rebellion much more forceful and louder than Russolo's performances, because Dada used the reaction of the audience as a feedback for the creation of noise.

Raoul Hausmann, however, changed this Dada assessment of noise and recognized that the question of noise is intrinsically connected to technology, namely the ability to produce strong signals. To do that, he tried to patent an amplification and sound pickup mechanism for the gramophone that was also supposed to limit the occurrence of side noises. Hausmann was much more interested in noise reduction and optimal data transmission than his Dada colleagues, and in the 1931 text "The Overbred Arts"[12] he contested that the future of music and noise experiments would be in electronic signal processing.

The noise experiments are of special significance for an investigation of the avant-garde. Russolo's art of noises and Dada bruitist poetry appear as the Dionysian nucleus that enabled the eruptive power of these movements. In the following, however, I want to show that the avant-garde reflections on noise, especially Russolo's attack on classical music, did not simply embrace chaos and disorder, but reflected on media historical developments. Not only was the ability to create, store, transmit, and reproduce noise unique to Dada or Futurism, but also the central technological ability of phonographs, telephones, the radio, and vacuum tubes. The noise experiments constituted the first in-depth involvement of avant-garde artists with technology. Russolo developed his ideas explicitly through a critical examination of nineteenth-century physics and described his work as an endless engineering venture.[13] Also, Hausmann's design of a gramophone pickup system was mainly driven by a technical fascination and focused on high fidelity. These attempts continued the parasitic abuse of media through the avant-garde; Futurism as well as Dada created feedback loops through their media performances that were supposed to amplify the noise of modernity that was already present. They just took the disturbances and complexities of the emerging media ecology and threw them back on the technological and social possibilities to create noise. In this way, they tried to construct a presence of artificially created noise in all media channels.

NOISE INTONERS

There is no doubt that Russolo had a wide knowledge of acoustics and that at the base of his "art of noises" stood a deep involvement with the mechanics of sound. Not surprisingly, Russolo's youth was marked by a great exposure to music. His father, Domenico, not only ensured that he studied violin and organ,[14] but might also have provided, as an organist and teacher at the local music school, the technical and theoretical background for the later sonic escapades of his son.[15] However, when one looks at the *intonarumori*, Russolo's famous noise intoners, one is not so much reminded of classical musical instruments as of a gramophone. In fact, the composer Igor Stravinsky remembered them as "[f]ive phonographs standing on five tables in a large and otherwise empty room [which] emitted digestive noises, static, etc."[16] These devices used a simple horn for sound amplification, and all these mechanisms were activated by a manual lever. Also internally, there was probably a similarity between the sound amplifying systems in phonographic devices and in Russolo's intoners. Identifying these similarities, however, is difficult, because Russolo's instruments were black boxes that concealed their internal structures, unlike phonographs and gramophones, which proudly presented their cylinders and disks (see figure 4.1).

Every close investigation of the mechanical nature of the *intonarumori* faces the problem that none of Russolo's instruments survived the Second World War. In 1977 attempts were made to reconstruct the *intonarumori*,[17] and the musicologist and composer Luciano Chessa rebuilt these instruments and performed a series of concerts in 2009.[18] There also exist four contemporaneous recordings of the *intonarumori*. In the performance of *Risveglio di una città*, *intonarumori* are played. The musical pieces named *Coralle* and *Serenate* performed by Russolo's brother Antonio also contain the sounds of noise intoners, and in a short sequence of the opera *L'Aviatore Dro* by the Italian composer Francesco Balilla Pratella, the *intonarumori* were accompanied by an orchestra.[19] However, the most important source for understanding the *intonarumori* is Russolo's book *The Art of Noises* (1916), in which he documented his theory, ideas, and reflections about his Futurist music. In this book, Russolo provided some general descriptions of his devices:

> Externally, the noise instruments take the form of boxes of various sizes, usually constructed on a rectangular base. At the front end, a trumpet serves to collect

and reinforce the noise-sound. Behind, there is a handle to produce the motion that excites the noise.

On the upper part, a lever with a pointer is moved along a scale graduated in tones, semitones, and fractions of a tone. Through its displacements, this lever is used to determine the highness, that is, the pitch of the noise, which can be read on a graduated scale.[20]

This description is mostly concerned with the outside of the *intonarumori*, and we learn how a musician would have played the noise intoners: Russolo points out that the noises could be manipulated—depending on the *intonarumore*—along a spectrum of up to two octaves[21] and be changed without any interruption.[22] While moving the handle rapidly created a greater sound intensity, the pitch could be altered by moving the lever on the upper part.

Although there are not many descriptions of the interior, it can be assumed that *intonarumori* were boxes that hid a rotating mechanism that excited a wire, which in turn transmitted impulses to a diaphragm that produced certain sounds. The membrane in the interior of the *intonarumore* was a drum skin mounted on a frame. The wire attached to the skin was able to vary the tension of the diaphragm and, therefore, the pitch of the noise intoners.[23] This constructive idea was not new; in fact, it had similarities to a musical instrument called "hurdy-gurdy."[24] A hurdy-gurdy is a musical instrument resembling a violin that was

Figure 4.1 Photograph of Russolo and *intonarumori* from *l'arte dei rumori* (1916)

already used in medieval times. The difference to a violin is that the strings are not excited by a bow, but by a rotating wooden disc.[25] Luciano Chessa emphasizes that the *intonarumori* had even more Renaissance predecessors. He recognizes similarities to the musical instruments that were designed by Leonardo da Vinci and that also used diaphragms and mechanical levers.[26] Certainly, when it comes to noise-producing elements, there were many constructive influences, and Russolo emphasized that his search for noises was an endless engineering venture.[27] However, I would like to assert that the basic design of the *intonarumori* was based on phonographic media, and this had probably a very simple reason: the amplification system (the horn) and the driving mechanism (the lever) were mass-produced items that were easily accessible, because they were widely used for gramophones. The difference is, while a gramophone used different disks as sound source, Russolo designed different noise-producing systems. However, all these systems were like the gramophone disk ultimately connected to a membrane transmitting the sound to a horn.

As I pointed out, Russolo applied various mechanisms and materials to the design of various *intonarumori*. For example, the *intonarumori* called "howler" (*ululatore*), "roarer" (*rombatore*), "crackler" (*crepiatore*), and "rubber" (*stropiccatore*) used a rotating wood or metal disks for generating sound-noises.[28] In another *intonarumore*, the *ronzantore*, Russolo used a small steel ball mounted on a spring wire or constantly moved by an electrical motor that vibrated against the drum skin or the wire connected to the drum skin. The "whistler" was an even more sophisticated *intonarumore* that employed resonating tubes for transmitting vibrations on the membrane.[29]

All these mechanisms had in common that they produced precisely those acoustic phenomena that should have been excluded from a phonographic apparatus. An article in the *Phonographische Zeitschrift* in the founding year of Futurism, 1909, reported the various reasons for why a gramophone would not produce a clear sound. It warned the gramophone user against an abuse of the device and demanded a regular replacement of needles, of the sound pickup system, and of the driving mechanism's spring. But not only these things affected the gramophone; the author identified a great variety of mechanical elements from cogwheels to lose screws as parasites intervening into a clean sound reproduction.[30] With this report in mind, Russolo's *intonarumori* appear as "abused gramophones" that explored and extended the possibility of ill-maintained phonographic equipment.

Russolo introduced the parasitic effects that created the unpredictable static in phonographic recording into the sound amplification system of his *intonarumori*. The *intonarumori* were not designed as sound-reproducing devices, but their task was to amplify the parasitic noise that was supposed to be excluded from technical recordings and music. Russolo already did what Caleb Kelly in his book *Cracked Media* recognized as typical for phonographic art in the later twentieth century: use of phonographic media to play broken records or no records at all.[31] Kelly understands John Cage as the first to use cracked and distorted phonographic media for compositions. He points out that in the 1960 composition *Cartridge Music*, Cage replaced the needle of a phonographic cartridge with foreign objects such as pipe cleaners, wires, feathers, slinkies, matches, toothpicks, and the like. Various objects were rubbed against this modified sound pickup system, and the sounds produced in this way were amplified by a speaker.[32] This practice mirrors precisely Russolo's abuse of phonographic equipment, because it used this technology for the exploration and for the reproduction of sound and noise. The *intonarumori*, however, not only had a technological similarity to phonographic media but shared the ability with the phonograph to potentially incorporate the whole dimension of acoustic sensations, and not simply the sound of musical composition.

SOUND-NOISE

Friedrich Kittler pointed out that the "phonograph does not hear as do ears that have been trained immediately to filter voices, words, and sounds out of noises; it registers acoustic events as such."[33] This statement is highly problematic, because Kittler leaves aside the fact that (especially the first) phonographs were not able to record all frequencies and therefore were not completely neutral recording devices. Mark Katz argues more concretely in his book *Capturing Sound* that the phonograph had a constructive effect that greatly changed practices of producing and listening to music.[34] For example, he points out that the average length of a song (three minutes) was designed to fit on a record,[35] and he asserts that recording techniques had developed their own aesthetic that made recorded music categorically different from live performances.[36] I agree with his assessment that phonographic media did not simply record but shaped practices of music production. However, even if Kittler overstates the "neutral" character of phonographic media, he correctly identifies phonographic devices as "noise machines"—not because they were, owing to their technical immaturity, contaminated with side noises, but because they did not differentiate between noise and sound. Russolo's project mimics precisely this aspect of phonography and tries to be immune to a distinction between musical sound and nonmusical noise.

The decisive element of the *intonarumori* was to create a technology that would attack the distinction between sound and noise. According to nineteenth-century physics, sound is determined by an even and uniform sine wave, whereas noise consists of an irregular wave pattern. Russolo rejected this clear-cut distinction and criticized the acoustics of the German physicist Hermann von Helmholtz in the chapter "Physical Principles and Practical Possibilities,"[37] included in his *The Art of Noises*.[38] He argued that music was not limited to a fixed set of sounds, but could continuously be expanded. While traditional music only uses regular sound—determined pitches—as material for its compositions, Russolo wanted to overcome this restriction through a constantly developing system of sound-noises, *suono-rumori*,[39] and the *intonarumori* were the technological base for achieving this goal.

In chapter 9 of *The Art of Noises*[40] there is a longer description of the sound-noises produced by the *intonarumori*: the "howler" (*ululatore*) sounded like a siren or a string instrument. The "roarers" (*rombatori*) produced a noise reminiscent of thunder. Russolo was unable to find a comparison for the metallic crackling of the low-pitched "cracklers," while he compared the sound of the high-pitched version to the grunting of a pig being skinned. The "rubbers" (*stropicciatori*) had a timbre of metallic rubbing. There are varieties of the *intonarumore* called "burster" (*scopitatori*) that produced noises like the bursting of objects or that resembled the sound of moving cars. The "hummer" (*ronzatore*) was reminiscent of electric motors and dynamos. The whistling of the wind came close to the sound emitted by the "whistler" (*sibilatore*), and the "gurgler" (*gorgoliatore*) produced a timbre like water running through a rain gutter.[41] In his descriptions of the sound-noises, Russolo especially emphasized the different timbres of the machines. The "roarers" had a timbre "quite rich in harmonic sound," and the same was true for the "cracklers." Russolo stated that "the timbre of the hummer includes some very charming harmonics" and added that the "gurglers" had "a group of harmonics that correspond in a certain way to the minor tonality."[42] It is this emphasis on the differentiated harmonics in the sounds of the *intonarumori* that was of real importance for his noise aesthetic. The description of the sounds of the noise intoners by means of analogy—for example, that the "cracklers" sounded like pigs being skinned or that the "bursters" approximated moving cars—was only an attempt by Russolo to give an idea of the sound. It did not indicate that he tried to create an art of noises that would reproduce the soundscapes of nature and the industrialized world. Russolo tried to design sound-noises and not to imitate actual noises.

Russolo's emphasis on timbre casts in particular a critical perspective on Helmholtz's distinction between noise and sound. The timbre (the quality of a tone) is, after volume and pitch, a central category used to describe a musical sound. When a note is played on different instruments such as a piano or a flute, the distinctive character of each instrumental sound is called timbre.[43] Russolo and Helmholtz assign timbre a specific place in their theories. Helmholtz states: "It is unnecessary to explain what we mean by the force and pitch of a tone. By the quality of a tone we mean that peculiarity which distinguishes the musical tone of a violin from that of a flute or that of a clarinet, or that of the human voice, when all these instruments produce the same note at the same pitch."[44] Helmholtz already understood timbre—the quality of a tone—as an individualizing element that posed problems. Timbre has a problematic place in an abstract classification of sounds, because it does not refer to a symbolic order of tones but to a material referent, the instrument. Russolo interpreted this structure of timbre as a distortion in instrumental music. It was the material parasite that constantly irritated every idea or perception of a pure music or sound. Every sound produced by an instrument contains minimal irregularities, which at the same time specifically characterize that instrument. These irregularities cannot simply be described as a mere distortion of the sound. They provide the character, and atmosphere, of a specific tone. Timbre itself is also not an object of musical notation but hangs on to a composition like a supplement. This parasite complements a sonic experience, although it stands outside of the symbolic system of music.

Phonographic media were supposed to exclude any timbre. Gramophones and phonographs are, unlike voices, flutes, and violins, not allowed to have a timbre of their own. As mere reproduction devices, they should be completely neutral and should only reproduce the timbres contained in the recording. However, parasitic noise can never be completely excluded, and when one uses the phonograph without a recording, one turns it into a timbre machine that only produces parasitic noise. This is precisely the point where the *intonarumori* emerged.

The increasing importance of timbre, however, is not unique to Russolo's aesthetics. Rather, a greater interest in the timbre of musical instruments is typical for the musical aesthetics of the nineteenth and twentieth centuries. For example, timbre can be seen as an important aspect in the development of the modern orchestral music with its growing number of musical instruments.[45] It is also crucial to the development of electronic music, especially the construction of synthesizers, which differ from other musical instruments in that they are able to generate an entire spectrum of different timbres electronically and thus sound like different music instruments.[46] In fact, the *intonarumori* can be understood as a mechanical pre-form of synthesizers that "sample" different

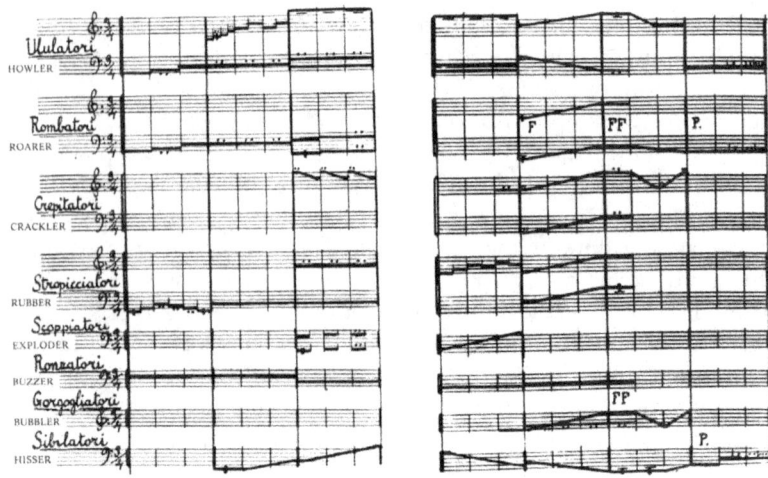

Figure 4.2   "Sveglio di una città" score from *l'arte dei rumori* (1916)

timbres. This becomes apparent when Russolo asserts that the noises of the *intonarumori* were not simply chaotic, but tuned: "*Every noise has a pitch, some even a chord, which predominates among the whole of its irregular vibrations.* Now, from this predominant characteristic pitch derives the practical possibility of assigning pitches to the noise as a whole."[47] This quote complicates the parasitic nature of timbre in Russolo's art of noises. The Futurist noise sound is a sound parasite and does not break with musical tradition; it even can be integrated into a specific system of musical notes, as a score in his book demonstrates (see figure 4.2).[48]

It is quite disturbing that Russolo explicitly refers to this sonic structure of his music and does not recognize it as a drawback for his art of noises. Instead, he acknowledges that "beyond enlarging the field of sound with new timbres, the noise instruments expand the chromatic-diatonic scale without destroying it."[49] For Russolo, the ordering system of musical tone does not indicate a restriction of his sound-noise. Rather, through a structural feedback, the Futurist implements microtonal structures that overcome a musical system based on segmented tones. From this conception of a sound-noise, it becomes clear that Russolo did not simply intend to destroy music, but to implement parasitic noises as ubiquitous phenomena into the discourse of modern music. His goal was not only to expose humankind to a completely new array of sonic phenomena, but also to educate humans so that they would expand their conception of music. The *intonarumori* were the training systems that should handle a psychoacoustic reeducation.

Constructing Feedback

> The ear of the Eighteenth Century man would not have been able to withstand the inharmonious intensity of certain chords produced by our orchestra (with three times as many performers as that of the orchestra of his time). But our ear takes pleasure in it, since it is already educated to modern life, so prodigal in different noises.[50]

The quote indicates that the construction of a sound-noise was not simply an aesthetic project, but connected to the evolution of the senses that, according to Russolo, was based on the development of the technologies of modern life. Russolo's art of noises intended to accelerate this evolutionary development of humankind through a structural feedback that created an abstract pattern based on environmental noises, which were amplified in their complexity. The machine noises that adjusted practices of hearing to new standards served for Russolo as a structural model to create different acoustic patterns. However, Russolo did not intend to simply reduplicate the noisescape of cars, factories, or heavy artillery.

Russolo constructed an abstract model of timbre in order to integrate it into musical composition. This meant not only that noise from the "outside" of music could be integrated, but also that a feedback loop of the materiality of sound became possible. It is important to recognize that Russolo's project was essentially nonmimetic. The art of noises was built on a feedback that took the distortions of musical sound and attempted to reintroduce them into a musical performance. That this feedback loop stood behind the art of noises becomes clear through Russolo's emphasis on the nonmimetic capacities of his noise art. He explicitly denied that his art of noises was supposed to be a representation of the modern world and claimed instead that he developed an abstract art capable of enriching the realm of acoustic pleasures.[51]

> As I pointed out in the manifesto, noise that comes from life we immediately restore to the same life (contrary to that which makes the sound) reminiscing quickly in our minds about the things that produce the determined noise that we hear. The restoration to life has, therefore, a character of an impressionistic fragmented episode of the same life. But as in every art, and thus also in the Art of Noise, we must not limit ourselves to an impressionistic fragmented reproduction of life.
>
> ...
>
> Well then, although the resemblance of timbre to imitated natural noise is attained in these instruments, almost to the point of misleading, nevertheless,

as soon as one hears that noise varies in tone, one becomes aware that it quickly loses its episodic, uniquely imitative character. It loses, that is, all its character of *result* and *effect*, tied to *causes* that produce it (motor energy, percussions, rubbings produced by speed, clashes, etc.) and that are due to and inherent in the same purpose of the machine or of some other thing that produces the noise.

It loses this character of effect by transforming itself into *element* and into *primary material*.[52]

In this passage, Russolo discusses the problem that noise evokes impressions from the environment and acknowledges that his instruments are in fact capable of recreating the noises of daily life. He also claims that his instruments had the capacity to undermine this referential structure. From a semiotic perspective, this referential structure is based on the indexical nature of noise. Noise, like smoke that refers back to a certain fire, has a causal, "natural" relationship to its referent. When we hear a loud bang, an irritating screeching, or some unknown sound, we look for the source. This is an essential difference to musical sound. We can hear musical sound without reference to the source. The practice of listening to music established that one listens to a musical composition and not to a violin, piano, and so on.

Russolo intended to suppress the indexical structure of noise. He claimed that his noise intoners were able to "eliminate the character of result and effect" from noise through the manipulation of the pitch of the sound-noise. Russolo's sonic structures did not simply refer to their source and did not construct an iconic resemblance of the modern world. They were rather conceptualized as a feedback loop without indicating an origin. What Russolo wanted was a sound-noise that did not represent anything. He intended to engineer complex acoustic patterns that were able to irritate, to provoke, and—in the end—to calibrate the ears of the listeners.

Intonarumori were instruments for generating such noise patterns, which had both a complex timbre and a determined pitch. It is significant that the *intonarumori* did not generate random noise events of unpredictable volume or pitch but were able to regulate sonic structures such as pitch and volume. They did not produce a stochastic sequence of unpredictable acoustical events but determined sounds that differed in their complex overtones from classical instruments. This complexity, together with their ability to generate microtonal transgressions, was supposed to challenge and recalibrate the sensory capacities of the audience gradually. Furthermore, Russolo's work stood close to scientific discourses.

Russolo's shift from note heads to a note-line corresponds to the representative technologies of the nineteenth-century physiological laboratories. As the media theorist Stefan Rieger points out, the transcription of data in graphical curves became the hegemonic practice in the emerging life sciences that needed to organize all the empirical data that they received from a multitude of studies.[53] Kittler also pointed out in *Gramophone, Film, Typewriter* that the shift from notating sound in musical scores to recording acoustic events in the analog images of curves creates a central moment of data processing, where signal technology opens up to real-time processing.[54] In Russolo's time this shift had its breakthrough. In the early twentieth century, media not only processed symbolic signs but also were able to record and reproduce the mere analog impact of physical phenomena. Russolo's new notation that replaced discrete noteheads through a note line highlights this shift from symbolic to analog media.[55]

The chapter about the "grafia enarmonica"/"Enharmonic Notation"[56] in *The Art of Noises* demonstrates that the shift from discrete to continuous signs was not only a technical development but geared toward perceptual patterns. Russolo called for a form of musical notation that would enable an immediate synesthetic transformation. He suggested that his note-line could greatly accelerate the reading of music. The act of reading music became similar to the phonograph—a progressive scanning of a graphical line.[57] This is also something that still echoes in Laszlo Moholy-Nagy's concept of the gramophone as compositional tool that he developed in his text "New Plasticism in Music."[58] He recognized that the gramophone line was a graphical line that could be creatively designed to generate all kinds of sonic events. The gramophone was for Moholy-Nagy a synesthetic system that shortcut acoustic and visual data. The phonographic line could not only be heard but also be drawn.[59]

What is important about this connection between the graphical modeling of phonographic media and the art of noises is that the graphical representation could now be inverted and fed back into media technology that formerly produced these lines only as traces of the real. Generating these lines led to a simulation of the real.

SIMULATING PARASITIC NOISE

Friedrich Kittler famously connected Jacques Lacan's triad of the real, the imaginary, and the symbolic to the media technologies of the gramophone, film, and typewriter.[60] While the typewriter was able to notate the symbolic with discrete signs, and the film constructed technologically the imaginary of dreams, the gramophone was able to record the real by analog inscription of impulses. This was a form of writing that worked without interpretation and was therefore free from any cognitive contamination that human subjects produce through thinking or imagination. Kittler, however, suppresses in his argumentation that the real does not only consist of the recording of impulses but also includes the materiality of the medium—that is, parasitic noise. Thus, phonographic media were no simple storage devices, but turned in the hands of avant-garde artists into machines for the creation of the real. Moholy-Nagy most famously suggested that gramophones be used for the production of sound,[61] and Ernst Mach emphasized the distorting and productive function of time axis manipulation that turned understandable, recorded speech into mere noise.[62] As discussed, Russolo likewise conceptualized his noise intoners as inverted phonographs that rewrote the traces of the real through feedback loops.

Russolo points out in *The Art of Noises* that initially his experiments were understood as an imitation of the noises of the modern world, as an imaginary reproduction of cars, streets, trains, and the like in a cacophonic symphony.[63] He rejected this response as a misapprehension of his art and emphasized that his noisy glissandi did not refer to the mechanical noises of engines, but rather constituted abstract acoustic patterns. This account testifies to the difficult aesthetic status of Russolo's art of noises. On the one hand, Futurist music carried traces of the noisy environment of cities and battlefields; on the other, Russolo's goal was a genuine composition of musical noise. The art of noises was thus confined to a struggle between imitation and abstraction, and Russolo tried to find a position that left imitation behind. The Futurist designed instruments for generating noise patterns that corresponded to or even surpassed structurally the noises of modern cities or warfare.[64] His project, however, was no mimetic duplication of these modern industrial processes. Instead, he aimed at a simulation of a complex acoustic environment for aesthetic and sensory training.

Simulation is a term strongly connected to technological modeling processes. In this context, simulation is understood as the execution of a model that does not have an external reference, but is solely based on its internal rules, structures, and parameters. The media theorist Bernhard Dotzler describes "simulation" in the following way[65]: "Simulation is . . . the function of semiotic processes in which not the representation or reflection of things external to these processes is at stake, but in which the reflection itself takes the place of these things."[66] According to Dotzler, simulation processes a set of signs that do not refer to anything outside of the simulation itself. The signs circulate only in the medium that produces them. Similarly, the complexity of noises in Futurist music increases not because of an irritation from the environment—for example, by new machines—but because the noises of the *intonarumori* themselves determine and extend the complexity of Futurist music. Russolo emphasizes this nonreferential character: "It will not be through a succession of noises imitative of life but through a fantastic association of the different timbres and rhythms that the new orchestra will obtain the most complex and novel emotions of sound."[67] Here, Russolo acknowledges that the increasing complexity of the modern soundscape does not fuel the art of noises. Rather, the technical abilities implied in the *intonarumori* themselves trigger the development and recognition of sound patterns.

Simulations, as well as the art of noises, have no immediate relationship with the reality they simulate.[68] Accordingly, simulations, similar to the sound-noises provided by the *intonarumori*, do not actually have to correspond to the reality of the world, but they have to be a model that can be manipulated in its complexity. The Futurist composer should have been able to engineer more and more complicated noise sounds and to generate a composition of complex acoustic phenomena. Only in this way could Russolo, or the Futurist composer in general, offer his audience structures that were more complex than the noises the city dwellers experienced in their daily routines.

Russolo's noise simulation was central to the construction of a Futurist *sensibilità*: the simulation of complex noise patterns was supposed to provide an auditory training ground that sensitized human beings to the acoustic structures implied in the noises of warfare and mass traffic. In Russolo's opinion, the living environment of the early twentieth century displayed an increasing complexity through the extension of industrial production.

> This evolution of music is comparable to the multiplication of machines, which everywhere collaborate with man. Not only in the noisy atmosphere of the great cities, but even in the country, which until yesterday was normally silent. Today, the machine has created such a variety and contention of noises that pure sound in its slightness and monotony no longer provokes emotion.[69]

The composer's task was to increase the variety of acoustical phenomena through the art of noises.[70] What Futurist music presented was, therefore, not the status quo of industrial production. Instead it constructed a complexity that was not supposed to have echo in the actual world. Such an increased complexity should enable humankind to appreciate more and more dissonant structures.

Complex acoustic structures—noise—became understood as musical material and thus integrated into the sphere of musical sounds. Thus, the human sensorium continuously adjusted itself to increasingly complex structures and finally processed them as simple, not very interesting sensations. Accordingly, the art of noises was an instrument that triggered the senses and programmed brains for more complex forms of pattern recognition. It was not only supposed to calibrate aesthetic judgment, but also capable of training humans for technologies and wars to come. In *The Art of Noises*, war had a special place and Russolo acknowledged that the noises of war were by far the most complex.

> Marvelous and tragic symphony of the noises of war! The strangest and the most powerful noises are gathered together there! A man who comes from a noisy modern city, who knows all the noises of the street, of the railway stations, and of the vastly different factories will still find something up there at the front to amaze him. He will still find noises in which he can feel a new and unexpected emotion.[71]

War offered the greatest variety of noises in modernity, and thus Futurist music could be seen as a preparation for the battlefield. One chapter of Russolo's book is dedicated exclusively to the noises of war.[72] In this chapter he emphasized the importance of the auditory sense on the battlefield: "In modern warfare, mechanical and metallic, the element of sight is almost zero. The sense, the significance, and the expressiveness of noises, however, are infinite."[73] He acknowledged that the glissando—the most important feature of his *intonarumori*—was also the dominant noise on the battlefield, because, while traveling through the air, all shells created a decreasing scale.[74] Further, Russolo identified the development of a certain musical sensitivity to the sounds of the battlefield as the most fundamental survival technique. Only if one was able to distinguish certain "sounds" from the noisy background, one could predict the size and trajectory of a flying object, and act accordingly.[75]

> From noise, the different calibers of grenades and shrapnels can be known even before they explode. Noise enables us to discern a marching patrol in deepest darkness, even to judging the number of men that compose it. From the intensity of rifle fire, the number of defenders of a given position can be determined.... Whatever the caliber of the shell, the whistling that it makes in the air is the same in one respect: from the moment the shell leaves the cannon until its arrival, it falls in pitch until the explosion. This difference in pitch can equal or even exceed two octaves in a long trajectory. The passage from the highest pitch to the lowest through all the steps of the scale is made *enhamonically*, that is, it is a true *shading* from the highest to the lowest pitch.[76]

Russolo's noise design was not an imitation of the battlefield, because it had no mimetic similarity to it. Yet, as his remarks about the noises of the shrapnel show, he recognized his *intonarumori* as capable of producing structures analogous to the noises of the battlefield, such as the glissando. The *intonarumori* exhibited a variety of noises, which the audience should try to filter and organize. The adjustment to Futurist music corresponded to the auditive demands of the battlefield: in both instances the listener should have identified complex sound patterns on a noisy background. This simulation of the war zone through *intonarumori* inverts Kittler's thesis of the abuse of military equipment. Instead of military technology that is used for entertainment purposes, the musical instrument of the *intonarumore* was supposed to train the sensorium of the listeners, so that they became accustomed to the art of noises and able to adjust more efficiently to the noise of war and traffic.[77]

Such a simulation demanded powerful media technology for provoking and training the audience. It is therefore significant that Russolo's project was undermined, because his *intonarumori* did not have the power to overwrite the given reality—that is, the *intonarumori* were not loud enough to compete with the noises of engines and cannons, or even of the audience: "As can be seen, the difficulty of performances with the orchestra of noise instruments is not so great as it would seem at first sight. The only great difficulty seems to be the bestiality of the public that does not want to hear it."[78] The problem of the art of noises was not the difficulty of performance but, ironically, noise itself. Russolo complained that the noise produced by the audience was the most disturbing factor for his *intonarumori* performances. The simulation failed at the moment when the noise intoners were not able to challenge the irritations produced by the outside world, because the machines were simply not loud enough. Reportedly, the mere presence of his *intonarumori* caused the audience to rebel, even before Russolo had the chance to begin his performance.[79] As a result, they could not hear the noise performances. Russolo certainly did not develop the aesthetics of a rock concert in which the amplified sound produced on stage overwrites the loud, yelling crowd. Quite the opposite, his compositions still presupposed a quiet symphony audience.[80]

The composer Edgar Varèse pointed out such technological and aesthetic problems with Russolo's machines by characterizing the *intonarumori* as "noisemakers that made so little noise."[81] Although Varèse primarily addressed the *intonarumori*'s inability to produce a great scale of tones, he also pointed to the central problem that the volume of the *intonarumori* was not loud enough to block the response from the audience. Lacking modern technologies of amplification, Russolo was unable to overwhelm his audience.[82] This experience not only makes the Futurist experiment somewhat ludicrous, but also clearly demonstrates that the art of noises had to become an environment that would be strong enough to control the reactions of the audience. In fact, the reports of the *serate* indicate that with its protests the audience was actually the much more successful noise artist.

The parasitic noise that Russolo squeezed out of his intoners was supposed to transcend its status as mere accidental disturbance. However, it did not lose its parasitical character. It did not simply reprogram the audience, but caused an irritation and a reaction. The Dadaists were much more aware of the parasitic nature of noise art and consciously applied its subversive power.

Dada Noise

From the beginning of Dada in Zurich, noise belonged to the iconic elements of the movement. The explicit and sometimes even obsessive incorporation of noise in performances can be seen as a rebellion against the predominantly louder, more destructive, and more influential noisescape of the time—the battlefields of the First World War. However, the Dadaists' noises were, compared with the noises of machine guns, tanks, and heavy artillery not more (perhaps even less) than parasitic noise in a channel. Nonetheless, these parasitic irritations attempted to change and transform the modern society as much as the cannons at the Western Front. The Dada noise, however, was an explicitly nonmilitaristic phenomenon and not, like Russolo's art of noises, a simulation of the war zone. The Dadaist Hugo Ball even reflected about noise as an element that created a resistance to the emerging technoscapes of the early twentieth century. As I have outlined in Chapter 2, he understood Dada bruitism as a practice for reconstructing an individuality that got lost in the ubiquitous noises of modern media and technology. As he states, "[n]oises (an rrrr drawn out for minutes, or crashes, or sirens, etc.) are superior to the human voice in energy."[83] What Ball described resembles very much the acoustic capacities of Russolo's *intonarumori*, and also similar to Russolo, he recognized noise as a sign for the industrial background that determines human existence. He, however, did not dream of a feedback system that would entangle the human subject even more into industrial processes as Russolo did, but aimed at a poetic language that displayed and not simply affirmed the clash between the individual and the surrounding environment. Ball's sound poetry, although reminiscent of and influenced by Futurist poetry, tried to escape the channels of mass media and technology. It is decisive that Ball used the human voice and not media technology as the noise-generating source. Ball's poetry was explicitly human and not explicitly posthuman, as were Marinetti's and Russolo's artistic experiments. However, Ball also recognized that this human voice was only able to represent the incongruence between the individual and the machine. Ball's poetry is an exception within the Dada movement, because it was not geared toward an abuse of media but was intended to establish the "true" or "primal" use of the human voice.

Ball's understanding of a "primal sound" was probably the reason why the Dadaists—although they also integrated the noises of drums and other objects into their performances—primarily used the human voice and language in their noise experiments.[84] They also did not incorporate machines that had solely the function of generating noise—such as the *intonarumori*. Nonetheless, the Dadaists acknowledged the importance of the Futurist art of noises for their own noise art.[85] Most importantly, Richard Huelsenbeck portrayed himself as the inventor of noise performances that took on human articulation. He referred to articulatory compositions consisting only of vowels (*concert voyelles*) or to poetry that incorporated all kinds of uttered noises (*poème bruitiste*)—that is, articulations that were not identifiable as linguistic expressions. As inspiration for his own noise creations, Huelsenbeck alluded to the Futurists and especially highlighted Russolo's composition "reveil de la capitale," but his remarks in *En avant Dada* make clear that his understanding of noise aesthetics was quite different from Russolo's:

> From Marinetti we also borrowed "bruitism," or noise music, *le concerte bruitiste*, which, blessed memory, had created such a stir at the first appearance of the futurists in Milan, where they had regaled the audience with *le reveil de la capitale*. I spoke on the significance of bruitism at a number of open Dada gatherings. "*Le bruit*," noise with imitative effects, was introduced into art (in this connection we can hardly speak of individual arts, music, or literature) by Marinetti, who used a chorus of typewriters, kettledrums, rattles and pot-covers to suggest the "awakening of the capital"; at first it was intended as nothing more than a rather violent reminder of the colorfulness of life.[86]

The Dadaists took on the Futurist ideas, but Huelsenbeck transformed and strongly altered Russolo's concept of an art of noises. This becomes clear when Huelsenbeck ascribes the invention of the art of noises to Marinetti and not to Russolo. In fact, Huelsenbeck had only a very superficial knowledge of the Futurist noise experiments and understood them as mere imitations of the modern world—a mistake that, as we saw in the discussion of Russolo, was often made. Further, his assumption that the awakening of the city in Russolo's composition was represented through noises caused by objects from everyday life is wrong. Apparently, Huelsenbeck did not know the technologies of Futurist composition. He did not mention Russolo's *intonarumori* at all. Instead, he privileged human articulation in his own noise aesthetics and only acknowledged the simple instruments—such as drums, toy guns, and lids—that were integral parts of Dada performances in Zurich.[87]

Huelsenbeck recognized similarities between Marinetti's events and his own anarchic ideas for experimenting with noise, but he did not accept the Futurist ideology of power and war that stood behind Marinetti's incorporation of noise into Futurist aesthetics. In place of the cannons, trains, and cars of the Futurist noisescape, Huelsenbeck referred simply to toys, drums, and kitchen utensils. The militaristic background noise of Futurism was replaced in Dada by an anarchic rebellion of the small, common, and antiheroic.

Overall, Huelsenbeck gives a distorted account of the Futurist noise practices, replacing Futurist militarism with the anarchic rituals of the Dadaists themselves. Huelsenbeck, however, does not paint a completely false picture of Futurist activities. What he describes is not Russolo's art of noises but rather the parasitic noise emerging at the Futurist happenings. These Futurist events—in which Marinetti and his friends read poems, proclaimed manifestos, showed pictures, staged short sketches, and performed Futurist music—were known not so much as places for new artistic innovations as moments of scandal and public outrage. In fact, when Huelsenbeck described the noises of Dada bruitism, he was invoking Futurist performances and not Russolo's compositions.

The reason for Huelsenbeck's misapprehension of Futurist music is probably based on the representation of Futurist activities in the contemporaneous press. Journalists described Futurism mostly as a provocation of public scandal and riot and not as a new art movement. A journalist reported, for example, about one such evening:

> [T]he audience grew so furious towards the end the actors could hardly be persuaded to come on stage at all. Marinetti himself, who fought well for Italy during the war, supported the bombardment almost without flinching, although he was hit on the head several times by apples and tomatoes, and his dress shirt was spotted with tomato juice, but the company was not quite so brave. When Futurist artists came on the stage carrying paintings they had achieved they used their masterpieces quite frankly as shields.[88]

Indeed, these Futurist *serate* incorporated noises produced by a variety of everyday utensils, which the audience threw at the Futurists and vice versa. The journalist, however, strongly emphasized the militaristic nature of the event by highlighting Marinetti as a "war hero" enduring the attacks by the audience bravely. This militaristic undercurrent was not present in Dada reports. However, Huelsenbeck gave a description of the performances in the Cabaret Voltaire in which the outrage of the audience was strikingly similar to the reports of the Futurist *serate*: "Loud roars from the audience. 'We want our money back.' First tribute in form of apples, potatoes and rotten eggs. They press against the podium, shout, cry, weep: the dadaist spirit, which was later to spread like an epidemic, starts to infect them."[89] The outrage and the interjections of the audience were common themes of Futurist as well as Dada performances. While in Futurism this provocation appeared as a conflict in which the Futurists fought against the audience, in Dada, noise spread like an infection over the stage into the hall. This contamination aggravated the audience and eliminated the gap between active performers and passive audience. Huelsenbeck's concept of noise performance was not so much inspired by an ideological "noise" program as by the uncontrollable and omnipresent parasitic disturbances created through the interaction between stage and audience. This is precisely the point where Huelsenbeck's and Ball's noise aesthetic diverged. While Ball envisioned noise as a performative element that would attempt through the human voice to reestablish a true or primal form of communication, Huelsenbeck consciously abused noise as an amplification system.

Dada Feedback

Departing from his understanding of Marinetti's noise performances, Huelsenbeck developed a noise aesthetic that configured noise as a hint at the colorful interplay of life ("reminder of the colorfulness of life"). In a passage from his book *En avant Dada*, Huelsenbeck outlines how he understood the use of noise in Futurism and also presented his theory of noise:

> Consequently Marinetti and his group love war as the highest expression of the conflict of things, as a spontaneous eruption of possibilities, as movement, as a simultaneous poem, as a symphony of cries, shots, commands, embodying an attempted solution of the problem of life in motion. The problem of the soul is volcanic in nature. Every movement naturally produces noise. While number, and consequently melody, are symbols presupposing a faculty for abstraction, noise is a direct call to action. Music of whatever nature is harmonious, artistic, an activity of reason—but bruitism is life itself, it cannot be judged like a book, but rather it is part of our personality, which attacks us, pursues us and tears us to pieces. Bruitism is a view of life, which, strange as it may seem at first, compels men to make an ultimate decision. There are only bruitists, and others. While we are speaking of music, Wagner had shown all the hypocrisy inherent in a pathetic faculty of abstraction—the screeching of a brake, on the other hand, could at least give you a toothache.[90]

For Huelsenbeck, noise was a parasitic element that hung on every development. "Life in motion" was always connected to noise that emerged from change. The Dadaist's vitalistic understanding of noise corresponds to Serres's theorem that complex systems, because they are complex, always generate something that was not intended, but just happened. The complexity of life has for Huelsenbeck, and also for Serres, a performative quality that cannot be contained or predicted. Noise constitutes an escalation that emerges from the side effects of life and cannot simply be stopped. It is an invasive, transgressive, and productive element that is on the base of transformation, and thus the ideal stimulus for avant-garde art. The Futurist admiration of war was directed precisely at this fascination with escalating complexities.

Huelsenbeck identified Futurist art and especially its incorporation of noise as an attempt to deal with the "problem of life," that is, complexity. Accordingly, Huelsenbeck deciphered the Futurist fascination with war ("war as the highest expression of conflict") not solely as the love for all things new and modern, but rather as the admiration of antagonistic and ultimately escalating situations. However, for Dada this fascination with struggle did not remain bound to the battlefield; it rather crystallized in aesthetic practices like the "simultaneous poem" (as Huelsenbeck pointed out) and also echoed in the tumult at the serate.[91] According to Huelsenbeck, the Futurists pursued an aesthetic operation, in which they translated the struggle as experienced on the battlefield into their art for representing conflict, but also for provoking tumult.[92] Huelsenbeck recognized a feedback loop that was already important to Russolo's art of noises. The noises of the industrial world or from the battlefield constituted the raw material for the design of an aesthetic transformation of noise. These noise patterns (either Russolo's sound-noise or Huelsenbeck's noise poetry) were fed back to the crowd and amplified by the outraged voices of the audience.

Further, Huelsenbeck shared the Futurist belief in the disturbing function of noise. His model of noise followed the lines of Marinetti's performance aesthetics—it, however, differed somewhat from Russolo's art of noises. While Russolo constructed his noise aesthetics on the basis of and in opposition to Helmholtz's acoustics, Huelsenbeck's concept was based on a vitalistic thinking centered on performance and the integration of the audience.[93] It was central to Dada bruitism that noise was a phenomenon that opened up an immediate access to the world that was not prestructured by a symbolic system. When Huelsenbeck compares the organized system of music to unorganized noise, he emphasizes precisely this character of noise. His reflection on music mirrors Russolo's critique of Helmholtz's acoustics. Huelsenbeck related music to reason and harmony, whereas noise indicated life and nature. Noise is a parasite that emerges as unintended side effect that blocks the iterability required by symbolic sign systems. Noise does not belong to a symbolic order, but to a phonographic reality that can only be captured by analog data processing. It is the object of the continuous curve and not of the discrete sign. Russolo's "note-line" already indicated this proximity between noise and the transcription systems of modern life sciences.

Noise is not a sign, but it is an impulse caused by a process in the world. This concrete physical quality of noise can have the power to affect the perceiving subject physically. The noise of a loud car not only indicates an automobile, or warns pedestrians, but also hurts the ears. By attesting that the noise of a brake may have the power to cause toothache, Huelsenbeck clearly recognized this physical power of noise.

For Huelsenbeck noise was a transgressive and escalating event able to provoke the audience physically. Accordingly, the use of noise in the Dada theater constituted an invasion of physical stimulation into aesthetic performances. The audience could no longer perceive the performance as something distant. The spectators were physically aggravated by disturbances and responded on their side with the demolition of the theater. The physical energy projected by Dada noise entered a feedback loop: the aggravations of the stage irritated the audience, who threw them back on the stage. This initiated a circle that amplified the force and complexity of the Dada performance through an integration of a multitude of new performers, namely the spectators. They no longer behaved like a tame theater audience, but rather became, as an angry mob, part of the performance or, in more technical terms, an amplifier based on feedback loops.

A report about a "scandalous soirée" from 1919 demonstrates the parasitic exploitation of the audience through the Dadaists. The reporter of the *Basler Nachrichten* commented with astonishment the calm and relaxed attitude of the Dadaist Walter Serner: "It was whistled, screamed, small coins, orange peels and cuss words were thrown on the stage and one stamped with feet and chairs. One has, nonetheless to admire the tranquility of the speaker, who remained seated within this hail of objects and noises."[94] Tristan Tzara's reaction was similar: "Already after the first stanza the tumult started again. Herr Tzara, however, read as long undisturbed as he was booed out. In spite of the rain of coins and cigarettes, he remained bravely on the stage."[95] The journalist clearly portrayed the parasitic nature of these two performances. Both artists sent out a small impulse into the communication channel. This impulse, however, was, as I have discussed in the manifesto and poetry chapter, not a meaningful sign but an irritant. It was a noise that could not be integrated into a hermeneutic understanding. This irritation provoked a reaction by the audience, and this reaction was significantly stronger than the initial provocation. Tzara and Serner just leaned back and observed how the chaos emerged. Without adding anything than an incomprehensible noise to the communication, they created and amplified a chaotic chain reaction.

Dada's aim, as frequently pointed out, was the destruction of borders.[96] This annihilation was not done by the Dadaists alone, but constituted through a feedback of the audience. To provoke such a dynamic was one of the major aims of Dada art, not solely as an attempt to challenge established aesthetic values but also to amplify the Dada noise on a very literal and that means technical level—that is, to make it louder. It is important that this was done in a parasitic way, because the Dadaists would have not been able to create such massive energies on their own. This is a central difference to Russolo. For him, the feedback of media technologies was supposed to exclude the audience; they were merely outside observers. Russolo aimed at a structural feedback that would increase the complexity of noise through a continuous reflection of noises already present. The technology enthusiast Raoul Hausmann apparently understood the problem of the Futurist art of noises. He recognized the importance of amplification for the avant-garde, and one of his first technical designs was an amplification system for the gramophone that ironically was connected to a noise reduction system.

Hausmann's Gramophone

As I outlined, the early Dada noise experiments in Zurich were not based on media technology, and the following excerpt from a report about a Dada soirée demonstrates the quite complicated relationship to phonographic media in Dada Berlin.

> Then there sounds out a gramophone "Little Doll you are my precious darling." As the record nears its end, a second gramophone begins to play the same melody. The Dadaists-Extras listen carefully. Hands at the ears. But the audience knows already what to do. One screams "down with the gramophone" and as the performance ends, one applauds.[97]

This quotation underlines the parasitic dynamic that was already established in Zurich. For creating a strong response, the Dadaists only had to offer a minor irritant, in this case the two simultaneously played gramophones, to provoke a positive feedback from the audience. The author of these lines, Frank Schulz, displayed the Dadaists as connoisseurs of phonographic noise, but he also implied that the Dadaists only abused noise to create an impulse in the audience to reject technology. The scene, thus, presents an ambivalent relationship to the gramophone, and the attitude of most Dadaists in Berlin to phonographic media probably resembled the simultaneous rejection and fascination of mass-produced items that also resonates in their collages. Hausmann, however, was keenly interested in this technology.

While Huelsenbeck represented the essence of Dada as a noisy celebration, Hausmann meditated already in the Dada time about the consequences of noise and the ways to eliminate disturbances that were intended in Dada art from technical equipment. The parasitic noise that haunted the dreams of electrical engineers also occupied Hausmann's mind. In 1922, Hausmann sketched down the construction of a new sound pickup for gramophones.

His notes for the "transversally vibrating sound pickup"[98] started out with a clear diagnosis of the technical standard of his time: "The commonly used gramophone sound pickups connected to a bell mouth do not produce a clean sound."[99] Hausmann was right in this respect. Early phonographic devices were not able to reproduce sound in a very high quality, because the materiality of the gramophone was still apparent and did not completely vanish as, for example, in today's MP3 players. The Dadasoph, however, did not celebrate this subcutaneous and subversive potential of technology; he even did not recognize an aesthetic value in the white noise of phonographic reproduction. Unlike Russolo he was not inspired by the parasite that was creeping out of the bell mouth, and unlike Huelsenbeck he was not fascinated by an amplification of these disturbing noises. Hausmann adopted the attitude of an engineer who clearly distinguished between sound and noise and identified two problems of the gramophones of his time. First, he recognized that the way in which vibrations were transmitted through the needle to a membrane was inefficient and created rather than eliminated disturbances.[100] Second, Hausmann was disappointed by the sound volume of the gramophone and criticized the mode of amplification.[101]

Apparently, Hausmann was aware of the problem that Russolo faced, namely that the phonograph was not loud enough to cause an avant-garde revolution. The sound in a gramophone was simply transmitted from the needle to the membrane, and the sound was merely amplified by a horn. Hausmann suggested in his design that one horn was not enough and that an amplifier element was needed in a gramophone. As a solution for this problem, Hausmann mimicked the stage-audience feedback that amplified the noises of the Dada evenings. This amplifier element was simply mechanical. Instead of one horn, Hausmann intended to employ two sets of horns ("Trichterfelder").[102] The first set contained 14 and the second 52 horns. Hausmann imagined that the sound would be fed from one amplifier system into another of the same structure, thereby increasing its volume. This resembled the projection of noise into the audience, which would in return amplify noise through many voices. Even if this appears as a simplistic and not very original idea, Hausmann's design was not so far off from other work that was done in electrical engineering in his time.

Amplification through feedback had already become possible through vacuum tubes in 1912. Edwin Howard Armstrong developed a regenerative circuit that consisted of an amplifying vacuum tube with its output connected to its input through a feedback loop.[103] Lee De Forest claimed to be the first to have developed such feedback amplification, an assertion that started a long patent fight.[104] This parasitic abuse of ideas is, however, here not of concern. It is rather more significant that amplification through feedback was an established practice in 1922,[105] and Hausmann was probably at least partly aware of such developments. It is, nonetheless, odd that he tried to mimic the function of electronic systems through a mechanical construction. In the early twenties, Hausmann was already very much interested in questions of electricity and electrical engineering. In fact, the other part of the patent for the gramophone system, a noise-reducing sound pickup, seems to allude to an electroacoustic paradigm.

Hausmann asserted that the way in which the needle and the sound-transmitting membrane were connected, amplified "noises caused through the needle."[106] The disturbing noises were here clearly understood as a material index of the sound-processing equipment. He recognized that the parasite was not easily divorced from the signal, but that noise and sound stemmed from the same source. Hausmann's strategy of noise reduction was based on reconstructing the gramophone in a way that these material perturbations were not produced in the first place. To do that, he suggested that the needle be turned 45 degrees and the membrane 90 degrees in the usual layout of a gramophone. Hausmann asserted that this tweaking would improve the quality of sound transmission, because the vibrations were no longer transmitted "longitudinal," but "transversal."[107]

This simple adjustment might or might not have helped, but what is interesting about this design is that he uses the distinction between longitudinal and transversal vibrations. This distinction is associated with the difference between mechanical and electromagnetic waves. Mechanical waves, for example sound waves, are considered as longitudinal waves that propagate through a medium. The waves are created through an alternating pressure that is exercised on the carrying medium, for example air. Electromagnetic waves and light consist of transversal vibrations. Transversal waves travel perpendicular to the direction of wave propagation. Although there are mixed forms—for example, water waves propagate transversal and longitudinal—electromagnetic waves are only transversal. I assume that Hausmann believed that a "transversally" swinging membrane would be an improvement, because in his thinking it was related to an electromagnetic paradigm that is based on ether. In a notebook from 1922, he explicitly refers to sound as a transversal and longitudinal wave and recognizes through that an analogy between sound and light waves.[108] This analogy is the basis for his optophonetic art, which I will discuss in the following chapter.

Technically, Hausmann's idea was very simplistic and probably would not have greatly improved the sound. It, however, points toward an understanding of a synesthetic art in which light and sound coincide. With his emphasis on transversal vibrations, Hausmann also tried to show that he understood that the improvement of sound-reproducing equipment and media art could not be found in simple mechanical systems, but in electrical engineering. At this time, he did not have the means to work on this path, but he tried to simulate it in his gramophone design. In fact, Hausmann's design was soon outdated by the new sound pickup invented by Electrola that started the electrification of the gramophone, and that was mentioned by Hausmann in a letter to his friend Daniel Broido as the final reason why he did not peruse patenting this design.[109]

Even if his improvements of the gramophone were never constructed, never patented, and already outdated when he invented them, the patent design indicates that the avant-garde interest in noise and amplification resonate in his technical work. As I will outline in the last chapter, Hausmann used technological constructions as tools for reflecting on aesthetic and anthropological ideas. The gramophone improvement is one of the earliest documents in Hausmann's estate that point toward such a relationship between his thinking and technology. This involvement with media engineering should continue. Hausmann recognized that mechanical systems would not be able to realize the aesthetic dreams of the avant-garde, but that modern electronics would provide the technological flexibility that a true art of noise required.

HAUSMANN AND THE VACUUM TUBE

The shift from the mechanics of noise to the electronics of sound was in the air when Hausmann designed his sound system. In fact, Hausmann's gramophone was dramatically behind contemporaneous developments. One of the first electric musical instruments was the Telharmonium or

Dynamophone that the American engineer Thaddeus Cahill constructed in 1901. It was an enormous sound-producing system that supposedly weighed about 200 tons. It generated sound through mechanical oscillators consisting of rotating tone wheels or "rheotomes" that produced differently oscillating currents through alternate sections of conducting and insulating material.[110]

In fact, this design is not so completely different from Russolo's construction. The "rheotomes" produced, like the rotating disks in the *intonarumori*, a continuous vibration, and the oscillating current was connected to a telephone circuit, which translated the electrical frequency into a sound. The significant difference between the Telharmonium and the *intonarumori* lies in the electrification, and the *intonarumori* can be recognized as a mechanical alternative to electrical oscillators. Like Russolo's noise intoners, the Telharmonium had no significant amplification system and therefore demanded huge generators that would produce a great amount of power, so that a significant volume could be emitted by the speakers. In contrast, modern audio systems take the signal from the sound source and amplify it much more efficiently through vacuum tubes or, today, through transistor circuits. However, the connection to the telephone and the reliance on impressive dynamos established the two different names, "telharmonium" (telephone + harmonium) and "dynamophone" (dynamo + telephone), of Cahill's first electroacoustic instrument.[111]

Clearly, this device was not intended for mass production. Its enormous dimension made it completely impractical for individualized mass use. Cahill, however, envisioned a mass distribution of the telharmonic sound through telephone networks, and his performances in New York in 1906 were in fact transmitted through cables to numerous restaurants in the neighborhood.[112] It is an ironic coincidence that in 1907 the American engineer Lee De Forest worked together with Cahill on a wireless transmission of the telharmonic sound[113]—ironic because De Forest's invention of the Audion, which he patented in the same year, would soon open up the way to much smaller and simpler electronic sound machines.

De Forest's Audion was a vacuum tube designed to function as an antenna for radio transmission that also could be used as an oscillator. An electrical oscillator is able to create determined frequencies, which when connected to a speaker can be transformed into sound. The Audion was very significant because it enabled a reliable, secure, and continuous emission of radio waves at an economic price and therefore provided the breakthrough to the transmission of audio through radio channels.[114] De Forest's Audion Piano, which he patented in 1915, employed an Audion tube as an oscillator to create sound vibrations, and this device constitutes the first musical instrument that used vacuum tubes for sound generation.

This development was recognized by artists of the time, and in 1923 Moholy-Nagy gave a comprehensive account of the possibilities of electronic music. The text "New Plasticism in Music," which became very famous for its suggestion to use the gramophone as a means of music production, opens up with a discussion of the new possibilities of the vacuum tube. Moholy-Nagy acknowledges that the Futurist project to create new sounds was now being fulfilled through new amplifier tubes that produced all kinds of acoustic sensations.[115] As I pointed out, these technologies were already known at the time, and it is quite late when Hausmann recognizes, in 1931, in a similar manner as Moholy-Nagy, the continuation of the Futurist noise project through the vacuum tube. Particularly, in his text "The Overbred Arts" he discussed such developments toward a new music.

In this text, Hausmann rejected at first new compositional methods such as Schönberg's atonal pieces.[116] For Hausmann, these steps would not break through the restriction of music and would not achieve a "physiological sound."[117] It is not entirely clear what Hausmann meant by "physiological sound," but it seemed to allude to a synesthetic, or "optophonetic," form of perception, which I will discuss in detail in the last chapter. However, the text identified Russolo's art of noises as a first fundamental step toward a complete reorganization of music, but rejected it as full of individual arbitrariness. It is also quite unclear what Hausmann meant with this criticism, but I assume that he alluded basically to Moholy-Nagy's article about the gramophone, which made very similar assertions: Mohloy-Nagy takes the idea that future music had to negotiate between individual and universal content from Piet Mondrian.[118] Moholy-Nagy asserted that the new electronic music enabled such a sound. New musical instruments should open up the way toward these new perceptual dimensions.[119] Hausmann followed precisely this track and referred in his text to such different devices as the Clavilux developed by Thomas Wilfred, the Elektrophon designed by Jörg Mager, and the Theremin named after his inventor Lev Theremin. The Clavilux, however, does not really fit in this enumeration. Wilfred designed a system that would only produce an interplay of colors and not of sounds.[120] This instrument had something to do with Hausmann's ideas about synesthesia, but it was not an acoustic instrument that employed vacuum tubes. In contrast, the Theremin, whose sound is familiar with fifties' and sixties' science fiction movies, and the Elektrophon can appropriately be described as "howling radio sets"[121] that used the technologies of modern electrical engineering, or in the German terminology that Hausmann used, "Nachrichtentechnik." "Nachrichtentechnik" refers to the field of signal processing within electrical engineering, and Hausmann correctly pointed out that the vacuum tube was at the basis of this discipline in the twenties. Hausmann acknowledged further that this technology enabled an astonishing modulation of sound.

> Its [Nachrichtentechnik] most valuable invention is the radio tube. In that vacuum, incredibly sensitive, practically de-materialized, vibrations are possible, so much so that with such technology a sound can be richly altered in its three "dimensions" (namely, pitch, volume, and timbre), in ways that were simply unthinkable with the instruments available up to this point. With a small rotary capacitor, for example, in conjunction with a jamming transmitter, one can—in a fraction of a second—not only run through several octaves [note by note] but also play micro-intervals, like quarters, sixths, or eighths of a tone, as easy as you like.[122]

This description brings us back full circle to Russolo. Modulation of sound through vacuum tubes enabled an active design of sound; it was also possible to play rapid glissandi and microtonal intervals. An explosion of unheard, nonreferential acoustic sensations was achievable, and that too at a considerable volume. Russolo's dream had come true. However, Hausmann emphasized another possibility of modern electronics and described something that would have been Russolo's nightmare: "It is, however, possible to influence electroacoustically the overtones of a sound in such a way that the single overtones are simply eliminated through a ‚sifting' "[123] Here, the Dadasoph completely turned away from noise. The timbre or overtones that constituted the foundation of Russolo's art of noises could now be cancelled out. It is interesting to see that Hausmann's gramophone was based on a "positive" feedback that would have amplified everything, including the parasitic noise—precisely in the same way as the Dada performances did. In the age of the vacuum tube, however, "negative" feedback became possible that consisted in filtering the parasitic elements. Positive feedback increased the power of a signal—also its unintended properties. A negative feedback striped down unintended detritus and reduced unintended complexity. The vacuum tube was thus not only the beginning of a new electroacoustic music, but also the end of the ubiquitous parasite in phonographic media.

Hausmann's explorations in the field of sound and noise show that the avant-garde artists of the twentieth century did not simply embrace the chaotic nature of something that Helmholtz classified as noise. Especially Hausmann was highly sensitive to developments in technology that reconfigured an understanding of communication. Hausmann was fascinated by the possibility to create acoustic sensations on the basis of semantically hollow media loops. The indexical noise of the early Dada performances turned in the age of signal processing into sound modulations that simulated the escalating dynamic of the Dada performance in a simple oscillating electrical circuit.

Noise and Modernity

Dada and Futurism recognized noise as an integral part of modernity. However, the noises of the avant-garde did not concentrate so much on the loud blasts that the war machines of the First World War produced, as on the parasitic noises that were accessible as irritations of communication channels. The American physician and antinoise lobbyist John H. Girdner came to a similar assessment of the importance of parasitic irritations and in 1896 had already identified[124] the disturbances of the city life as ubiquitous and highly problematic.

> The act of hearing should not require attention. Under ordinary circumstances, no effort calling out consciousness of the operation is elicited. The vibrations, or sound waves, are conducted to the sensorium, where they are interpreted and duly considered. But when a Bale of discordant sounds and noises of every degree of harshness and force is poured into the auditory canals, an effort, indeed, is required to catch the sounds we wish to interpret, and to eliminate those which are not only of no consequence, but positively painful. This sustained effort of selection and elimination is an incalculable strain and source of exhaustion to our nervous energy. The fact that persons who live in the midst of confusing and discordant noises, as do the dwellers in large cities, become in time accustomed to them, is no proof that the noises are any the less destructive and exhausting to the brain and nervous system. Such persons have only become expert in discriminating and selecting the sounds in which they be interested at the moment.[125]

For a noise-free channel, Girdner called for a media environment that would enable the proper reception of input. The perception of information through the senses was supposed to happen without attention, that is, without environmental distraction that forced the subject to select the correct message from a perturbed channel. The environment of the modern city—in this case New York—demanded a very high degree of attention from the nervous system, a fact that Girdner recognized as a cause of stress, which then became a factor in illness and death. Girdner's understanding of noise—as something that complicated receptive processes—corresponds to Serres's conception of the parasite. Noise is a ubiquitous factor that makes it hard to select the correct message in a communicative situation. The avant-garde artists understood Girdner's diagnosis very well. However, their goal was not to reduce the complexity of the environment, but to increase the pathogenetic effects of the side noises. Russolo used his sound noise for a recalibration of the senses, and Huelsenbeck as a productive aggravation of the audience.

Noise was no longer conceptualized by the avant-garde as part of the environment but entered the channel as a signal. This is where the Futurist simulation of noisecapes started. Everything that blocked high fidelity in early gramophones was used by Russolo to design new timbres, or sound-noises. Noise was here not conceptualized as an invasive outsider, but as something that emerged from the media system itself. Russolo's dream was to increase the presence of noise so much that it would overwrite the presence of machines: "Our multiplied sensibility, having been conquered by futurist eyes, will finally have some futurist ears. Thus, the motors and machines of our industrial cities can one day be given pitches, so that every workshop will become an intoxicating orchestra of noises."[126] Noise should develop from a pollution of the communication channel into the actual signal that was sent by the information source. However, Russolo's noise technologies were so weak and imprisoned in a mechanistic paradigm that they were nothing more than the initial impulse for noises produced and amplified through a feedback loop initiated by the audience.

The Dadaists implemented a similar feedback intentionally, but without media technology—they simply used their audiences to echo the Dada noise. The technology freak Hausmann quickly realized that feedback loops were not only artistic tactics but also technological strategies to amplify sound and noise. However, his gramophone would have only created a positive feedback that would have greatly increased all the parasitic noise as well. Therefore, he recognized the importance to minimize all the side noises produced by the gramophone needle. Nonetheless, he also instinctively believed that electronics would overcome the sheer mechanical nature of the early-twentieth-century attempts of an art of noise. The radio tube would soon realize a sound and noise modulation that would surmount even Russolo's wildest fantasies. Hausmann's insights further indicate that the initial fascination with noise that can be found in Dada as well as in Futurism was not geared toward as simple celebration of the chaotic and uncontrollable. The goal of the avant-garde was not only to generate disturbing structures, but also to regulate and shape this chaos.

The noise experiments of the avant-garde are of special significance for a media historical approach, because they constitute the point where Dada and Futurist artists transcended established media channels. Helmholtz identified noise as the opposite of sound. The phonograph changed this situation conceptually and technologically. Noises could now be integrated into music, because they became reproducible in controllable setups. The phonograph also opened up to the possibility to reflect about every acoustical event (and not only a musical tone) as a signal processed by a media device. Noises and sounds were now processed and created by media technology. This is the foundation of modern signal processing, and it is quite an important insight of Hausmann to recognize that the vacuum tube constituted the end of a sheer mechanistic art of noises, because it enabled the infinite creation and modulation of sounds and noises electronically.

The parasitic noises of the phonograph and the audiences stood at the beginning of the avant-garde experiments. The goal of artists such as Hausmann or Russolo was to expand and manage the realm of noise that they understood as one of the most significant phenomena of their time. Their strategies to control and generate noise were innovative in the sense that they generated a feedback system that short-circuited the noises of the performances with the noise-producing sources of the environment. Technologically, however, they were stuck in a mechanistic paradigm. This is quite astonishing, because their arts of noises developed precisely at the same time as the foundations for modern electronic music emerged. The exchange between aesthetics and electrical engineering, however, would improve in the twenties, when Hausmann and Marinetti took off to the ether of radio transmission.

CHAPTER 5

ETHER PARASITES

THE RADIO ENDED IT ALL. CERTAINLY, the invention of the radio by the British Italian engineer Guglielmo Marconi in 1895 even predated the avant-garde, but the German and Italian fascist regimes implemented radio as a ubiquitous media only in 1933—a time when Futurism faded out and Dadaists fled Germany from Hitler's menace. However, this political use of the medium was not the reason that the avant-garde experiment vanished in the ether. The Futurists as well as the Dadaists recognized the ability to broadcast data wirelessly as a clear sign that the future had arrived and a new human being would emerge in this media ecology that even superseded the technological fantasies of the avant-garde. The radio manifesto "La Radia" of 1933 documents this assessment of the wireless.[1] In it, Marinetti claims that this medium represents the ultimate means to achieve the Futurist goals, thereby cannibalizing all previous achievements such as *parole in libertà* or *l'arte dei rumori*. The radio becomes for Marinetti the instrument of a permanent, omnipresent contact with the audience. It does not wait for its listeners; it rather always broadcasts and constantly demands that everybody congregate in front of a receiver. This technical but intimate connection to the audience will be the model for Marinetti's radio plays that want to connect the Italian people through a mere physiological shock aesthetic to the apparatus.

This work in radio art is a culmination of Marinetti's ideas of an immediate form of communication, which is based on tactility and which Marinetti had developed in two manifestos titled "Tattilismo."[2] This search for a new form of perception is closely connected to Marinetti's desire to dehumanize the human body and to reread it in analogy to modern media technology. This discourse about tactility constitutes also a direct exchange between the Futurist and Raoul Hausmann. Hausmann wrote a manifesto titled "Présentismus,"[3] which he sent to Marinetti, whose response, however, clearly showed that the Futurist did not care much about the Dadaist's thoughts. This non-engagement is apparent, because Marinetti joyfully thanked Hausmann for the manifesto in his letter of acknowledgement.[4] This is something that he certainly would not have done if he had read the text, because Hausmann openly rejected the Futurist ideas and even directly insulted Marinetti, while he developed a counterprogram to the art of tactility established by Marinetti.

This exchange between Marinetti and Hausmann predates Walter Benjamin's famous discussion of tactility in the artwork essay by ten years. It shares, however, Benjamin's reflection that tactility is recognized as an interface between human physiology and media technology, but whereas Benjamin discusses tactility mainly in regard to film, Hausmann and Marinetti recognize it as a form of hypersensitivity that leads to a potential interconnection between human bodies and all kinds of media technology, including the wireless. The Futurist's as well as the Dadasoph's approaches to tactility start out from a desire to enhance human physiology by bringing together technology and the human sensorium and end up in a celebration of radio technology or, in more scientific terms, electromagnetic waves. While Marinetti expands through tactility his ideas of a physiological, nonhermeneutic form of poetry and theater to the ether, Hausmann's concepts of a new haptic art are based on his experimentation with technological equipment that started out with his work on a new sound pickup system for the gramophone (which I have discussed in Chapter 4) and culminated in his work with synesthetic, or in Hausmann's terminology *optophonetic*, machines that were based on the relatively new technology of the photocell.

This turn toward instruments that process light, or electromagnetic waves, remains for Marinetti and Hausmann connected to an understanding of the ether as a medium in which these phenomena propagate. This is interesting not only because artists conceive of their aesthetic programs in a scientific terminology, but also because the ether was, after Albert Einstein formulated his theory of relativity in 1905, quickly ruled out as a scientific hypothesis and only used by radio engineers as a simplification to explain the propagation of radio waves. Actually, in the case of Futurism, the ether was only embraced as a technological radio space of communication and not as an ontological foundation. Marinetti envisioned using the radio ether for his aesthetic purposes in a similar way as the totalitarian regimes of the thirties did for crowd control, and he intended to abuse the established technology of the fascist radio network. The fascist radio apparatus no longer had the democratic ability to send and receive, which the German playwright Bertolt Brecht has celebrated so much,[5] but was a sheer receiver that could convey commands to its subjects, and did not accept any feedback from its listeners.

Marinetti exploits exactly this deterministic nature of the radio, and he comes at least technologically close to the radio engineer Hans Bredow, whom Friedrich Kittler described as a parasite that abused military communication equipment to broadcast news and music into the trenches of the First World War, thereby establishing the foundation of the modern broadcasting industry.[6]

While Marinetti tinkered around with the radio as a technopolitical medium, Hausmann engaged with the radio or the electromagnetic spectrum in general on a much deeper and epistemological level. His optophonetic art had the ultimate goal to demonstrate that the human system is connected to the ether and thus could be conceived as a radio station. Hausmann's engagement with the ether can be appropriately described as an anthropotechnical exploration. From 1922 on, the Dadaist developed an understanding of the interplay between human physiology and technology that assumed that technologies do nothing else than represent innate organic functions of the human body that humankind just had not actualized. Technology, especially the radio and the photocell, became for Hausmann media art in the sense that by studying these apparatuses, one would not only learn more about technology, but more importantly one would gain insight into the unfulfilled potentials of the human body. Hausmann envisioned that the human organism could literally function as a radio receiver, so that at a certain point radio technology would disappear, because the human organism functioned like this technology. So, Hausmann's engagement with technology can be characterized as parasitic abuse of emerging technologies in order to conceive of the hidden physiological capacities of humans.

The turn toward the radio by the avant-garde also let the tactics of the parasite arrive historically in the context from where Michel Serres ultimately took it, namely communication engineering.[7] Interestingly, however, while noise in the sense of the disturbance of communication is so central for avant-garde poetry, music, manifestos, and visual art, it has hardly a place in Hausmann's and Marinetti's discussion of radio transmission or hypersensitive perception. The radio becomes rather the medium of a constant and uninterrupted transmission of impulses. The reason for this lies in the fact that Marinetti as well as Hausmann did not conceive the radio as a system that transmits hermeneutically coded messages. What the radio transmits can be both noise and signal; both artists were not too much concerned about the difference. What is more important, however, is interruption. The disturbance they conceive of is not a garbled signal, but the interruption of the transmission. The goal was not to subvert established media discourses, but to create a completely new media ecology.

The logic of the parasite that the avant-garde adopts under the radio paradigm is thus not so much concerned with irritation as with ubiquitous presence. The radio is always on and everywhere, it invades every space, and it is for Hausmann always already present in the brain as the basis of sense perception. The parasite is no longer an intruder, but rather constitutes the new media ecology into which the users are switched. While up to this point Dada and Futurism primarily engaged with existing media such as poetry, music, collage, and the newspaper, the development of a tactile, radiophonic, or optophonetic art was geared toward establishing its own hegemonic media environment, which the avant-garde created rather than subverted.

Marinetti's Tattilismo

In 1921 and 1924, Marinetti published manifestos on tactility. In these texts, he announced the importance of the sense of touch and also formulated a program for discovering new modes of perception and interconnection between the human sensorium and its surroundings.[8] Marinetti represents such a reinvention, acceleration, or enhancement of the human sensory apparatus as a new wave, a new beginning in Futurism.[9] This comes with a crucial transformation of an understanding of sensitivity, human relationships, erotics, and contact. Accordingly, the manifesto on Tattilismo begins by proclaiming the dawn of a new era, a new *sforzo* of Futurism—one that nonetheless remains connected to the old achievements such as *l'arte dei rumori* or *parole in libertà*, but one that will overcome all these ventures.

The entire manifesto is made up of a fast-paced staccato of different textual components. It opens with a familiar enumeration of the characteristics and achievements of Futurism, such as a hate of museums, a love for speed, the Futurist sculpture, and the variety theater.[10] This introductory part promptly ends in a little story that Marinetti weaves into his reflections on the society of his time.[11] He tells the story of the invention of Tattilismo and constructs a new founding myth for this new phase of Futurism by relying on motifs from older texts. Marinetti describes how he spent the summer in Antignano, where he was swimming off the coast, naked in the sea. Similarly to the first founding manifesto that ends with a bath in industrial mud, this scene connects elements of birth and procreation.

> I was naked in the silken waters lacerated by foaming rocks, sharp-edged like scissors knives razors, swimming among beds of seaweed saturated with iodine. I was naked in a sea of flexible steel, rippling against my body in an animated,

manly, fertile fashion. I drank from the sea's cup, which was filled to the very brim with genius. The sun, with its long blistering flames, vulcanized my body and bolted the keel of my brow, in full sail.[12]

This scene alludes to several motifs in the Futurist tradition.[13] First, Marinetti displays himself as the sunburnt, naked archetype of Futurism and refers in this way to the African tribe leader of his first novel, *Mafarka*. Second, the first Futurist manifesto already celebrated the bath in an inspiring liquid. In the Tattilismo text, however, it is not industrial oil and mud, but a sea of "flexible steel," full of hard edges that engrave their traces into Marinetti's body—hard edges that write the Tattilismo into Marinetti's skin. Similar to the first manifesto, Marinetti appears as a parasite that uses its environment as a host; he drinks from the surrounding liquid and inhales the genius from the environment.[14] As in the first Futurist manifesto, the birth of the art of tactility is connected accordingly to a transformation of Marinetti's body itself. Marinetti is both the subject and the object of his own invention. He is irritated by tactile stimuli and produces them at the same time. This bathing/creation/procreation scene is then interrupted by a short satirical dialogue, which condenses Marinetti's theory of tactility:

> A girl from the common people, who smelled of salt and hot stones, smiled when she looked at my first tactile panels: "You're enjoying yourself making your little boats, aren't you!"
>
> I answered her:
>
> "Yes, I'm building a boat that will bear the human spirit toward unknown regions."[15]

This little scene says a lot about Marinetti's project: a peasant girl misunderstands Marinetti's revolutionary tactile tables or panels (boards covered with a material such as sandpaper that evokes complex tactile sensations) as little toys. This moment brings to mind not so much Marinetti's chauvinistic attitude toward women as a communicative problem that is central to his theory of tactility.

Marinetti analyzes the lack of communicative capacity as the most profound problem of his time: there is no real communication between human beings or between the sexes.[16] For Marinetti, the model of human interaction is rooted in communication at a distance, where acoustic or visual signs dominate the communicative exchange. According to Marinetti, these forms of interaction fail to convey intimate impressions.[17] Accordingly, the girl cannot understand what Marinetti is doing, because she merely sees the small boats and speaks with Marinetti about them.

She perceives them but only from a distance. To understand Marinetti's discovery, one has to touch the tactile tables.[18]

The communication between the girl and Marinetti fails, the necessary connection—the contact through touch—does not exist between them. Textually, Marinetti uses the breakdown of this conversation to outline his sociopolitical analysis: "These were my reflections as I swam in the waters:"[19]

Marinetti continues the manifesto by describing the "pathological" state of postwar Italy. He criticizes the general crowd as well as the intellectual minority of the Italian people. He attacks the majority for their interest in material satisfaction and condemns the intellectual elite for escaping in a dream world of drugs and narcotics. He claims that the society is weak, numb, sick, and in a pathological state of decay.[20] As a remedy, Marinetti calls for a recalibration of communication and demands an intensification of "communications and association among human beings"[21] by destroying "distances and barriers that separate them in love and friendship."[22] He issues a command: "Give fullness and total beauty to these two vital aspects of life, Love and Friendship."[23] Marinetti recognizes a desensitization of society and tries to intensify the interactions among human beings. Most surprisingly, this time Marinetti does not adopt a technological approach, but calls out instead the most intimate modes of human communication: love and friendship. These forms of communication are distorted by the medium of spoken language. Marinetti criticizes all modes of distance communication, because they struggle to convey intense intimacy.

> From my careful, unconventional observations of all the erotic and sentimental factors that unite the two sexes, and of the no less complex features of friendship. I have realized that human beings speak to one another with their mouths and their eyes, but that they never quite manage to be totally sincere, because of the insensibility of skin, which is ever a poor conductor of thoughts.[24]

This statement signifies a crucial shift in Futurist thinking. The abandoned and condemned values of love and friendship have become the foundation for a reinvention of Futurism in the spirit of tactility.[25] Communication based on physical contact, so as to avoid noise in the channel, becomes the central idea for rebuilding postwar Italian society.

THE TACTILIST

Marinetti asserts that the sensibility of humankind is weak and, to extend the possibilities of the human body, he outlines six categories of tactile values.[26] These categories represent an increasing educational scale and show that Marinetti wants not merely to intensify the tactile sense, but also to construct a system of tactile signs—a tactile language. The scale is categorized according to tactile values such as "smooth" or "rough." But Marinetti adds more varied connotations to these values. The smooth surface of silver paper would, for example, evoke the connotation of "abstract," or for Marinetti the soft structure of hair suggests "human."[27] In a way similar to Russolo's organization of noises, this scale is only a first attempt to classify tactile values, and Marinetti implies a greater variety of tactile categories. In fact, *l'arte dei rumori* and Tattilismo are similar in several respects. Like Russolo's sound-noises, Marinetti's tactile tables represent training devices for calibrating and extending sensory capacities. The education of the senses is in both cases geared toward the recognition of superfine structures that would otherwise be dismissed as mere noise.

Marinetti differentiates between different types of tactile panels.[28] At first he has simple tables prepared with various tactile materials such as sandpaper, silk, or wool for training the sense of touch to recognize different tactile structures. Second, Marinetti refers to abstract or suggestive tactile tables. These panels are covered with materials of several textures, so that these *tavole tattili* become something like a symphony for the sense of touch. As an example for such a composition, Marinetti refers to an already designed table called Sudan-Paris that is prepared with materials denoting certain landscapes. For example, sandpaper indicates a desert; silver paper, the ocean; and velvet, the city.[29] The third kind of panel— "tactile panels for the different sexes"—is used by a man and a woman who feel the table and experience the different haptic textures together. Marinetti extends his tactile project further and demands the design of tactile pillows, furniture, chambers, and even streets.[30]

Marinetti aims at the recognition of very delicate structures. On the one hand, he claims that the aim of his ventures is a deep understanding of matter even on a subatomic level: "With Tactilism, we intend to penetrate better the true essence of matter."[31] On the other hand, he uses tactile matter for evoking certain impressions, pictures, and analogies. This becomes apparent from Marinetti's use of tactile tables as devices for the improvisation of *parole in libertà*. As Marinetti explains, the "Tactilist will announce the different tactile sensations that he experiences during the journey made by his hands. His improvisation will take the form of Words-in-Freedom, which have no fixed rhythms, prosody, or syntax. These improvisations will be succinct and to the point, and as nonhuman as possible."[32] The tactilist is dehumanized (becoming "as nonhuman as possible") and is transformed into a kind of gramophone so that we might even be able to speak of a human being "reading" a phonographic disk directly, without the mediation of a mechanical device. By using his fingers, he literally reads the surface of the table, thereby (re)producing the tactile qualities of the *tavola tattile* in free-word expressions. As Marinetti emphasizes, it is an improvisation in *parole in libertà* and therefore it is connected to the ability of the tactilist to be sensitive to the tactile material and to translate these sensations into a highly condensed language. What is at stake is a sensitivity capable of retrieving information from complex and "noisy" structures without the help of media technology—the senses should become hypersensitive interfaces. This is a utopian thought that Marinetti further develops in his second manifesto on Tattilismo.

Clearly, the *tattilista* is derived in a parasitical transformation from the technology of the gramophone, something that Russolo already had prepared for with his implementation of a note-line that enables the reading of music in an immediate way. What is more, however, technology is no longer understood as something that is external to the body, but becomes the body itself. The body of the *tattilista* is not the receiver of a message; it becomes media itself. In the second manifesto on Tattilismo, Marinetti expands his fantasies about a possible transformation of the human physiology based on the sense of touch:

> Just suppose the Sun leaves its orbit and forgets about the Earth! Utter darkness. Men blundering into one another. Utter terror. Then, the beginnings of a vague sense of security settling in. Caution from the epidermis. Life feeling its way. Having attempted to create artificial lights, men become used to the darkness. They feel a respect for the nocturnal animals. Dilation of human pupils, which react to the tiny amount of light present in the darkness. The attentive powers of the optic nerve are built up.
>
> A visual sense is born at the tips of fingers.
>
> An intervisionary sense develops, and some people can already see inside their bodies. Others dimly perceive the interiors of nearby bodies. Everyone feels that sight, smell, hearing, touch, and taste are but modifications of one very active sense, namely that of touch, split in different ways and localized at different points.
>
> Other localizations are necessary. And here they are. The center of the abdomen can see. The knees can see. Elbows can see. Everyone admires the variations in speed that differentiate light from sound.[33]

This apocalyptic fantasy is highly revealing. The deprivation of human senses is not caused by a failure in the sensory system itself, but rather by an environmental change. The sun disappears and humankind remains helpless because of its inability to see in the dark. Men and women fall down on their knees; the environmental change forces them to go back in their evolutionary development. Now, to regain their ability to walk upright, they have to adjust their senses. Marinetti does not favor a technological solution—"having attempted to create artificial lights, men become used to the darkness"—and imagines instead a physiological adjustment of the senses. But he also alludes to technological innovations such as X-ray vision ("an intervisionary sense") to describe the newly developed senses. Indeed, these transformations change the human body into a highly sensitive antenna. The transformation of the *tattilista* into a media technological device is extended to humankind as such. Technology is no longer something that supplements the human organism, but becomes an essential part of the human being.

What Marinetti diagnoses in this nightmare scenario is the status quo in the Futurist understanding and not a dark utopia of a world to come. The modern human is blind; it is not possible to read properly the line inscribed in a gramophone disk by means of visual or even tactile senses—modern technologies such as phonography disconnect humankind from data. The proper decoding of analog data without a technological medium is not possible for human beings.

Now, Marinetti's tactility project intends a calibration of the human sensorium to the different sensory challenges of modern society. Marinetti understands the human body as a medium that can extend and differentiate its sensory abilities infinitely. The Futurist concept of tactility is to be perceived not only from the position of the sensory receiver, but also from the perspective of the Futurist artist who addresses the body of the recipient. The intensification of the sensorium is necessary for the Futurist artist who requires a multiconnectedness for his or her multisensorial art. Only the further development of sensory interfaces creates the possibility of extending the framework of Futurist art; this extension enables the Futurist artist to find new materials that address the advanced sensory capacities of Futurist human beings.

Marinetti claimed that "sight, smell, hearing, touch, and taste are but modifications of one very active sense, namely that of touch, split in different ways and localized at different points,"[34] and he recognized, therefore, that tactility is a "super"-sense that constitutes a common interface for all sensory input. "Tactility" not only describes the sense of touch, but also opens up Futurist art to an all-encompassing sensation, a *Gesamtkunstwerk* aesthetic that crystallizes into Tattilismo. But this "tactile" quality of Futurist art is already apparent in the Futurist theater and also becomes of great importance to Marinetti's radiophonic experiments.

Total Theater

Futurism had from its beginning an all-encompassing, escalating dynamic that used public spaces to create a provoking impact that would forcefully include its spectators. Especially the theater represented for Marinetti a laboratory for experimenting with the transgression of borders. It is legendary that the first Futurist performances, so-called *serate*, were accompanied by an advertisement campaign that tried to include an entire city in the Futurist spectacle. In fact, it seems that Marinetti and his friends invested more energy in these advertisements than in the show itself. They drove through the main streets with cars painted in wild colors, or disturbed public events such as theater performances, where they distributed their flyers and manifestos.[35] The actual *serata*, which consisted of a heterogenous program that included the recitation of poems, theoretical texts, political proclamations, music, and short plays, was just the culmination of the Futurist performance. The Futurists abused the infrastructure of a community in order to promote their program; public places, theaters, cafes, and cinemas became the unwilling host for their parasitic intervention. Like a parasitic disturbance in a complex system, the Futurist theater could happen everywhere and at any time. The construction of exactly such a presence was a fundamental goal of Futurism.

This all-encompassing logic, however, was directed not only at social discourses but also at the physiology of the spectators. The Futurist theater is based on sociopolitical subversion as well as on sensorial overload. Thus, the ideas that Marinetti develops in the context of Tattilismo also find their articulation in the theater manifestos. Accordingly, in the manifesto on the variety theater, Marinetti abolishes a clear distinction between stage and hall and embeds the sensorium of the audience in an extremely stressful situation. The audience cannot sit back and relax, but is forced into a nervous state of mind, and is constantly provoked to react.

> Introduce surprise and the need to move among the spectators of the orchestra, boxes, and balcony. Some random suggestions: spread a powerful glue on some of the seats, so that the male or female spectator will stay glued down and make everyone laugh (the damaged frock coat or toilette will naturally be paid for at the door)—sell the same ticket to ten people: traffic jam, bickering, and wrangling—offer free tickets to gentlemen or ladies who are notoriously unbalanced, irritable, or eccentric and likely to provoke uproars with obscene gestures, pinching women, or other freakishness. Sprinkle the seats with dust to make people itch and sneeze, etc.[36]

The theater affects the spectators in a direct and all-encompassing tactile way. The varieté uses all the spatial and temporal dimensions of the theater and communicates with all the senses of the audience members. As Kirby emphasizes, the variety theater brings all the elements together that were important for the "new sensibility" of Futurism.[37] Smell, itching powder, glue, smoke, and the stage act are equal parts of the theater. Thus, the entire theater is affected by surprises. Marinetti develops a further understanding of the structure of these surprises in his manifesto on the synthetic theater (1915). "Synthetic. That is very brief. To compress into a few minutes, into a few words and gestures, innumerable situations, sensibilities, ideas, sensations."[38] "Sintetico," the central point of this conception, is linked to his theory of *parole in libertà*. Similar to the free-word poetry, the "synthetic" acts on the stage are supposed to compress surprises and sensations into a short moment.

The synthetic theater is a theater of shocks, for it is not understanding but instead reaction that is expected from the audience. His reference to itching powder or glue makes clear that direct physical involvement is of great importance in the variety theater. The entire body is supposed to be affected and embedded in a multisensory performance. The sensations in the variety theater should provoke an immediate response, similar to stimuli such as the ringing bell in Pavlov's famous experiment with dogs or the military command directed at the soldier. The stimulus provided by the Futurist stage performance does not offer room for discussion and provokes a reaction instead. The dichotomy of input/no input constitutes—as I will go on to discuss—the system that the Futurist dramatists adopt in their theatrical performances. Such a switching with the human psyche is the central aesthetic or rather neurological operation in Futurist theater, devoted to the purpose of constructing an immediate connection to the recipient. Cangiullo's play *Lights* and Marinetti's radio plays are examples of this pursuit.

> The curtain rises. The apron, stage and auditorium of the theatre are in darkness. Dark pause. Until someone shouts LIGHTS! (Still darkness.) Then two spectators shout LIGHTS! LIGHTS! (Still darkness.) Then four, then the impatient shout becomes magnified, contagious, and half the theatre shouts: LIGHTS LIGHTS LIIGHTSSS! The entire theatre: LIIIIGHTSSSS!!! Suddenly, the lights come up everywhere on the apron, stage, and in the auditorium. Four minutes of blazing fear. CURTAIN. And everything is clear.[39]

This play is very short and simple. The most striking feature of this play is its medial structure. The "main character" is light. Light establishes the dramatic conflict. This conflict is no longer a staged problem between characters. It lies with the possibility of the stage play itself. Without light there is no stage. The play does not refer as much to cognitive assumptions of the spectators as to their physiological setup—they cannot see in the dark. Cangiullo does not assume that the audience will start a discussion on the apparent failure of the play to begin, as happens in the romantic plays of Ludwig Tieck such as *The Booted Cat*. In the Futurist theater, the audience simply manifests a reflex. The utterance "light" is not the result of a cognitive reflection. It is an instinctive reaction to the lack of light.

What comes together in the Futurist theater is the condensation of sensations and a totalizing, transgressive force. It incorporates the same logic of data compression as *parole in libertà*. The Futurist poetry has the same synthetic, shocking, and aggravating intention as the stage performance, and it is not surprising that the recitation was an integral part of the Futurist *serate*. The other aspect of the Futurist stage is that it consumes its audience and does not constitute a border but a dynamic, expanding space. The medium of the radio will fulfill this expansive logic, and it is only logical that Marinetti published in 1933, the same year when he developed a radio aesthetic, a manifesto about a "Total Theater."[40] This total theater includes all media technology that could possibly be employed such as telephones, cinematographic projections, light shows, and even smells. More importantly, the spectators are embedded in this theater that consists of multiple rotating stages and confront the audience with a great number of simultaneous performances.[41]

Marinetti describes this as a new breakthrough, a culmination of the Futurist aesthetics; however, this total theater was an anachronistic concept still rooted in an ontology bound to the stage presence. The virtual space of the radio ether was clearly the paradigm that finally fulfills the Futurist dreams of a total, all-encompassing form of art.

RADIO PLAYS

Marinetti undertook the development of radiophonic *sintesi* in 1933, the year Hitler introduced the "people's receiver" (*Volksempfänger*) and the Italian government promoted the distribution of radios to the underdeveloped countryside. These sociopolitical interactions became crucial for Futurist radio aesthetics, because they constituted radio as a medium that could reach an entire *Volk* simultaneously. In his radio manifesto "La Radia" (1933) Marinetti emphasizes the capacity of the radio to send signals almost anywhere, and he understands this as the next step toward the Futurist aim of the compaction of space and time.[42]

As Marinetti points out in his radio manifesto, neither space nor time disturbs the radio signal. The equal presence of a signal at every receiver at all times is no longer a problem. Indeed, it becomes the specific feature of the medium. Radio is the medium of constant and immediate contact. Moreover, distortions and interferences between radio stations are not understood as disruptions, but are part of the signal "radio transmission" and even highlight the simultaneous presence of different places. This is an effect that Marinetti explored more thoroughly in his radio play *Drama of Distance*,[43] where he planned to transmit sound bits of 11 seconds in length from different places all around the globe, such as religious music from Tokyo, a boxing match in New York, or a military march in Rome.[44] In this play it is not the story but the specific structure of the medium radio that is central. What Marinetti stages is the medial quality of wireless communication, for the actual messages transmitted through the ether are secondary. Marinetti's radio plays are self-referential systems that highlight the technology of wireless transmission and try to embed the spectator's physiology into this media spectacle. The two radio plays *Silences Speak among Themselves* and *A Landscape Heard*[45] attempt this experiment by addressing the audience through a binary logic that was already present in Canguillo's play *Lights*:

> 15 seconds of pure silence.
> Do-re-me on a flute.
> 8 seconds of pure silence.
> Do-re-mi on a flute.
> 29 seconds of pure silence.
> Sol on a piano.
> Do on a trumpet. 40 seconds of pure silence.
> Do on a trumpet.
> 10 seconds of pure silence.
> Do on a trumpet. Ne-ne-ne of a baby.
> 40 seconds of pure silence.
> Ne-ne-ne of a baby.
> 11 seconds of pure silence.
> 1 minute of rrrr of a motor.
> 11 seconds of pure silence.
> Amazed oooo's from an eleven-year-old little girl.[46]

In place of a narrative, Marinetti's play *Silences Speak among Themselves* creates an alternating structure between silence and a variety of acoustic phenomena—the pattern of no-input and input thereby duplicates the binary structure of early wireless telegraphic communication. As in Canguillo's play *Lights*, no specific story is narrated; instead, the sheer possibility of the medium is exposed. The radio transmits silence and all kinds of different acoustic sensations. The listeners do not receive continuous information, but they are listening to silence and wait in front of the radio for the next stimulus. Similar to Cangiullo's play, the audience is forced to wait actively. The audience is not merely receptive. On the contrary, the audience is proactive, remaining in a kind of standby mode. While in *Lights* the spectators are exposed to only one forceful positive stimulus, the listeners of Marinetti's radio plays have to hear several impulses slowly dropping in through the ether.

The different sounds and noises of the radio *sintese* are created only to keep the listener interested. It is enough that the signals are only sensations with different acoustical values. To interpret the sensations can only mean that listeners recognize a pattern allowing them to predict subsequent inputs. If listeners could do this, the play would lose its shock value and become boring. But the listener is incapable of leaving the play and remains in front of the radio, like a soldier in his trench waiting for the next attack. This aesthetic of binary switching is also of paramount importance for the radio play *A Landscape Heard*. Although Marinetti does not work with the binary opposition of silence and sound, he alternates between the two acoustic sensations of lapping water and crackling fire. Only in the end does the twittering of a blackbird appear:

> The twittering of a blackbird, envious of the crackling
> of fire leads to ending the chattering of water
> 10 seconds of splashing
> 1 second of crackling
> 8 seconds of splashing
> 1 second of crackling
> 5 seconds of splashing
> 1 second of crackling
> 19 seconds of splashing
> 1 second of crackling
> 25 seconds of splashing
> 1 second crackling
> 25 seconds of splashing
> 6 seconds of twittering of a blackbird[47]

Marinetti stages this play as a struggle between the acoustic phenomena of lapping, crackling, and a blackbird's twittering. For the listener, however, the acoustic experience is quite similar to *The Silences Speak among Themselves*: sound bits of different length are interrupted by an exact second of a different noise. Binary logic is central here also. The difference, however, is that the final sound (the blackbird), in its categorical divergence from the prior sounds, signals the end of the play, so that the listener can withdraw from the radio receiver, a liberty that the audience of *The Silences Speak among Themselves* does not have. Here, the listener is not capable of deciding whether the silence following the play denotes the end of the play or whether it is still a pause and thus part of the *sintese*. This strategy is also a central aesthetic feature in *Battle of Rhythms*:

> A careful and patient slowness expressed with a tick-tock of a water drop, cut-off first than killed by
>
> A soaring and arpeggiating elasticity of notes from a piano cut-off first then killed by
>
> A jingle of an electric bell cut-off first and killed by
>
> A silence of three minutes cut-off first and then killed by
>
> A struggle of a key in a lock ta "trum ta trac" followed by
>
> A minute of silence.[48]

In a way similar to *A Landscape Heard*, this play stages the struggle among different acoustical phenomena. Although this play represents a rather random selection or "struggle" of different noises and sounds, silence also performs here a decisive function. The introduction of silence into this play, ironically, does not close, but rather opens up the play infinitely. Since Marinetti uses silence as an aesthetic element within the play, the listener, like the soldier in a trench, is left alone to wait for the next impact provided by the ongoing battle of rhythms.

Marinetti experimented with different ways to use the radio; however, the binary logic seems to be of central importance for the conception of his radio plays. With the exception of *Violetta and the Airplanes*,[49] the radio *sintesi* do not unfold a complicated narrative, but adopt an absolutely minimalistic aesthetic based on alternating sounds, noises, and silence.

The radio becomes omnipresent in a latent manner—for at any time it could disseminate inputs. The radio signal is not aimed at a single destination, but instead addresses all radio receivers. Marinetti uses exactly this potentiality of the radio to transmit a stimulus to all at any time in order to connect the listener to the radio. Accordingly, he does not send a specific aesthetic content, but rather exhibits through his radio play the medial structure of the radio itself. He does not stage a story or transmit a message, but merely takes advantage of the radio's capacity to send any kind of acoustic phenomena regardless of their meaning.[50] This exhibition of merely technical qualities demonstrates the technical specifications of the radio, but at the same time it is reminiscent of earlier wireless technology. Because of the high degree of distortion caused by environmental noise, the radio could initially only transmit simple signal systems. The language of the first wired and wireless telegraphs was Morse code, which was based on the alternating absence and presence of a signal, thereby creating an essentially binary code.

In his radio experiments, Marinetti brings the most advanced use of radio technology (to transmit all kinds of acoustic data) in contact with the primary function of wireless telegraphy (to transmit a simple binary code). Marinetti thereby constructs an immediate contact between audience and machine based on a process of on/off switching. The construction of tension is based on the fact that the stimulus that is turned off can be turned on any time. Marinetti's reliance on this on/off structure results in a constant involvement of the audience. The audience functions as a simple detector, because its primary task is to distinguish between on (input) and off (no input)—it is no longer a cognitive entity external to the media, but hardwired into the broadcasting system.

The main intention of Futurist poetics—in plays made for both stage and radio—is to involve the audience. Futurist theater and radio establish a contact with recipients that they cannot break. Now, the audience becomes the parasite internalized in the circuit of Futurist art. The variety theater was a first scenario for such an attempt. Marinetti transcends the distinction between hall and stage in order to create a permanent contact to the audience. In addition, the endless row of acts appearing on stage keeps the spectator in a constant state of alert. The radio increases this effect: while the variety guests are embedded in the performance only so long as they are in the theater, the radio creates the possibility of a permanent, never-ending show—even when it is off, it is on because the receiver (mechanical and human) is in standby mode. It constitutes the environment for the mass media audience that depends, like a parasite, on the host and does not give anything in return.[51] Marinetti's radio show displays the most essential ability of broadcasting technology: to transmit signals or not. Through this binary structure, Marinetti intends to generate a permanent tension in the audience. Physiological irritation functions as a strategy for connecting human receivers to the radio system. They wait for new input, in the same way as a telegraph office accountant has to wait for incoming messages from the ether, or the soldier for the next bomb shell. Radio transmission finally enables a constant contact to the "Volkskörper," as Dominik Schrage points out in his book *Psychotechnik und Radiophonie*: "Radiophony stands for a new kind of coupling of sense impressions and social reality, and thus brings about a new, highly abstract facet of artificial reality: radio-publicity."[52] Everybody becomes part of the radio public and remains receptive at all times. Marinetti's twenties' program of, as it were, calibrating the senses by means of tactile media—using the tactile tables, for example, as a means of refining one's sense of touch—is replaced in the thirties by a new emphasis on radiophonic contact: permanent connection to the state and its technological media. The radio public represents the form of intimate immediacy that Marinetti was heading toward in his manifesto on tactilism. McLuhan clearly understands this paradoxical situation, which overlays a highly anonymous medium with a private experience:

> Radio affects most people intimately, person-to-person, offering a world of unspoken communication between writer-speaker and listener. That is the immediate aspect of radio. A private experience.... This is inherent in the very nature of this medium, with its power to turn the psyche and society into a single echo chamber.[53]

This connection between psyche and society is central to Marinetti's phantasmagoria of direct contact. On the one hand, his radio plays are supposed to be transmitted to individuals in front of their radio receivers, and the radio performances should constitute a personal and immediate contact to every subject of society. On the other hand, these signals are transmitted to the entirety of the Italian population without any distinction between or reflection on individual needs and desires. As McLuhan acknowledges, the radio connects an entire society in one echo chamber. The direct contact that Marinetti fantasized about is not established through direct physical touch, but through the omnipresent control of the radiophonic ether.

What Marinetti rehearsed with the *tattilista*—namely to turn the human subject into a media device, that is, a mediary station in a communicative situation—is expanded through the radio on a mass scale. The radio does not address the listeners as the simple endpoint of transmission. They are understood as an integral part of the entire network. They hang on to the technological system like parasites; they constantly participate in the broadcasting through a one-directional channel and never give anything back in return. This corresponds precisely to the economy of the parasite as outlined by Serres,[54] and the modern media users become parasites par excellence, because they are an integral part of the system without engaging in the communication in a direct sense. However, the medium of the radio carries also parasitical attributes itself: it exploits the sheer presence of the listeners. Further, on a technological basis the radio constructs the ubiquitous presence of Serres's parasite, because it—like the parasite—does not occupy a specific place but constructs a relationship.[55]

Hausmann's Présentism

Like Marinetti, Hausmann comes to think of the sense of touch as a central interface that enables a general reflection on human sensory abilities. The discussion of tactility begins to enter his texts in the early twenties. For Hausmann, tactility is not a particular sense, but a mode of immediate contact with the world that is not restricted to the sense of touch. It is, in fact, the basis of all forms of human sense perception.[56] In what follows, I will explain what Hausmann means by this assertion. It is important to note that Hausmann's explorations and discoveries in the field of tactility are closely linked to his overall project of developing a new art form capable of incorporating new perspectives and modes of expression that emerged with modern technologies. Like Marinetti, Hausmann acknowledges that media technological innovations altered perceptual abilities. The interplay between the human sensory apparatus and its historically changing environment is also central to Hausmann's writing.

Texts such as "Optophonetik"[57] and "Présentismus"[58] display the complex connection between anthropology and the technoscientific discourses of the time. Various scientific discourses from physics to biology fueled Hausmann's attempts to renovate human society by way of "reprogramming" the human sensory apparatus. These texts reflect on science and human perception from a sociohistorical perspective and constitute a sociopolitical commentary. The difficulty of these texts consists in the fact that Hausmann presents to the reader a technical and very colorful amalgam of a wide array of diverse theories. Hausmann was a great admirer of Hanns Hörbiger's "Welteislehre" and an eager reader of the neo-Kantian philosopher Ernst Marcus—two thinkers whose theories are forgotten for the most part on account of their unusual presuppositions. In addition to his interest in these rather esoteric theories, he was well informed about early electronics and behavioral biology. He parasitically participated in these discourses and reassembled a wide array of such obscure theories in his own ideas about an optophonetic extension of man. As in Marinetti's texts, media technology is here not something that is external to the human being—the human being is rather conceptualized as a media technological system.[59]

One of Hausmann's most central texts on the topic of a new sense is "Présentismus," which was written in response to Marinetti's first "Tattilismo" manifesto. Hausmann published this text in the Dutch art journal *De Stijl* in 1921 and sent a copy to the Futurist. In this manifesto, instead of siding with Marinetti, Hausmann criticizes the Italian and rejects his concepts as random, scarcely innovative nonsense. "From Italy, the news of Marinetti's tactilism reaches us," says Hausmann. "He has defined unclearly the problem of haptic sensation, and spoiled it! We find Marinetti, the most modern person in Europe, disagreeable, because he takes chance as his starting point, and not superior awareness."[60] Although Hausmann's verdict on Marinetti's project is clearly negative, the Dadaist recognizes the achievements of Futurist painters.[61] Nonetheless, he starts out by criticizing the Futurist ideology. Hausmann attempts to finesse Marinetti's binary code of Passatism or Futurism with a new "Présentismus," a fresh attitude toward the world that focuses on the present moment and not on the future or the past: "Let us sweep away all the prejudices that yesterday something was good or that it will be better tomorrow, no! Let us grasp the today by the second!"[62] The title of the manifesto, "Présentismus," refers to exactly this focus on the present moment, thereby opposing both Futurist ideology and the traditionalism of Weimar society. Hausmann intends to abolish any temporal transcendence: human activity should orientate itself to the present moment, not to the future or to the past.[63] This ideology of the present not only attacks the worldview of Italian Futurism, but also clears the way for Hausmann's theory of art and sense perception. For him culture is not isolated from the physiological and biological development of humankind, but needs to incorporate art and technology on a physiological level. A first step to do that is to acknowledge how technologies have determined the present state of the senses:

> Why aren't we able today to paint pictures like Botticelli, Michelangelo, or Leonardo and Titian? Because in our understanding man has completely transformed himself, not only because we have telephones, airplanes, and the electrical piano or a revolving lathe, but because our entire psychophysis is transformed through this experience.[64]

In the beginning of the twenties, Hausmann develops this understanding of the historical determination of the senses. In texts such as "The New Art" ("Die neue Kunst")[65] or "Art and Time" ("Die Kunst und die Zeit"),[66] he formulates his theory of the historical development of art and calls for new artistic enterprises that would correspond to the actual demand of the age.

The focus on the ability of modern technology to change the perceptual capabilities of human beings is likewise prominent in Walter Benjamin's artwork essay. In a way that bears comparison to Freud, Benjamin speaks of the "optical unconscious" that might be revealed by certain technologies giving men access to new optical dimensions.[67] This new perceptual "knowledge" determines perception in such a way that human understanding becomes more sensitive even without the help of technological gadgets. Humans are seen as parasites that profit from the new media technologies. Like Hausmann, Benjamin embeds this discussion in a historical thesis. Drawing on the art historian Alois Riegl, Benjamin refers to the historically changing patterns of perception.[68] Benjamin formulates this connection ten years after Hausmann. The Bauhaus movement presents a more contemporaneous context for Hausmann's concepts. In his book *Painting, Photography, Film*,[69] Moholy-Nagy claims that "we have—through a hundred years of photography and two decades of film—been enormously enriched.... We may say that we see the world with entirely different eyes."[70] In fact, Moholy-Nagy acknowledged Hausmann as a predecessor who would have been one of the first to conceptualize a new modern theory of sense perception.[71]

Hausmann brings the term "optophonetics" for such a physiohistorical transformation into play. He, however, did not invent it. Around 1910, the English engineer Fournier E. E. d'Albe developed a device called the optophone, which was an instrument that detected light sensitivities through a photocell and represented it through a corresponding sound; d'Albe soon developed it further into a device for transforming writing into sounds.[72] Hausmann never mentioned d'Albe or any other source for the word, but he might have picked up the term from the physicist Christian Ries, who heavily published on photoelectric devices in Weimar journals.[73] What is central to this idea is that different forms of sense perception can be converted into one another. For example, light can become audible or sound visible. These experiments do not simply elaborate artistic practices or technologies, but are based on a theory of perception that enabled the emergence of this modern form of art as called for by Hausmann and Moholy-Nagy.

Ether Perception

> Let us not forget that the sense of touch, the haptic sense, is an element in or the almost decisive foundation for all our senses.[74]

As outlined in the text "Présentismus," Hausmann's theory of perception is centered on tactility.[75] Actually, the Dadaist prefers the term "haptism" to "tactility" in order to differentiate his project from Marinetti's.[76] Hausmann develops his ideas about haptism in response to the works of the philosopher Ernst Marcus. A judge in the industrial city of Essen (Westphalia), Marcus studied the works of Kant intensely and was closely connected to the Berlin scene around the philosopher Salomo Friedländer.

Especially important to Hausmann is Marcus's book *The Problem of Eccentric Perception and Its Solution*,[77] published in 1918 by the Sturm-Verlag. Marcus develops a theory of perception in which the subject constructs its experiences through a sense-physiological reaction to stimulus. In his theory the perception of the outside world functions in the following way: objects emit vibrations that travel through the ether. Through the retina, these vibrations affect the nerve of the eye. This irritation does not yet produce the sensation of light, but the stimulus is transmitted through the nerve to the brain—or, as Marcus calls it, the central organ. Triggered by the stimulus, the central organ itself produces ethereal vibrations, which project the sensation of the object outside of the body. Through this theory, Marcus tries to solve the problem of "eccentric perception"—that is, the problem that although the perceived object is generated by our sensory organs, we experience it as external to them, outside of our bodies.[78] As Marcus explains, experience (especially visual and acoustic experience) appears largely as transsomatic,[79] and the only form of experience that is seemingly somatic and therefore immediate to the body is tactile sensation. Marcus's theory, however, presupposes a direct, "tactile" contact for all forms of sense perception.

Marcus recognizes the brain as a universal sensory interface that processes different sensory inputs. The "central organ" transforms "objective" vibrations that are sent out from the object into "subjective" vibrations, projected as a reaction by the subject. The brain is a constructive device that examines and creates its environment. Marcus develops the concept that the ambit of the sensorium is extended through the connection of the central organ to the cosmic ether:

> We assume that the central organ not only consists of a solid anatomical matter, but that this matter is also organically connected to an ethereal matter constantly in flux. This matter is an integral part of the central organ, just as the solid matter is. Thus, both components are dependent on each other in their states.[80]

Marcus makes it explicit that the central organ is not simply a physiological substratum, but rather an extended perceptual system that is part of, but not limited to, the corporeal unity of the body. The anatomic matter of the central organ is in direct, one might say, "tactile" contact with the ether and thereby creates experience. The brain constructs its environment by sending out rays, which let the objects emerge in perception outside of the body. In this way, the immediacy of touch is part of every sensation. All sensations are derived from the direct connections that the senses establish through the ether to the objects they perceive.[81] Marcus thus claims that experience is dependent on the ether and not on the sensory organs: "Thus, the phenomena of the senses are not, as one assumed until now, attached to the bodily organs, located in the nerves, in the center of the nervous system (brain), but are connected to the organic prime ether."[82] The subjectivity of experience, which is fundamental for the Kantian philosopher Marcus,[83] does not lead to the conclusion that the world constitutes itself in the perceiving subject, but the process of perception projects the perceived objects outside of the body. The decisive point is that this idea gives Marcus the ability to claim that there is direct contact between the object of the outside world and the perceiving subject.[84]

Marcus's theory was without doubt the most important source for Hausmann's optophonetics; however, two more sources strongly influenced the Dadasoph, namely the retired artillery lieutenant Karl Koelsch[85] and the Berlin-based electrical engineer Johannes Zacharias.[86] Both theorists did not much engage with a theory of perception, but defended a theory of ether against Einstein's relativity. Zacharias mainly focused his research on magnetism and electricity and attempted to describe these phenomena by assuming the existence of different pressure distributions in the ether. For example, he explained the polarity of an electric current by asserting that at the negative pole there is less pressure than at the positive pole.[87] Koelsch's theory transgresses this focus on electrical engineering and attempts to design a new cosmological model. At the center of Koelsch's considerations stands the thought that light waves propagate in a spiraling form and are ejected from the sun through a pulsating movement that consists of an alternating process of extension and contraction.[88] Light is for Koelsch, and Hausmann will adapt this notion soon, a cosmic breath travelling through the ether. Hausmann combines Marcus's, Koelsch's and Zarcharias's positions in the manuscript "Attempt of a Cosmic Ontography"[89] to give a generalizing theory that represents the foundation of his optophonetic worldview. This cosmotechnological paradigm is essential for an understanding of his engineering ventures, because for Hausmann the ether not only is a phenomenon that can be used through technology, and is connected to the senses, but it also places the human subject as a breathing being amid the dynamics of the cosmos. The ether represents the true new ecology in which a technological being lives. The radio is just a technology that reminds of this physiological capacity, and this is the reason why Hausmann becomes deeply involved in media technology from the early twenties on.

Optophonetic Media

Hausmann uses the term "optophonetics" to describe his research in synesthesia, but this concept—which denotes the interplay between different sensory sensations—emerges also in his poetics. He claims that his optophonetic concrete poetry and letter constellations signify the starting point for his work on an intermedial form of art as well as his research on the perceptual capacities of the human psyche.[90] Optophonetic poems such as "OFFEAH," however, did not elaborate on the distinction between hearing and seeing, but merely reflected on the different medial qualities of pictures and writing.[91] The iconic and the symbolic qualities of letters fluctuate here in a dynamic interplay. Hausmann's goals went further than the elaboration of semiotic structures and made connections with media technology, and from the early twenties on, he developed various apparatuses such as a sound pickup of the gramophone, an endoscope, and, finally in the early thirties together with the engineer Daniel Broido, a calculating machine.

However, it needs to be acknowledged that Hausmann was not singularly original with his constructions and technological ideas. The machines he planned had already been built by engineers such as Fournier E. E. d'Albe and Ernst Ruhmer, or discussed in periodicals such as *Der Mechaniker* and *Electrician*. In one of his initial reports about an attempt to build a synesthetic apparatus (he first spoke about the construction of such a device in 1921), Hausmann refers already to a common practice of the early film industry. This text, "From the Talking Movie to Optophonetics," deals with the construction of a "sound film": "In a way similar to Ruhmer's construction, the new speaking and singing film transforms acoustic vibrations into light frequencies, which are stored through photography on a film strip and reproduced as sounds."[92] "Sound Film" has to be understood in a very literal sense. The optical medium of film is used for storing acoustic data. This "sound-on-film" system was attached to a film carrying optical data, so that the simultaneous reproduction of sound and visual data was possible. In the sound-on-film system, a microphone transforms sound into electrical impulses; these impulses are transferred to a high-frequency lamp that represents the different impulses by changing light intensity. The lamp is filmed, and in this way the film stores the optical signals, which correlate to the acoustic data. The reproduction functions thus: the film is projected onto a potassium cell[93] that transforms the light input into electric currents, which go to a speaker that retranslates the currents into acoustic signals.[94]

The film scholar Corinna Müller states that this system was much debated in the twenties by engineers and film artists, as well as by the general public.[95] She emphasizes the point that the sound-on-film system was not favored so much for its technological superiority as for its ability to store sound in an optical medium—which allowed it to be perceived as an almost spiritual force.[96] This ubiquitous discussion did influence Hausmann,[97] but the most pivotal source for construction plans of synesthetic machines was Ernst Ruhmer's book *The Selenium and Its Importance for Electrical Engineering*.[98] The photocell represents the central technology for all of Hausmann's synesthetic experiments, because the selenium cell brings light and sound intensity in an analog relationship to each other.

In "About Color Pianos," Hausmann gives a concise account of this data transformation: "Color pianos are technical devices for the transformation of sound into color values and vice versa."[99] Indeed, the color pianos already constitute a form of Hausmann's "optophone," an instrument that is specifically designed for converting acoustical into optical data and vice versa:

> The optophone transforms induced light phenomena into sounds again with the help of the selenium cell and through the microphone that is connected to the circuit. What appears in the recording station as a picture is in the transmitter already sound and, when the processes at the source are being recorded, they will produce sounds in the telephone and vice versa. The series of optical phenomena transformed into a symphony, the symphony into a living panorama.[100]

Although Hausmann represents these ideas as new discoveries, they in fact reflect well-established standards in electrical engineering at that time. Devices that transformed data with the help of photocells were already used in the beginning of the twentieth century. As already mentioned, d'Albe even had constructed an optical apparatus that he called the optophone, and Ernst Ruhmer's book of 1902 contains an entire collection of inventions that use photocells for a variety of applications—from the transmission of visual data to the selection of coffee beans.

The construction of a "directly writing phonograph" was another example already proposed in the *Phonographische Zeitschrift* in 1901. This device was supposed to transform continuous speech into the discrete code of writing. It operates according to a principle similar to Hausmann's optophone: acoustic data are transformed into light data and these light data have an influence on a photocell. As with the phonograph, a horn is connected to a membrane, which moves according to the sound frequency. An optical lens is attached to this membrane. A light beam is projected onto the lens, and this beam is focused into a finer beam. Further, the kinetic energy of the membrane moves the light beam according to the sound input. The light ray hits a photocell, which conducts a certain electrical current at the moment when light strikes it. This current activates a certain letter, which is printed on a piece of paper. The device has to be calibrated in such a way that the movement of the light ray corresponds to a certain position, which activates the intended letter. The problem of such an invention is apparent. Speech does not simply correlate to the discrete system of writing. Even if one does not take the individual differences of different speakers into account,[101] the device can hardly be capable of handling the complexity of human speech.

The "directly writing phonograph" adopts the technological setting that is also common to Hausmann's optophone, but Hausmann's device uses the technology in a different way. While the earlier apparatus attempted to transform continuous into discrete data, Hausmann's optophone displays one form of data simultaneously in both an acoustic and optical form. Hausmann's gadget is much simpler than the proposed phonograph and relies on the capacity of the selenium cell to conduct a current with the exact ratio of the light that is projected onto the photocell. The input thus corresponds to an output on the same level. The "singing arc lamp"—as mentioned by Ruhmer[102]—functions according to this principle, and Hausmann recognizes this device as analogous to his optophone: "When a telephone is connected to the circuit, the light arc transforms itself in response to the acoustic vibrations that are transmitted through the microphone into vibrations that correspond exactly to the acoustic vibrations. This means that the ray of light, as far as its form is concerned, modifies itself in relation to the acoustic vibrations."[103] The analog proportionality of the light input and the electric output is important not only because of an equivalent translation from the one into the other, but also because of the selenium's ability to process the entire range of possible data. The optophone does not segment the input in the manner of a digital device. The comparison to the "directly writing phonograph" makes this point clear. This "phonograph" was supposed to encode acoustic data as discrete signs; the intensity of the current conducted by the photocell is not important. For the optophone the entire spectrum of the light input should be processed and represented by the electric current and displayed in sound.[104] This apparatus is constructed for generating a light and sound performance simultaneously. Hausmann describes such an optophone or color piano as an instrument with a keyboard of 100 keys.[105] The keys are connected to 100 optically prepared fields that are able to produce various reflections, and the light is simultaneously projected onto a screen and a selenium cell. The selenium cell transforms the light into a certain current, which again is used for producing a sound. This apparatus most literally produces a "sound color"—the sound produced by the optophone is nothing other than a color transformed through a light-sensitive converter into an acoustical emission.[106]

The most important aspect of this machine is that it enables Hausmann to represent one form of complex data simultaneously as a visual and acoustic sensation. Nonetheless, it is not the construction of the apparatus that is in and of itself so innovative—the technology was already well known. Instead, the physical preconditions that Hausmann postulates imply the innovative potential of his machines.[107] His texts speak often to the idea that the frequencies of light and sound have the same structure in principle and can therefore be translated into one another:

> Our sounds, starting from singing, vibrate in the spectrum of 32 to 41.000 [vibrations per second] for the musical sounds. Light vibrates from 400 trillion [vibrations] per second for the slowest red up to 800 trillion for violet within the color ranges of red, orange, yellow, blue, green, and violet visible to us.
>
> In the reduction of the vibrations slower than the infrared, however, there has to be a possible transformation towards the sound, towards acoustics.[108]

Hausmann understands the frequencies of light and sound merely as parts of one continuous spectrum. Although electric and mechanical waves have in common that they are waves, they differ in that sound waves need a medium in which they can propagate, whereas light also travels through a vacuum. Hausmann's entire concept is based on the idea that light waves, similar to sound waves, travel through a medium. Hausmann, in accordance with nineteenth-century physics, postulates the existence of an ether in order to explain the propagation of light waves. Twentieth-century physics, in the vein of Einstein, abolishes the ether as a medium and claims that both frequency patterns are fundamental in respect to the medium in which they propagate. Moholy-Nagy's student Walter Brinkmann—after studying Hausmann's optophonetics—provides a more careful analysis of how mechanical and electromagnetic waves can be correlated with each other. He agrees with the observation that these types of waves are fundamentally different from each other, since "sounds are 'vibrations of air' " and "light is 'vibrations of ether'."[109] Nonetheless, he argues that optics—with light perceived as an electromagnetic phenomenon—represents a part of the theory of electricity, and thus he suggests that electrodynamics may serve as a unifying theory that incorporates the study of mechanical as well as electromagnetic waves. As he says, "we no longer baldly assert that any kind of 'correspondences' between the two [sound and light] must be totally impossible."[110]

Hausmann too had based the correspondence between different physical phenomena on the theory of ether—the old form of electrodynamics. Hausmann is more radical than Brinkmann in his assumption because, in accordance to Marcus's theory of perception, he holds that all physical phenomena are fundamentally based on ether waves. Hausmann believes that undulations of the ether generate the sensation of sound (mechanical waves) as well as light (electromagnetic waves). Hausmann's synesthetic apparatus tries to simulate a basic cognitive ability of humankind that makes no fundamental distinction between mechanics and electrodynamics. For Hausmann, the optophone is, therefore, not simply a synesthetic apparatus, but also the duplication of a sensory organ: "Obviously, other living beings do not have separate organs for seeing and hearing. For example, bees have both in one organ, they have a wonderful optophone."[111]

ANTHROPOTECHNOLOGY

The active role of the subject is what made Marcus's theory so attractive to Hausmann. The Dadaist found in Marcus a theorist who based the contact of the subject to its surrounding environment on a constructive operation and also presupposed one basic form of sense perception that constitutes a common denominator for auditory, visual, olfactory, and tactile sensations.[112] Therefore, when Hausmann is speaking about haptic perception he does not mean to refer literally to the sense of touch, but rather to a basic mode of operating that is common to all senses and establishes physical contact with the perceived world. Hausmann turns the human sensorium from a simple receiver into a medial system. In accordance with Marcus, Hausmann also understands seeing as a haptic operation that is in immediate contact with the perceived object.[113] This form of contact represents the core mode of all sense experience. Perception is not a differentiated system that constructs knowledge of the world on the basis of heterogeneous data from different sensory channels, but a single mode of projecting objects into the world.[114] Like Marinetti's tactilist, the human subject is in this model not the final receiver, but a station in a media network.

In general, Marcus's theory implies an externalization of sense perception and subjectivity. The inner self is no longer an internal system and is instead a dynamic system receiving information from and sending it to the ether—that is, a medium. Hausmann makes this understanding of the human being as a media device explicit:

> Marcus still ascribes haptic emanations to the cones of the visual center, but it has to be assumed that the activity of the cones consists in a modification and partial absorption of the concentric beam. The activity of the rods consists in ejecting the eccentric beam into space, similar to a "Marconi Station,"

which after being charged with a certain amount of electricity emits it in short intervals as diminished waves.[115]

Hausmann criticizes Marcus's theory because it lacks a discussion of the transforming capacity of the perceptual organs. Hausmann suggests that the central organ receives energy from the environment and processes it to generate the sensation of the world. The technological model Hausmann uses is the electric medium of the radio ("Marconistation") that transmits electromagnetic waves.[116] The connection between electricity and human perception is central to Hausmann's ideas about art, technology, and sensation. He proclaims that electricity is the medium capable of converting any sense emanation into one another.[117] For Hausmann's adaptation of Marcus's theory, electricity is the force that enables a projection of subjectivity onto the outside world. In this respect, the medium of radio imitates the process of human sensibility. Hausmann's concept becomes an example for Marshall McLuhan's thesis of an extension of man through electric media. McLuhan claims that "with the arrival of electric technology, man extended, or set outside himself, a live model of the central nervous system itself."[118] McLuhan sees in the dawn of electric media an inversion of human subjectivity. Perception, communication, and any other contact to the outside world are no longer internal processes that reinforce a clear distinction between inside and outside, but are externalized through media reaching out and connecting the body to its environment. The expansion of electric networks is understood as the expansion of nervous systems into the world. Hausmann differs from McLuhan only in that, although he recognizes media technology as an extension of man, he implies that these machines are only crutches that could be replaced at some point by the properly trained organic functions of the human sensory system. Again, tactility is for Hausmann, but also for McLuhan, the fundamental sense that corresponds and fits to the new conditions of mass media. Tactility is not the sense of touch but rather the central interface that brings human beings into contact with their environment. As Ina Blom points out in her essay "The Touch Through Time," Hausmann's haptic sensation and McLuhan's extension of man imply a radical redefinition of the spatiotemporal presence of the physical body.[119] This redefinition is based on the tactile quality of electricity. "Electricity offers a means of getting in touch with every facet of being at once, like the brain itself. Electricity is only incidentally visual and auditory; it is primarily tactile."[120] This statement from McLuhan corresponds precisely to Hausmann's belief in the possibilities of electric media. Electricity as "undulation of the ether" points to the vibrations that create the immediacy of human perception. For McLuhan as well as for Hausmann, electricity becomes the emblematic structure for all human extensions into or interactions with the world. It also constitutes the central interface through which different forms of sensation can be translated into one another. As he puts it, "electricity enables us to transform all our haptic emanations into mobile colors, noises, into a new kind of music."[121] Electricity stands at the basis of synesthesia.

The linkage of technology and sense perception explains the growing hegemony of all things technical in Hausmann's thinking, starting in the early twenties. The assumption of an "eccentric" or tactile form of perception enables him to consider the possibility of a common basis of all forms of sense perception because every sense perception depends on the "undulation" of the ether. Therefore, Hausmann and Marcus postulate the existence of an interface that can transform one form of sense perception into another.[122] Hausmann attempts such transformation of sensory data through special electric devices: he tries to construct an optophone that has the capacity to translate acoustic into visual data and vice versa.

The optophone is not a perceptual organ, but rather a transforming system, and the construction of optophonetic machines mirrors the optophonetic sense in human perception. Marcus and Hausmann formulate their ideas within a technological and scientific imaginary. They abuse ideas drawn from the technological realm with concepts of human perception. This correlation generates hybrid theories in which subjects become parasites on the border between man and machine. And it is central to Hausmann's position that he attempts to resolve a distinction between art and engineering: "Mechanics as science, technology, and machine is not simply an increased economy of work, but leads in the end—similar to the sensory achievements of art—to the heightening of the organic functionality of mankind."[123]

The organic function of human beings and the technological capacities of machines engage in a phantasmagoric exchange. The idea that there is a uniform type of data in the world—the vibrations of the ether—brings Hausmann to a meditation on the human sensorium that leads him to the construction (or at least planning) of machines that may prove or may process the stipulated physical reality of the ether.

Hausmann constructs an exchange between media and man that has a media hermeneutical agenda. For Hausmann, organic functions and machine operations coincide. Hausmann uses thus his devices as hermeneutic strategies for understanding the construction of the human perceptual system. Or, more precisely, he abuses devices that do not merely extend human capabilities but also simulate the functions of human cognition, not for understanding media, but for understanding man.

ETHER ECOLOGIES

To assert that the radio ended the ventures of the avant-garde means that this medium realized the ecology of total communication that Dadaists and Futurists envisioned in the beginning of their movements. The radio ether embodied for Marinetti and Hausmann a sphere of immediate and constant contact, and the radio broadcasting system was perceived as a machine that is permanently, at least ideally, in operation. Certainly, the use or abuse of the radio paradigm through Futurism and Dada greatly differed. Futurism did actually not engage in an abuse of the medium, if we follow Friedrich Kittler's anecdote of the radio engineer Hans Bredow.[124] Bredow's abuse consisted in using radio equipment for a purpose that was not intended by the military organization, namely to transmit entertainment programs to the soldiers in the trenches. Marinetti's use of the radio, in contrast, is in complete accordance with a fascist paradigm of the radio. In Marinetti's radio plays there is no place for feedback or listener participation. It is a bombardment with sheer physiological stimuli that are supposed to prepare the people for the passive tension and monotony of trench warfare. Mussolini's and Hitler's radio politics differed, however, from Marinetti's in the sense that the Futurist did not conceptualize the radio as a sheer technology of communication. Whereas the fascist leaders used the radio to convey political orders to its people, the Futurist recognized it as a new form of ambience in which the distinction between host and parasite became increasingly complex, because it could no longer be identified if the listeners are participating in the radio program as parasites, taking something without giving anything in return, or if the radio intervenes as a continuous irritation in the intimate space of the household.

Hausmann's ether ecology literally goes deeper than Futurist radio politics—it becomes part of the human organism itself. This also entails a decisive difference between Hausmann and Marinetti. While Marinetti thinks about the radio as a one-directional communication system, Hausmann radicalizes Bertolt Brecht's vision of the radio as a multi-connected sender-receiver network.[125] For the Dadasoph, the human organism itself is a radio station, constantly sending and receiving data. This rooting of media technology in the human body undermines every attempt of a state control of media channels, because every subject has unlimited means of constant communication. The Dada performances with their dynamic feedback, in which the difference between stage and audience is annihilated, find here their media physiological realization. According to Hausmann, the exploration of technology carries the promise to turn the liberating Dada project of borderless communication without hierarchies into a physiological condition of humankind. Exploring modern media technology is nothing more for Hausmann than to unveil this innate human capacity and to develop a society that is based on this total mode of communication.

To establish a difference between host and parasite is here no longer possible, because if every subject is simultaneously a sender and a receiver, everybody creates and intervenes into the radio chatter that a communicating society creates. In a media ecology of total communication the parasite is not only the intruder but also the source of such an escalating environment.

The radio becomes for the avant-garde the manifestation of pure communication. It transcends the possibilities of dissemination that are given by the newspaper, the cinema, and stage performances. It rather turns the entire life-world into a permanent theater constructed and permeated by a constant mass media bombardment.

Conclusion: Odradek and the Future of the Parasite

This study traced how the avant-garde movements of Futurism and Dadaism interacted with, used, and influenced the media discourses of their time. My intention was to demonstrate that the work of Futurism and Dada was intrinsically connected to the new technological and communicative possibilities of the early twentieth century, and I described this relationship between the avant-garde and media as parasitical.

I did this because the notion of the parasite enabled me to analyze the avant-garde in a more complex way that made it possible to show how these movements can be characterized as agents that were able to influence greater hegemonic structures through minor irritations. This view opens up a new approach that does not fall back into a narrative that ends up in a glorification of the individual artist, who opens the way for the liberation of the masses. The parasitic irritations of the avant-garde did not establish a new revolutionized and utopian world—it needs to be spelled out in all clarity that Marinetti and Hausmann, the leaders of Italian Futurism and Berlin Dada, were not successful revolutionaries, although they clearly voiced such an agenda. Marinetti's aesthetics and politics did not trigger a great change, but were subsumed in Mussolini's fascism, which, with its adoration of the Roman Empire, can hardly be described as truly Futurist. Hausmann's project of an optophonetic art was interrupted or ended not only because the Dadasoph had to leave Hitler's Germany but also because his agenda of a renovation of the senses was not based on politics, but on a misconception of science, and new technological developments such as the vacuum tube that rendered his work outdated.

The true value of the avant-garde movements does not lie in their radical transformative agenda, but in the fact that they were relatively unimportant agents within a greater cultural industry and nonetheless constantly injected small irritations into the public discourse. Such a manipulation of sociotechnical contexts was not revolutionary, because it was connected to this environment as its host. The avant-garde could not work without using the established communicative channels of a society. They intervened in the newspaper production, fantasized about hijacking the networks of the radio and human physiology, and reassembled preexisting visual material in their complex collages, but they did not simply destroy or attack them; rather, they accelerated and parodied these media networks. This engagement with media is not a revolution; it is a subversion and an abuse of existing conditions. Again, these interventions did not cause a great shift in mass media or media engineering; nonetheless, they introduced minor irritations that forced media systems to create a reaction, a feedback.

The origin of both movements, namely the performances in variety theaters, displays this situation quite clearly. The avant-garde performances were created to provoke audiences to generate an expansive field of interaction where they themselves fed back their irritations into the spectacle, meaning the visitors of the theater ended up screaming and shouting at least as loud as the artists on stage. As I have analyzed, similar feedback loops can be found in the media technologies constructed by Futurists and Dadaists, such as Luigi Russolo's *intonarumori* and Hausmann's amplifier system for the gramophone. However, while through a structural feedback Russolo attempted the diversification of the timbre, Hausmann aimed to reduce noises and to decrease the complexity of the produced acoustic signal. This negotiation with the complexity of a signal is central to a comparative study of Futurism and Dada, and as I have outlined, the general strategy of Futurism was to increase the power of the signal while simultaneously decreasing the amount of complexity, that is, the noise it carried—Russolo's art of noises was here a significant exception. Dada, on the contrary, attempted to increase the ambiguity, the noise, and the complexity of a transmitted message. In the manifestos, it should become increasingly unclear what "dada" meant, and a Dada poem would not contain an ultimate meaning, but rather confront the reader with a list of equally meaningless letter constellations that could only be used, as Friedrich Kittler had pointed out, in psychophysical test laboratories for memory experiments or for testing the transmission rate of communication channels.[1]

Futurism, in contrast, hijacked communication channels in order to transmit a forceful and extremely simple message to everybody. In fact, the message was supposed to be so simple that it should be "understood" on a mere physiological level, as a mere nervous impulse, as an alarm. In this way, the Futurist aesthetics left the human being behind and conceptualized the receiver of poetry, art, and performances as an almost mechanical system whose behavior and reaction could be manipulated on a noncognitive level. Again, the avant-garde did not try to overthrow the media ecology of its time but attempted to push it to its ultimate possibilities. What was at stake in Futurism as well as Dada was not an aesthetic revolution but a new form of communication design.

The avant-garde is a parasite, because it cannot be divorced from its contemporaneous media ecology. The relationship of the avant-garde to its environment is neither revolutionary nor supportive, but avant-garde practices constitute a tactical abuse that attempts to push established practices beyond its limits. There is, however, another reason to describe the avant-garde as parasite that is not so much linked to the biological notion than to Michel Serres's interpretation of the term. Serres took the notion of the parasite not only from biology, but also from communication engineering, where it describes disturbances in a communication channel; for example, the static in a radio transmission. For Serres, the origin of such a disturbance is not clearly identifiable, but is rather a by-product of every communicative interaction—it emerges in tandem with the transmission of a signal. This means that the parasite is everywhere, not in the sense that it is actually at every conceivable place, but that it can intervene at every moment—that every communication is threatened by the spontaneous intrusion or emergence of a parasite. The parasite is ubiquitous. The avant-garde shares this all-encompassing logic of the parasite. Again, it does not mean that the avant-garde were everywhere, but that they potentially could intrude at every time, at any place. I outlined how the Futurist manifesto production was geared at precisely this aim and how the nonsense of Dadaist manifestos intended to create a constant presence in the daily press. Also, the surprise tactics involved in Dada and Futurist performances had the goal to turn every public place into a potential site of an avant-garde event. Finally, the ether of radio transmission was the ultimate medium to construct such a total presence.

The parasite/avant-garde is a constant intruder that feeds on an established media discourse and endangers the stability of this order. That this interpretation of the avant-garde is not simply a postmodern reading that takes into account communication theoretical models becomes clear when one looks at Franz Kafka's 1920 text "The Cares of a Family Man."[2] This text describes a strange object called "Odradek," which does not fit into any discursive order. The narrator starts out by acknowledging that it is impossible to trace the origin of this word; then the story continues to describe this object as a flat and strange yarn spool, including an antenna-like extension, and the literary scholar Wolf Kittler carefully remarked in his text "Schreibmaschinen, Sprechmaschinen"[3] that it could point to Odaradek's nature as a radio device.[4] However, the narrator of Kafka's story cannot ascribe a specific use to the object. Rather he attests that Odradek appears as if it had a certain use but now is just broken. The narrator also rejects this understanding because he cannot identify any ruptures or breaks in its structure,[5] and thus re-capitulates something that coincides precisely with Dada aesthetics: "the whole thing looks senseless enough, but in its own way perfectly finished."[6] Like the Dada aesthetics, Odradek represents a ruptured totality that withdraws from hermeneutic understanding. This fleeting quality is reiterated in Odradek's spatiotemporal behavior.

The story continues by outlining that the observation of Odradek is very problematic, because this strange object is highly mobile and can appear everywhere in the household. On interrogating him about his place of living, he simply responds, "No fixed abode."[7]

Odradek is a parasite not only because it fits into Serres's description that points to the ubiquitous and unpredictable presence of the parasite, but also, literally, because it invades the living space of a host, namely the family man who tells the story of this object. Odradek constantly irritates its host without fundamentally disturbing it. However, the family man is intimidated by this apparently harmless intruder, because he fears that, after he has passed away, this object will outlive him and continue to influence his family sphere: "He does no harm to anyone that one can see; but the idea that he is likely to survive me I find almost painful."[8] Odradek's power lies not in a forceful confrontation but in a constant lingering that cannot be excluded or ended.

To understand the outbursts of Dadaists and Futurists along this line is certainly not without provocation. This reasoning turns these movements into agents with minor impact, but comes with a great advantage. The avant-garde is highly adaptive, because Futurism and Dadaism attempted to construct an identity that could not simply be subsumed under an established discursive order. However, they also did not establish a new order on their own, but acted as constant irritations to the hegemonic discourses; they tried to enact an unpredictable, nonlinear behavior that corresponds to the partisan tactics of Odradek. As the family man outlines, "I ask myself, to no purpose, what is likely to happen to him? Can he possibly die? Anything that dies has had some kind of aim in life, some kind of activity, which has worn out; but that does not apply to Odradek."[9] Odradek constantly withdraws from any meaning and always presents an irregular behavior that apparently does not have an ultimate goal. This lack of orientation, however, is not a weakness, but constitutes the particular strength of this object. It does not engage in an open conflict, but creates a permanent state of exception. The sheer complexity of Odradek's behavior endangers the stability of the household, a phenomenon that resonates in the media guerrilla tactics of the avant-garde.

In fact, as a figure of subversion the parasite is close to the partisan. As the political theorist Carl Schmitt has outlined in his epochal "Theory of the Partisan,"[10] the partisan destabilizes warfare through an unpredictable, nonlinear, irregular behavior. These tactics make it extremely hard to establish countermeasures, because they transcend the regularity of a war that is based on confrontation of two regular armies. The partisan is not simply a different army, but a constant intruder that emerges in the moment when a power is occupying a territory. The partisan is not simply the opponent of an enemy, but becomes created through enemy intervention. It is not a preexistent army, but an emergent force. Accordingly, Schmitt claims that one can only start to speak of guerrilla war or partisans when a regular form of warfare is established.[11] Only the regularity of a hegemonic power enables an irregular subversion of this order. The partisan does not fight against an adverse power, but attempts to irritate the integral structure of the enemy. He does not destroy, but transforms the enemy. In this sense, the partisan is also a parasite. Like Odradek, the partisan is not simply opposed to an order, but becomes a part of the order that it is attacking or inhabiting.

This constitutes the true power of the parasite: it never disappears. It is not to separate from the order to which it is opposed. Like Odradek, it might disappear for a certain time, or stay dormant, but it can possibly reappear everywhere at any time. This uncanny constancy describes the true power and impact of the parasite. For the avant-garde and their media subversion this means that it will never disappear; it only lies dormant in the evolving discourses—ready to come back to life at every time at every moment. This does not necessarily have to happen in the art scene. The radio ether, as I have argued, constitutes an endpoint for Marinetti's and Hausmann's visions, but viral strategies of social networks seem to carry the promise to connect to this early history of media subversion that the avant-garde pioneered.

NOTES

PRELIMS

1. Peter Bürger, *Theory of the Avant-Garde* (Minneapolis: Minnesota UP, 1984), 22.

INTRODUCTION

1. The letter is part of the Raoul Hausmann estate in the Berlinische Galerie. Sources from this archive will be quoted with the archival signature "BG-RHA." The signature of Broido's letter to Hausmann is BG-RHA 1115. Most of the texts that I quote are forthcoming in my edition of Raoul Hausmann's scientific and technical writings (Raoul Hausmann, *Dada-Wissenschaft: Wissenschaftliche und Technische Schriften*, ed. Berlinische Galerie and Arndt Niebisch [Hamburg: Philo Fine Arts, 2012]).
2. Hausmann documented this interest in a new "optophonetic" form of perception in texts such as "Présentismus" (Raoul Hausmann, "Présentismus," in *Texte bis 1933*. 2 vols., ed. Michael Erlhoff [München: Edition Text + Kritik, 1982], II, 24–30), "Optophonetik" ("Optophonetik," Hausmann, *Texte*, II, 50–57), and "Die überzüchteten Künste" ("Die überzüchteten Künste," Hausmann, *Texte*, II, 133–145).
3. The work on this calculating machine is widely documented in the correspondence between Hausmann and Broido, which also contains several drafts for patents. These documents are also part of the Raoul Hausmann estate in the Berlinische Galerie. Hausmann and Broido received their patent for the construction in 1936 in Britain. The patent number is GB446338.
4. Hausmann, *Texte*, II, 214.
5. In a letter to Broido he mentions several inventions that he conceptualized in the twenties (BG-RHA 1079).
6. Hausmann describes in his text "Die überzüchteten Texte" the optophone (Hausmann, *Texte*, II, 143–144).
7. See, for example, a letter from the Reichspatentamt to Hausmann's patent lawyer (BG-RHA 1139).
8. Filippo Tommaso Marinetti, *Selected Writings*, ed. Robert W. Flint (New York: Farrar, Strauss and Giroux, 1971), 39–44.

9. Neil Postman is mostly recognized as the person who brought the term "media ecology" into the discourse. Most significantly, he established "Media Ecology" as a subject of study at New York University. There is a wide consensus that Postman was inspired by the Canadian media theorist McLuhan, who described, in *Understanding Media* (Marshall McLuhan, *Understanding Media* [Cambridge, MA: MIT Press, 1994]), media as something that "shapes and controls the scale and form of human association and action" (McLuhan, *Understanding Media*, 9). Lance Strate provides an overview of the development of the notion of "Media Ecology" that has a special focus on the work of Postman and McLuhan (Lance Strate, "A Media Ecology Review," *Communication Research Trends*, 23.2 [2004]: 1–48).
10. Matthew Fuller, *Media Ecologies: Materialist Energies in Art and Technoculture* (Cambridge, MA: MIT Press, 2005). Fuller does not so much rely on Postman's and McLuhan's notions of media ecology as an environment; he uses the term "ecology" to describe the "massive and dynamic interrelation of processes and objects, beings and things, patterns and matter" (Fuller, *Media Ecologies*, 2). Central for Fuller's account is the multi-connectedness of media systems that generate a complex field for interaction and innovation.
11. Michael Goddard and Jussi Parikka, "Editorial," *The Fibreculture Journal* 17 (2011): 1–5.
12. Goddard and Parikka, "Editorial," 2.
13. Bernard Matthews, *An Introduction to Parasitology* (Cambridge: Cambridge UP, 1998), 16–17.
14. In regard to the German physicist Helmholtz, the experiments of the Futurist composer Luigi Russolo, which I discuss in Chapter 4, are of special importance, because they constitute simultaneously a rejection and expansion of nineteenth-century acoustics.
15. Hausmann reflects in his notebooks about the similarity between planetary orbits and the orbits of electrons surrounding an atomic nucleus. See, for example, BG-RHA 1757.
16. I suggest that in his famous formulation "Time and Space died yesterday. We are already living in the absolute, since we have already created eternal, omnipresent speed," from the Futurist Manifesto, Marinetti partly alludes to Einstein's relativity, where the only constant is c—the speed of light. Marinetti also refers to Brownian motion, which Einstein used to prove the validity of atom theory (Marinetti, *Selected Writings*, 41). Also, the Dadaist Richard Huelsenbeck claims at one point that Dada is a phenomenon developing parallel to relativistic philosophies (Richard Huelsenbeck, *Dada-Almanach* [Berlin: Erich Reiss, 1920], 3).
17. The collection of essays *Hermes* provides a good first insight into Serres' work that is driven by a desire to build bridges throughout history and disciplines (Michel Serres, *Hermes: Literature, Science, Philosophy* [Baltimore: Johns Hopkins Press, 1982]).
18. Certainly this rehabilitation of errors as creative elements is not solely Serres invention. The fusion of noise, complexity, and creativity had its most

forceful articulation in late eighties/early nineties of the twentieth century, when cultural scholars showed an increasing interest in chaos theory and the nonlinear dynamic of complex system. These forms of scientific inquiry focused on the importance and productivity of systems that were previously disregarded as chaotic. Katherine Hayles provided in an edited volume an important overview of how chaotic structures contribute essentially to a literary aesthetic (N. Katherine Hayles, ed., *Chaos and Order: Complex Dynamics in Literature and Science* [Chicago: Chicago UP, 1991]). This interest in chaotic complexity as a source for aesthetic productivity, however, had its important theoretical predecessor in the informational aesthetic of Max Bense (Max Bense, *Einführung in die informationstheoretische Ästhetik: Grundlegung und Anwendung in der Texttheorie* [Reinbek: Rowohlt, 1969]), which was then of major importance to the development of concrete poetry and also for the aesthetic theory of Umberto Eco (Umberto Eco, *The Open Work* [Cambridge, MA: Harvard University Press, 1989]).
19. Michel Serres, *The Parasite* (Baltimore: Johns Hopkins UP, 1982).
20. The German media theorist Bernhard Siegert recognizes that the parasite is not only a communication theoretical reflection, but a figure that short-circuits information theory and anthropology. The parasite is Serres' way to describe relationships from communicative to economical exchange (Bernhard Siegert, "Cacography or Communication? Cultural Techniques in German Media Studies," *Grey Room* 29 [2007]: 26–47). Jacques Derrida also uses the term "parasite." Derrida, however, focuses not so much on the role of the parasite in communication, but on its role as a transgressive element (Jacques Derrida, "Subverting the Signature. A Theory of the Parasite," *Blast Unlimited* 2 [1990]: 16–21). An excellent introduction to Serres' understanding of the parasite is Stephen Brown, "Michel Serres, "Science, Translation, and the Logic of the Parasite," *Theory, Culture and Society*, 19.3 [2002]: 1–27.
21. Shannon, Claude, *Mathematical Theory of Communication* (Urbana: University of Illinois, 1949).
22. Shannon, Claude. "Communication Theory of Secrecy Systems," *Bell System Technical Journal* 28.4 (1949): 656–715.
23. The *Encyclopedia of Electronics* for example defines "Parasitic Oscillation" as an "undesirable oscillation [that] can occur at frequencies that differ from its operating frequency. These oscillations are called parasitic oscillations, or simply parasitic." Stan Gibilisco and Neil Sclater, *Encyclopedia of Electronics* (Blue Ridge Summit: Tab Professional and Reference Books, 1990), 627.
24. The biologist Bernard E. Matthews shares such a positive or productive interpretation of the "parasite." Similar to Serres, he recognizes that the fact that at least two distinct units, the parasite and the host, are involved adds greatly to the complexity of the relationship (Matthews, *Parasitology*, 16).
25. Serres, *Parasite*, 14.
26. Serres, *Parasite*, 7.
27. Luigi Russolo, *The Art of Noises* (New York: Pendragon: 1982), 29.
28. Marinetti, *Selected Writings*, 51.

29. Hausmann, *Texte*, II, 27–28.
30. Serres, *Parasite*, 51–55.
31. Friedrich Kittler develops this understanding explicitly in "Rockmusik: Ein Missbrauch von Heeresgerät," *Appareils et Machines a Représentation. MANA. Mannheimer Analytica* 8 (1988): 87–101. He formulates this thought also in *Gramophone, Film, Typewriter* (Stanford: Stanford UP, 1999), 94–105.
32. Kittler, *Gramophone, Film, Typewriter*, 140.
33. In his book *Kittler and the Media*, Geoffrey Winthrop-Young discusses critically Kittler's emphasis on war as father of all media; he asserts that this cannot be assumed for all media. For example, in case of video games, one can actually witness how entertainment electronics become adapted by the military for training soldiers. Winthrop-Young, however, points out that Kittler has a very extended understanding of war that recognizes modern civilizations in a constant state of mobilization that prepares them for sudden military actions and that undermines every clear-cut distinction between military and civil practices (Geoffrey Winthrop-Young, *Kittler and the Media* [Cambridge: Polity Press, 2011], 131–135).
34. Walter Benjamin, "The Work of Art in the Age of Mechanical Reproduction," *Illuminations*, ed. Hannah Arendt (New York: Harcourt, Brace and World, 1968), 219–253.
35. Benjamin, "Work of Art," 244.
36. Benjamin, "Work of Art," 244.
37. Benjamin, "Work of Art," 239–240.
38. Kittler, *Gramophone, Film, Typewriter*, 96.
39. Caleb Kelly, *Cracked Media: The Sound of Malfunction* (Cambridge: MIT Press, 2009).
40. Friedrich Kittler, *Discourse Networks, 1800/1900* (Stanford: Stanford UP, 1990).
41. Kittler, *Discourse Networks*, 206.
42. Kittler, *Discourse Networks*, 208.
43. Serres, *Parasite*, 63.
44. Peter Bürger, *Theory of the Avant-Garde* (Minneapolis: Minnesota UP, 1984).
45. Bürger, *Theory*, 32.
46. Jonathan Sterne, *The Audible Past: Cultural Origins of Sound Reproduction* (Durham: Duke UP, 2003).
47. Sterne, *Audible Past*, 7–8.
48. Nicholas Gane and Stephen Sale, "Interview with Friedrich Kittler and Mark Hansen," *Theory, Culture & Society*, 24.7–8 (2007): 323–329.
49. Gane, "Interview," 324.
50. For a detailed discussion of Kittler's post- or antihuman position, see Winthrop Young, *Kittler and the Media*, 120–124.
51. Kittler takes the term "Aufschreibesysteme" from the schizophrenic Senate President Daniel Paul Schreber, who recorded his mad visions in his book *Memoirs of my Nervous Illness* (Daniel Paul Schreber, *Memoirs of my Nervous Illness* [New York: New York Review of Books, 2000]). Discourse networks

represent for Kittler the central media structure of a society, a "network of technologies and institutions that allow a given culture to select, store, and process relevant data" (Kittler, *Discourse Networks*, 369).
52. In a chapter of his book, Winthrop-Young provides an overview of the most common criticisms voiced against Kittler. Significantly, this chapter starts out with the alleged media determinism (Winthrop-Young, *Kittler and the Media*, 120–146). I believe that this claim is not only the common topic of hot debates because it questions the status of the free subject, but because it includes one of the most important methodological shifts that Kittler brought about. A media theory in the vein of Kittler does not so much reject the human as it focuses on the discursive systems that create citizens, subjects, and human beings. Winthrop-Young also points out that within Kittler's work discourse networks are not exclusively technological constructs. For example, Romanticism, that is, the Discourse Network 1800, was not based on new technologies but on new reading pedagogies that implemented a new role of the written word (Winthrop-Young, *Kittler and the Media*, 121).
53. Friedrich Kittler, *Gramophone, Film, Typewriter*, xxxix.
54. This resembles a basic theorem of chaos theory or nonlinear dynamics, namely that minimal irregularities in initial stages contribute to an unpredictable and irreversible complexity in a system. Alan Beyerchen discusses this theorem in a convincing and accessible way on the basis of Carl von Clausewitz' notion of friction on the battlefield (Alan Beyerchen, "Clausewitz, Nonlinearity, and the Unpredictability of War," *International Security* 17.3 [1992–93]: 59–90).
55. In regard to the larger field of avant-garde studies my book traces the shift from art production to media engineering and psychophysics, and highlights the interplay of media technology and cultural production. This emphasis has become an important point of discussion in recent years. Brigid Doherty's important article "See: We Are All Neurasthenics!" (Brigid Doherty, "'See: We Are All Neurasthenics!' or, The Trauma of Dada Montage," *Critical Inquiry* 24 [1997]: 82–132) points to the correlation between trauma and photomontage. In parts of her book *"Dada Triumphs!" Dada Berlin, 1917–1923: Artistry of Polarities. Montages, Metamechanics, Manifestations* (New Haven: G. K. Hall, 1996), Hanne Bergius retraces the connection between Dada and early-twentieth-century sciences. With regard to Futurism, Jeffrey Schnapp reads Futurist poetics in its media historical context (Jeffrey Schnapp, "Propeller Talk," *Modernism/Modernity* 1.3 [1994]: 153–178; Jeffrey Schnapp, "Crash," *Modernism/Modernity* 6.1 [1999]: 1–49), and Lorenzo Mango establishes in his book *Alla Scoperta di Nuovi Sensi: Il Tattilismo Futurista* (Napoli: La città del sole, 2001) a connection between the sense of tactility and Marinetti's attempts to create an all-encompassing multimedia art. Also, the contributions by Timothy Campbell in his book *Wireless Writing in the Age of Marconi* (Minneapolis: Minnesota UP, 2006) and his article "'Infinite Remoteness.' Marinetti, Bontempelli, and the Birth of Modern Italian Visual Culture" (*MLN*

120 [2005], 111–136) demonstrate that Futurist aesthetics were fueled by contemporaneous media engineering as well as by experimental psychology. The art historian Matthew Biro brings the discussion of avant-garde and technology closer to posthumanist debates as they are carried out by Donna Haraway and Katherine Hayles (Donna Haraway, "A Cyborg Manifesto: Science, Technology, and Socialist-Feminism in the Late Twentieth Century," *Simians, Cyborgs and Women: The Reinvention of Nature* [New York: Routledge, 1991], 149–181; N. Katherine Hayles, *How We Became Posthuman: Virtual Bodies in Cybernetics, Literature, and Informatics* [Chicago: Chicago UP, 1999]). In his book *The Dada Cyborg: Visions of the New Human in Weimar Berlin* (Minneapolis: Minnesota UP, 2009), Matthew Biro explores how the Dada movement attempted to fuse man and machine based on the figure of the cyborg. He thereby not only focuses on the technological constructedness of Dadaist montage and collage, but also analyzes the social and gender theoretical implications of hybridization through the avant-garde.

56. Especially the relatively new field of auditory studies focuses on media historical investigation of media abuses of the avant-garde and their continuous history throughout the twentieth century. Especially, Douglas Kahn's study of noise and sound in the avant-garde (*Noise, Water, Meat: A History of Sound in the Arts* [Cambridge: MIT Press, 1999]) is of great significance in this regard, but also recent contributions such as Steve Goodman's *Sonic Warfare: Sound, Affect, and the Ecology of Fear* (Cambridge: MIT Press, 2010), a study of military and partisan uses of sound, and Caleb Kelly's *Cracked Media* focus on the constant transformations and abuses of sound equipment. *Cracked Media* is here of special interest, because it describes modern digital sound design explicitly as an attempt to abuse and distort the functioning of media technology, and therefore discusses the continuation of the media manipulation that was started by Marinetti and others.

CHAPTER 1

1. Marjorie Perloff, *The Futurist Moment: Avant-Garde, Avant Guerre, and the Language of Rupture* (Chicago: Chicago UP, 2003), 82.
2. Martin Puchner, *Poetry of Revolution: Marx, Manifestos, and the Avant-Gardes* (Princeton: Princeton UP, 2006), 13.
3. Karl Marx and Friedrich Engels, *Collected Works*, vol. III (New York: International Publishers, 1975), 481.
4. Marx, *Collected Works*, 481.
5. Uwe Spörl, "Manifest" *Reallexikon der deutschen Literaturwissenschaft*, vol. II (Berlin and New York: de Gruyter, 2000), 535–537.
6. Puchner, *Revolution*, 12.
7. Mary Ann Caws, *Manifesto: A Century of Isms* (Lincoln: U of North Nebraska P, 2001).

8. Neil Postman, *Amusing Ourselves to Death: Public Discourse in the Age of Show Business* (London: Penguin Books, 1985), 8.
9. Umberto Eco, *Apocalittici e Integrati: Comunicazioni di Massa e Teoria della Cultura di Massa* (Milano: Bompiani, 1964), 11.
10. Postman, *Amusing*, 8.
11. Niklas Luhmann, *The Reality of Mass Media* (Stanford: Stanford UP, 2000), 25.
12. Christina Poggi, *Inventing Futurism: The Art and Politics of Artifical Optimism* (Princeton: Princeton UP, 2009), 4.
13. Filippo Tommaso Marinetti, *Mafarka: An African Novel* (London: Middlesex UP, 1997).
14. Perloff, *Futurist Moment*, 89.
15. Gottfried Benn, "Probleme der Lyrik" Gottfried Benn, *Essays und Reden* (Frankfurt am Main: Fischer, 1989), 505–535.
16. Benn, "Probleme," 508.
17. This close connection between mass media and Futurism is widely recognized in the literature. Mary Ann Caws also emphasizes this event character of the manifesto (Caws, *Manifesto*, XX). Tisdall and Bozolla point out that the "determination to reach as wide an audience as possible is the key to Futurism" (Caroline Tisdall and Angelo Bozolla, *Futurism* [New York: Thames and Hudson, 1977], 7). Martin Puchner claims that, since Marinetti launched his texts, the genre of the manifesto is intimately connected to advertising (Puchner, *Poetry*, 159). An especially important article on the connection between mass media and Futurist manifestos is Claudia Salaris, "Marketing Modernism. Marinetti as Publisher," *Modernism/Modernity* 1.3 (1994): 109–127. She contests that from "the beginning... Marinetti possessed an uncommon capacity for using the media and forging public relations" (Salaris, "Publisher," 110).
18. Anna Lawton, "Futurist Manifestoes as an Element of Performance," *Canadian-American Slavic Studies* 19.4 (1985): 473–491; Puchner, *Revolution*, 87.
19. Hansgeorg Schmidt-Bergmann, *Futurismus: Geschichte, Ästhetik, Dokumente* (Reinbek bei Hamburg: Rowohlt, 1993), 68.
20. Salaris, "Publisher," 112.
21. Schnapp, "Crash," 5.
22. Clara Orban, *The Culture of Fragments: Words and Images in Futurism and Surrealism* (Amsterdam and Atlanta: Rodopi, 1997), 29.
23. Luhmann, *Reality*, 28.
24. Schmidt-Bergmann, *Futurismus*, 51–52.
25. Marinetti, *Selected Writings*, 39–40.
26. Luciano De Maria remarks that Marinetti's manifestos differ greatly in their aggressive and lyrical tone from other proclamative texts of that time (Filippo Tommaso Marinetti: *Filippo Tommaso Marinetti e il Futurismo*, ed. Luciano de Maria (Milano: Mondadori, 2000), XVI).

27. Perloff, *Futurist Moment*, 86.
28. This can also be recognized as homage to Marinetti's hometown, Milan, because the northern Italian cities were, because of the hydroelectic power from the water of the Alps, the first to receive electric street lightning and trams.
29. Marinetti, *Selected Writings*, 40. This quotation makes clear that the Futurist machine is not only an ally but also a dangerous unpredictable enemy.
30. Schnapp points out that this accident, which constitutes the *grande finale* of the introduction, is in fact a biographical reference. Marinetti had a car accident in 1908 that also ended in a ditch (Schnapp, "Crash," 6).
31. Marinetti, *Selected Writings*, 41.
32. For example, Marinetti mentions the concept of the Futurist immortality in his literary manifesto. The mortal is replaced by a mechanical cyborg that consists of spares (Marinetti, *Futurismo*, 84). For a very detailed discussion of the relationship between life and death see Timothy Campbell, "Vital Matters. Sovereignty, Milieu, and the Animal in Futurism's Founding Manifesto," *Annali d'Italianistica* 27 (2009): 157–174.
33. Marinetti, *Selected Writings*, 39–40.
34. Giovanni Lista, "The Activist Model or, The Avant-Garde as Italian Invention," *South Central Review* 13, 2/3 (1996): 13–34.
35. Lista, *Activist*, 17.
36. Lista, *Activist*, 20.
37. Kees W. Bolle, "Myth: An Overview" *The Encyclopedia of Religion*, ed. M. Eliade, Vol. 10 (New York: Macmillan, 1987), 261–273.
38. Roland Barthes, "Myth Today," Roland Barthes, *Mythologies* (London: Paladin, 1972), 109–159.
39. Barthes, "Myth Today," 109.
40. Barthes, "Myth Today," 114.
41. Barthes, "Myth Today," 121.
42. Barthes, "Myth Today," 155.
43. Marinetti, *Selected Writings*, 41.
44. Clara Orban stresses the closeness between Marinetti's ideology of speed and Einstein's theory that under extreme speeds time and space collapse (Orban, *Fragments*, 30–31).
45. Schnapp, *Crash*, 21.
46. Wolfgang Schivelbusch, *The Train Journey: The Industrialization of Time and Space in the 19th Century* (Berkeley: U of California P, 1986).
47. Stephen Kern, *The Culture of Space and Time 1880–1918* (Cambridge, MA: Harvard University Press, 1983).
48. Marinetti, *Selected Writings*, 94–96.
49. Marinetti, *Selected Writings*, 96.
50. Marinetti, *Selected Writings*, 96.
51. Marinetti, *Selected Writings*, 55–58.
52. Marinetti, *Selected Writings*, 56.

53. Marinetti, *Selected Writings*, 98.
54. Marinetti, *Selected Writings*, 67.
55. Filipp Tommaso Marinetti and Pino Masnata, "La Radia," Douglas Kahn and Gregory Whitehead, eds., *Wireless Imagination: Sound, Radio, and the Avant-Garde* (Cambridge: MIT Press, 1992), 265–268.
56. Marinetti, "Radia," 266–267.
57. Dr. Frosch, "*Was ist Dada.*" *Welt am Montag* quoted from Harriet Watts, ed., Dada and the Press (New Haven: G. K. Hall, 2004), 2.
58. Watts, *Press*, 56.
59. Watts, *Press*, 56–57.
60. Timothy Benson, "Conventions and Constructions. The Performative Text in Dada" *Dada. The Coordinates of Cultural Politics*, ed. Stephen C. Foster (New York: Hall, 1996), 93.
61. Otto Flake, "Züricher Kunstchronik (1919)," *Die neue Bücherschau*, 1.2 (1919). Quoted from Watts, *Press*, 2004, 50.
62. Karl Riha and Jörgen Schäfer, ed., *DADA total: Manifeste, Aktionen, Texte, Bilder* (Stuttgart: Reclam, 1994), 33.
63. Marx, *Communist Manifesto*, 519.
64. Watts, *Press*, 29.
65. Watts, *Press*, 34.
66. Raimund Meyer also points out journalists adopted and parodied the Dada language (Watts, *Press*, 14).
67. Watts, *Press*, 35.
68. Compare Benjamin's claim in the *Artwork* essay that Dada poetry would attack its readers like a projectile (Benjamin, "Work of Art," 240).
69. Serres, *Parasite*, 7.
70. Riha and Schäfer, *Dada Total*, 34.
71. Kahn argues that, for example, Ball's sound poetry was created because the Dadaists wanted to address the multilingual audience in the Cabaret Voltaire (Kahn, *Noise Water, Meat*, 48).
72. Martin Puchner emphasizes the importance of internationalism for Dada (Puchner, *Revolution*, 140–145).
73. That "Dada" is just an example for a more extended linguistic project becomes clear in the second part of Ball's Manifesto that consists of a Dadaistic poetics: "Ich will keine Worte, die andere erfunden haben. Alle Worte haben andere erfunden. Ich will meinen eigenen Unfug, ... " (Riha and Schäfer, *Dada Total*, 34).
74. *Neue Zürcher Zeitung*, July 18, 1916, Zweites Abendblatt, quoted from: Watts, *Press*, 29.
75. Quoted from Watts, *Press*, 18.
76. Watts, *Press*, 104–105.
77. Jean Baudrillard, *The Gulf War Did Not Take Place* (Bloomington: Indiana UP, 1995).
78. Richard Huelsenbeck, *Dada Almanach* (Berlin: Erich Reiss, 1920), 94.
79. Watts, *Press*, 106–107.

80. Johannes Baader, *Oberdada. Schriften, Manifeste, Flugblätter, Billets, Werke und Taten*, eds. Hanne Bergius, Norbert Miller, and Karl Riha (Giessen: Anabas, 1977), 11–17.
81. Baader, *Oberdada*, 48.
82. Bergius, "*Dada Triumphs!*," 49.
83. Bergius, "*Dada Triumphs!*," 50.
84. Watts, *Press*, 72.
85. Quoted from Watts, *Press*, 72.
86. Karl Riha, "Der Oberdada im Urteil der Dadaisten" in Baader, *Schriften*, 193–201.
87. Robert Motherwell, ed., *The Dada Painters and Poets: An Anthology* (Cambridge: Harvard UP, 1979), 244.
88. Motherwell, *Dada Painters and Poets*, 243.
89. Huelsenbeck uses the affirmation of war as a provoking strategy also in the Dada-Almanach (Huelsenbeck, *Dada Almanach*, 106).
90. Motherwell, *Dada Painters and Poets*, 244.
91. Riha and Schäfer, *Dada Total*, 93.
92. Motherwell, *Dada Painters and Poets*, 72.
93. Hausmann emphasizes the artificial and strategic character of the list of signatories, which was in reality just a fictitious collection of important names: "Zu unserem Erfolg nötig ist Reklame. Darum führen wir auf unserem Manifest die Namen der ausländischen Dadaisten an, um in der Oeffentlichkeit den Glauben zu erwecken, als wäre der Dadaismus eine ganz grosse, europäische Angelegenheit" (Raoul Hausmann, *Scharfrichter der bürgerlichen Seele: Raoul Hausmann in Berlin 1900–1933*, ed. Eva Züchner (Berlin: Hatje, 1998), 71).
94. Alfons Backes-Haase, *Kunst und Wirklichkeit: Zur Typologie des DADA-Manifests* (Frankfurt am Main: A. Hain, 1992), 75; Hanne Bergius, *Das Lachen Dadas: Die Berliner Dadaisten und ihre Aktionen* (Gießen: Anabas. 1989), 324.
95. Hausmann, *Scharfrichter*, 71.
96. Franz Schulz, "Das dressierte Publikum," *Prager Tagblatt*, June 17, 1919, quoted from: Watts, *Press*, 95–98.
97. Watts, *Press*, 95–96.
98. Watts, *Press*, 96.
99. Riha and Schäfer, *Dada Total*, 109.
100. Riha and Schäfer, *Dada Total*, 109.
101. Watts, *Press*, 96.
102. Watts, *Press*, 70.
103. Backes-Haase, *Typologie*, 11–12.
104. Luhmann, *Reality*, 28–29.
105. Bergius, "*Dada Triumphs!*," 72.
106. Watts, *Press*, 11.
107. Watts, *Press*, 12.
108. Benson, *Conventions*, 87.

CHAPTER 2

1. Riha and Schäfer, *DADA Total*, 29.
2. Hugo v. Hofmannsthal, *Das Märchen der 672. Nacht: Das erzählerische Werk* (Frankfurt am Main: Fischer, 1999), 102.
3. Filippo Tommaso Marinetti, *Futurismo Tommaso Marinetti e il Futurismo*, ed. Luciano de Maria (Milano: Mondadori, 2000), 77.
4. Hugo Ball, *Flight Out of Time: A Dada Diary* (New York: Viking Press, 1974), 71.
5. Günther Berghaus, *The Genesis of Futurism: Early Career and Writings, 1899–1909* (Leeds: The Society of Italian Studies, 1995), 4.
6. Berghaus, *Genesis*, 55–58.
7. Berghaus, *Genesis*, 58–72.
8. Berghaus, *Genesis*, 78–83.
9. Filippo Tommaso Marinetti, *Mafarka the Futurist: An African Novel* (London: Middlesex UP, 1997), VIII-IX.
10. Filippo Tommaso Marinetti, *Selected Writings*, ed. Robert W. Flint (New York: Farrar, Strauss and Giroux, 1971), 45–54.
11. Marinetti, *Selected Writings*, 84–89.
12. Umbro Apollonio, *Futurist Manifestos* (London: Thames and Hudson, 1970), 95–106.
13. Marinetti, *Selected Writings*, 89.
14. Marinetti, *Futurismo*, 85–86.
15. Marinetti, *Selected Writings*, 89.
16. Marinetti, *Selected Writings*, 87.
17. Apollonio, *Futurist Manifestos*, 100–103.
18. Apollonio, *Futurist Manifestos*, 105.
19. Campbell, *Wireless Writing*, 82.
20. Johanna Drucker, *The Visible Word. Experimental Typography and Modern Art, 1909–1923* (Chicago: U of Chicago P, 1994), 109.
21. Marinetti, *Selected Writings*, 84.
22. Jeffrey Schnapp, "Propeller Talk" *Modernism/Modernity* 1.3 (1994): 153–154.
23. Marinetti, *Selected Writings*, 84.
24. Marinetti, *Selected Writings*, 87.
25. Marinetti, *Selected Writings*, 84.
26. Marinetti, *Selected Writings*, 87.
27. Marinetti, *Selected Writings*, 87.
28. Marinetti, *Selected Writings*, 84.
29. Friedrich Kittler, "Im Telegrammstil" *Stil: Geschichte und Funktionen eines kulturwissenschaftlichen Diskurselements*, ed. Hans-Ulrich Gumbrecht and Karl Ludwig Pfeiffer (Frankfurt am Main: Suhrkamp, 1986), 359.
30. Marinetti, *Futurismo*, 108.
31. Marinetti, *Futurismo*, 108.
32. Marinetti, *Futurismo*, 88–91; Willard Bohn, *Italian Futurist Poetry* (Toronto: Toronto UP, 2005), 12–13.

33. Onomatopoeias can be called *iconic* signs, because they are *similar* to the sounds they represent. Just as a picture of a tree is similar to that tree, so also the word "squeak" is similar to the squeaking sound of a mouse.
34. Also Russolo emphasizes in the chapter "I Rumori di Linguaggio" from his book *L'Arte dei Rumori* the importance of onomatopoeias for Marinetti's liberated words (Luigi Russolo, *L'arte dei Rumori* (Milano: Edizioni Futuriste di Poesia, 1916), 51–57). Furthermore, he recognizes onomatopoeias as the central link between his art of noises and Marinetti's poetics.
35. Marinetti distinguishes in the manifesto "Lo Splendore Geometrico e Mecanico e la Sensibilità Numerica" between four kinds of onomatopoeias: (1) imitative; (2) indirect, complex, and analogical; (3) abstract; and (4) psychological onomatopoeias. These four types differ from one another in the degree that they represent concrete or abstract entities. Imitative onomatopoeias represent actual sensory sensations, while abstract onomatopoeias represent something like states of mind (Marinetti, *Futurismo*, 146). With this classification Marinetti emphasizes that onomatopoeias do not serve simply as direct representations of brute reality. On the contrary, he recognizes in them a device that is able to store and reproduce complex cognitive processes with a high efficiency.
36. Michael Kirby points out that many avant-garde films could be described as "cinematic *parole in libertà*" (Michael Kirby, *Futurist Performance with Manifestoes and Playscripts* (New York: PAJ Publications, 1986), 141).
37. Paul Virilio, *War and Cinema: The Logistics of Perception* (New York: Verso, 1989), 17; Friedrich Kittler, *Film, Gramophone, Typewriter* (Stanford: Stanford UP, 1999), 124
38. This event was of great public interest. The newest developments of aeronautics were displayed and the audience brought all kinds of technology enthusiasts together: D'Annunzio, Kafka, and certainly Marinetti were among the guests. Peter Demetz wrote a wonderful book, *The Flight Show at Brescia*, about this flight show. (Peter Demetz, *The Air Show at Brescia* [New York: Farrar, Strauss, and Giroux, 2002].) It is now tempting to recognize the speedy succession of objects as perceived in flight as the origin of Futurist poetics, and to argue that it attests to the interconnection, in *parole in libertà*, between flight surveillance and cinema as formulated by authors such as Virilio and Kittler. Although this connection is implied in Futurist poetics, it cannot be ascribed to the first lines of the technical manifesto directly. The reason is simple: Marinetti is not inspired by visual impressions, but rather by tactile and auditory sensations caused by the vibrating engine of the airplane. As Schnapp carefully and clearly outlines, Marinetti sits in a position where he cannot see anything except the sky above and the back of the pilot's head in front of him. (Schnapp, "Propeller Talk," 160–161.)
39. Virilio, *War and Cinema*, 11–30.
40. Marinetti, *Selected Writings*, 85.

41. Marinetti, *Selected Writings*, 85.
42. Marinetti, *Selected Writings*, 85.
43. Marinetti, *Selected Writings*, 86.
44. It would also be interesting to draw a comparison between Marinetti's analogy and analog media. In media-technology "analog" signifies all kinds of storage and transmission media that operate with immediate, noncoded impulses. It is, however, rather unlikely that Marinetti had this notion of the term "analog" in mind. The distinction digital/analog that constituted the terminology of analog media arose only shortly after World War Two. For the history of the digital-analog distinction, see: Jens Schröter and Alexander Böhnke, eds., *Analog/Digital—Opposition oder Kontinuum?: Zur Theorie und Geschichte einer Unterscheidung* (Bielefeld: Transcript, 2004).
45. Marinetti, *Selected Writings*, 85.
46. Willard Bohn, *Futurist Poetry*, 13.
47. Marjorie Perloff, *The Futurist Moment. Avant-Garde, Avant Guerre, and the Language of Rupture* (Chicago: Chicago UP, 2003), 60.
48. Marinetti transgresses, however, the limitation of film to the sense of sight. It is significant that Marinetti addresses all senses in his text and gives information about smell, noise, and heat.
49. Sergej Eisenstein, "The Dramaturgy of Film Form (The Dialectical Approach to Film Form)," *The Eisenstein Reader*, ed. R. Taylor (London: British Film Institute, 1998), 93–110.
50. Eisenstein, "Dramaturgy," 95.
51. Marinetti, *Futurismo*, 90.
52. Apollonio, *Futurist Manifestos*, 98.
53. Schivelbusch, *Train Journey*, 113–123. While Marinetti develops in his poetical text an aesthetics of shell shock before the WWI, that is, before the term came into use, Brigid Doherty observes a connection between war trauma and photomontage in Berlin Dada as an reaction to experience from WWI (Doherty, "Neurasthenics," 82–132). Doherty interprets a poem by George Grosz that displays a similar scenario as Marinetti's text. The poem "Kaffehaus" describes the experience of a soldier returning to the metropolis Berlin. The soldier comments on his impressions as follows: "I am a machine whose pressure gauge has gone to pieces!" (Doherty, "Neurasthenics," 95). The language of this poem is very close to Marinetti's descriptions. Shock is shown as a mechanical breakdown. Doherty comments: "The pathology of the machine thus described is internal. To repeat, a pressure gauge has blown, and the parts spinning inside do not know how or when to stop; that is the analogy drawn to neurasthenia or, more precisely, that is the condition whose description is meant to function, within the poem, as an example or a demonstration of neurasthenia and its ubiquity" (Doherty, "Neurasthenics," 97).
54. Linda Dalrymple Henderson points out in her essay "Vibratory Modernism" the importance of vibrations, electromagnetism and "ether waves" for modernist art. (Linda Dalrymple Henderson, "Vibratory

Modernism. Boccioni, Kupka, and the Ether of Space," *From Energy to Information: Representation in Science and Technology, Art, and Literature*, ed. Bruce Clarke and Linda Dalrymple Henderson [Stanford: Stanford UP, 2002], 126–149.) She also recognizes Marinetti's "wireless imagination" as a testimony indicating that this paradigm also influenced literary production (Henderson, "Vibratory Modernism," 129). In Chapter 5, I am going to discuss the importance of radio technology and forms of telepathic communication for the avant-garde in more detail.
55. Apollonio, *Futurist Manifestos*, 98.
56. Johanna Drucker also acknowledges this importance of electricity for Futurism in her book *The Visible Word*: "Marinetti moves immediately into the world of transmission, broadcast, and communication dependent on the new technology of electricity" (Drucker, *Visible Word*, 108).
57. William James, *Psychology* (New York: Henry Holt, 1908), 11.
58. Richard Huelsenbeck, *Phantastische Gebete* (Berlin: Malik, 1920).
59. Ball, *Flight*, 55.
60. Martin Puchner also emphasizes the uniquely theatrical quality that emerged out of the performances in the Cabaret Voltaire (Puchner, *Revolution* [Princeton: Princeton UP, 2006], 148).
61. Ball, *Flight*, 54.
62. Ball, *Flight*, 68.
63. Eckhard Philipp, *Dadaismus: Einführung in den literarischen Dadaismus und die Wortkunst des "Sturmkreises"* (München: Fink, 1980), 63; Wassily Kandinsky, *Concerning the Spiritual in Art* (New York: Dover, 1977).
64. Kandinsky, *Spiritual*, 15.
65. Ball, *Flight*, 70–71.
66. Riha and Schäfer, *Dada Total*, 29.
67. Ball, *Flight*, 57.
68. Seth Taylor, *Left-Wing Nietzscheans: The Politics of German Expressionism, 1910–1920* (Berlin and New York: de Gruyter, 1990), 166.
69. Friedrich Nietzsche, *The Birth of Tragedy and the Case of Wagner* (New York: Random House 1967), 36.
70. Nietzsche, *Tragedy*, 67.
71. Ball, *Flight*, 64–65.
72. Riha and Schäfer, *Dada Total*, 20.
73. Riha and Schäfer, *Dada Total*, 29.
74. See, for example, Tzara's "Negerlieder" published in the *Dada Almanach* (Huelsenbeck, *Dada Almanach*, 141–143).
75. A different example can be found in Christian Morgenstern's "Großes Lalula." In this poem a line ends with "(;)!" (Christian Morgenstern, *Werke und Briefe: Kommentierte Ausgabe*, ed. M. Cureau [Stuttgart: Urachaus, 1990], 61). This sequence of signs cannot be performed, because all the letters indicate functions of the written medium and do not indicate any vocal quality.

76. Karl Riha in his text "fmsbwtözäu pggiv-..?mü" also acknowledges that Ball's use of the poem title as an associative framing structure turns his poetry into a less radical form of poetical expression. Riha especially points out that Hausmann's lyricism takes a decisive step by neglecting organizational patterns such as titles, ordered print, use of stanzas, etc. (Karl Riha, "fmsbwtözäu pggiv-..?mü. Raoul Hausmanns optophonetische Poesie," *Raoul Hausmann*, ed. K. Bartsch and A. Koch, 31–42. (Graz: Droschl 1996).
77. Richard Huelsenbeck, *Mit Witz, Licht und Grütze: Auf den Spuren des Dadaismus* (Hamburg: Nautilus. 1991), 15.
78. Philipp, *Dadaismus*, 246.
79. Philipp, *Dadaismus*, 246.
80. Huelsenbeck, *Phantastische Gebete*, 7.
81. The activity of breathing as the physiological pre-condition for articulation is an important factor in Dada poetry. I will discuss this point more intensely in the context of Hausmann's poetics.
82. One might argue that this first part could be added to the text version of the poem and that the actual sound poem as it would have been performed in Zurich started after the line containing "Anfang."
83. Huelsenbeck, *Phantastische Gebete*, 7.
84. Huelsenbeck, *Phantastische Gebete*, 8.
85. Michael Erlhoff, *Raoul Hausmann, Dadasoph: Versuch einer Politisierung der Ästhetik* (Hannover: Zweitschrift 1982), 96.
86. Erlhoff, *Dadasoph*, 1982, 99.
87. Sybille Krämer, "Writing, Notational Iconicity, Calculus: On Writing as a Cultural Technique" *MLN* 118.3 (2003): 518–537.
88. Krämer, "Notational Iconicity," 520.
89. At first, the characters are quite different, but more importantly, the direction of reading is different in each alphabet. The Hebrew signs not only indicate the possibility of different alphabetic sign systems, but also refer to the conventionality of the reading direction.
90. Michel Serres, *The Parasite* (Baltimore: Johns Hopkins UP, 1982), 38–39.
91. Walter Benjamin, "The Work of Art in the Age of Mechanical Reproduction," *Illuminations*, ed. Hannah Arendt (New York: Harcourt, Brace and World, 1968), 240.
92. Raoul Hausmann, *Am Anfang war Dada* (Gießen: Anabas, 1980), 43.
93. Riha and Schäfer, *Dada Total*, 132.
94. Hausmann, *Anfang*, 43.
95. Rudolf Kuenzli, "The Semiotics of Dada Poetry" *Dada Spectrum: The Dialectics of Revolt*, ed. S. C. Foster and R. E. Kuenzli (Madison: Coda Press, 1979), 51–70.
96. Kuenzli, "Semiotics," 63.
97. The letter case that Hausmann used was designed for typesetting texts in the German language. Accordingly, "y" is one of the less frequently used letters.

98. Brigid Doherty argues that this poem would be "an abrupt and artificial return to sound and speech" (Doherty, "Neurasthenics," 125). It is true that Hausmann ascribes a synesthetic character to these posters that stimulates a verbal performance (Hausmann, *Anfang*, 43). But the posters include a variety of signs such as the pointing finger, which do not correspond to sounds. These poems do not exhibit speech, but expose the entropy of the letter case.
99. Stephen Budiansky, *Battle of Wits: The Complete Story of Codebreaking in World War II* (New York: The Free Press, 2000), 63–64.
100. Karl Riha makes a similar claim and refers to the deep structure of language when he acknowledges that the great number of consonants in Hausmann's "Plakatgedicht" is due to the fact that there are more consonants than vowels in the letter case (Riha, "fmsbwtözäu pggiv-..?mü," 35).
101. Hausmann, *Anfang*, 43.
102. Erlhoff, *Dadasoph*, 195.
103. Peter Demetz, "Varieties of Phonetic Poetry: An Introduction," *From Kafka and Dada to Brecht and Beyond*, ed. Reinhold Grimm et al. (Madison: U of Wisconsin P, 1982), 23–33
104. Demetz, "Varieties," 31.
105. Demetz, "Varieties," 32.
106. Hausmann, *Texte*, II, 69–70.
107. Demetz, "Varieties," 31.
108. This correlation between smoking and experimental poetry can also be found in Canguillo's poem "fumare" (see: Marinetti, *Futurismo*, 144). Here, the verb for smoking stands in for the extending cloud of smoke blown out by a traveler in a train compartment. Interestingly, Hausmann connects train travel with the experience of smoking and complains about the smoking restrictions. "Das Vergnügen des Rauchens wir dem Reisenden drakonisch untersagt" (Hausmann, *Scharfrichter*, 155–156).
109. Demetz, "Varieties," 33.
110. Hausmann, *Scharfrichter*, 208–212.
111. Rama Prasad, *The Science of Breath and the Philosophy of the Tattvas* (London: Theosophical Publishing Society, 1894).
112. Tristan Tzara, *Seven Dada Manifestos and Lampisteries* (London: Calder, 1977), 39.

CHAPTER 3

1. Friedrich Kittler, *Optical Media: Berlin Lectures 1999* (Cambridge: Polity, 2010), 118.
2. Walter Benjamin, "The Work of Art in the Age of Mechanical Reproduction," *Illuminations*, ed. Hannah Arendt (New York: Harcourt, Brace and World, 1968), 221.
3. Paul Virilio, *War and Cinema: The Logistics of Perception* (New York: Verso, 1989).

4. Filippo Tommaso Marinetti, *Selected Writings*, ed. Robert W. Flint (New York: Farrar, Strauss and Giroux, 1971), 62–63.
5. Benjamin, "The Work of Art," 239.
6. Friedrich Kittler's book *Gramophone, Film, Typewriter* is based on the premise that these media technologies correlate to the categories of the symbolic, real, and imaginary as identified by the French psychoanalyst Jacques Lacan. (Kittler, *Gramophone, Film Typewriter* [Stanford: Stanford UP, 1999], 15–16.)
7. Robert Brain points out the importance of the graphical method developed in the physiological laboratories of the late nineteenth century for symbolist and avant-garde poetry. He especially highlights the importance of phonographic transcriptions of spoken language in visual curves as central for the development of Futurist poetics. I completely agree with the observation that this graphical method had a great impact on the avant-garde. However, I see the resonances to this scientific method rather in the visual language of Futurist painters with their lines of force, in Futurist noise compositions (which I discuss in Chapter 4), and in the development of a tactile art (which I discuss in the last chapter). Certainly, Futurist poetry also adopts elements from this discourse, but Marinetti's *parole in libertà* still conserve a form of digital compression that is different from the "lines of force" in Futurist painting. (Robert Brain, "Genealogy of *Zang Tumb Tumb*: Experimental Phonetics and the Invention of Free Verse and Modernist Sound Art," *Grey Room* 43 [Spring 2011]: 88–117.)
8. Giovanni Lista, *Futurism and Photography* (London: Estorick Collection, 2001).
9. Gerado Regnani, "Futurism and Photography: Between Scientific Inquiry and Aesthetic Imagination," *Futurism and the Technological Imagination*, ed. Günther Berghaus (Amsterdam: Rodopi, 2009), 177–199.
10. Lista, *Futurism and Photography*, 9–16.
11. Filippo Tommaso Marinetti and Tato, "Futurist Photography," *Critical Writings*, ed. Günther Berghaus (New York: Farrar, Straus and Giroux, 2006), 392–393.
12. Marinetti, *Critical Writings*, 393.
13. For an overview of the history of chronophotography, see Marta Braun, *Picturing Time: The Work of Etienne-Jules Marey (1830–1904)* (Chicago: Chicago UP, 1992).
14. Marinetti, *Selected Writings*, 85.
15. Sarah Carey, "Futurism's Photography: From Fotodinamismo to Fotomontaggio," *Carte Italiane* 2.6 (2010): 221–217.
16. Umbro Apollonio, *Futurist Manifestos* (London: Thames and Hudson, 1970), 28.
17. Apollonio, *Futurist Manifestos*, 29.
18. Linda Dalrymple Henderson, "Vibratory Modernism. Boccioni, Kupka, and the Ether of Space," *From Energy to Information: Representation in Science and Technology, Art, and Literature*, ed. Bruce Clarke and Linda Dalrymple Henderson (Stanford: Stanford UP, 2002), 126–149.

19. Marta Braun points out that the preparation of the subject for photography was an important step in the development of Marey's experiments. He started out with a high contrast between the clothes and the background and continued with applying shinny buttons marking the joints, which were connected through metal bands. In this way, Marey focused more and more on the movement in the representation, and the actual subject vanished in the background; only the lines indicating the motoric apparatus remained visible (Braun, *Picturing Time*, 81).
20. Lista, *Futurism and Photography*, 14.
21. Kittler, *Gramophone, Film, Typewriter*, 152–156.
22. In his famous 1766 essay *Laokoon*, Gotthold Ephraim Lessing discusses the difference between poetry and visual arts and explicates, on the basis of the ancient sculpture of Laokoon, how the artist can display a gesture as if it was in motion (Gotthold Ephraim Lessing, *Laokoon oder über die Grenzen der Malerei und Poesie* [Stuttgart: Reclam, 1964], 114–115).
23. Paul Virilio, *The Vision Machine* (Bloomington and Indianapolis: Indiana UP, 1994).
24. Vrilio, *Vision Machine*, 2.
25. Apollonio, *Futurist Manifestos*, 24–27.
26. Apollonio, *Futurist Manifestos*, 27–28.
27. Henderson, "Vibratory Modernism," 126–149.
28. Stefan Rieger provided an in-depth study of the importance of the curve as a heuristic technology: Stefan Rieger, *Schall und Rauch: Eine Mediengeschichte der Kurve* (Frankfurt am Main: Suhrkamp, 2007).
29. Apollonio, *Futurist Manifestos*, 47.
30. Apollonio, *Futurist Manifestos*, 48.
31. Benjamin, "The Work of Art," 240.
32. Christoph Asendorf, "Parabeln und Hyperbeln: Über die Kodierung von Kurven," *Über Schall: Ernst Machs und Peter Salchers Geschoßfotografien*, ed. Christoph Hoffmann and Peter Berz (Göttingen: Wallstein Verlag, 2001), 357–380.
33. Peter Berz and Christoph Hoffmann, eds., *Über Schall: Ernst Machs und Peter Salchers Geschoßfotografien* (Göttingen: Wallstein Verlag, 2001), 156.
34. Asendorf, "Parabeln und Hyperbeln," 360.
35. In this context it is interesting that one of the central scientists who employed dynamic curve diagrams for the recording of physiological phenomena was the Italian physiologist who analyzed the fatiguing of human muscles after work. (Angelo Mosso, *Fatigue* [New York: G. P. Putnam's Sons, 1904].)
36. Apollonio, *Futurist Manifestos*, 38–45.
37. Apollonio, *Futurist Manifestos*, 38.
38. Apollonio, *Futurist Manifestos*, 43.
39. Apollonio, *Futurist Manifestos*, 39.
40. Apollonio, *Futurist Manifestos*, 39.
41. Apollonio, *Futurist Manifestos*, 40.
42. Benjamin, "The Work of Art," 239.

43. Jean Arp, *Collected French Writings* (London: Calder & Boyars, 1974), 85.
44. Apollonio, *Futurist Manifestos*, 66–70.
45. Malcom L. Grice, *Abstract Film and Beyond* (Cambridge, MA: MIT Press, 1977), 17–19.
46. R. Bruce Elder, *Harmony and Dissent: Film and Avant-garde Art Movements in the Early Twentieth Century* (Waterloo: Wilfrid Laurier UP, 2008), 124–125.
47. Hans Richter, "The Film as an Original Art Form," *The Film Culture Reader*, ed. P. Adams Sitney (New York: Prager, 1970), 15–20.
48. Richter, "The Film as an Original Art Form," 19.
49. Richter, "The Film as an Original Art Form," 19.
50. See, for example, the letter of Daniel Broido to Hausmann, where Broido asked for some magazines for leisure reading, because the Dadasoph owned so many. (BG-RHA 1115).
51. Wieland Herzfelde and Raoul Hausmann, *Erste internationale Dada-Messe: Katalog* (Berlin: Kunsthandlung Dr. Otto Burchard, 1920).
52. Quoted from: Dawn Ades, *Photomontage* (New York: Pantheon Books, 1976), 7.
53. In his catalogue *Die Fotomontage* Richard Hiepe provides a very detailed terminological and technical overview of the different techniques of collage and montage. (Richard Hiepe, *Die Fotomontage: Geschichte und Wesen einer Kunstform* [Ingolstadt: Stadttheater Ingolstadt, 1969].)
54. Maud Lavin, *Cut with the Kitchen Knife: The Weimar Photomontages of Hannah Höch* (New Haven and London: Yale UP, 1993), 230.
55. Matthew Biro, *The Dada Cyborg: Visions of the New Human in Weimar Berlin* (Minneapolis: Minnesota UP, 2009), 1.
56. Hanne Bergius, *"Dada Triumphs!" Dada Berlin, 1917–1923: Artistry of Polarities. Montages, Metamechanics, Manifestations* (New Haven: G. K. Hall, 1996), 131.
57. Brigid Doherty, "'See: We Are All Neurasthenics!' or, The Trauma of Dada Montage," *Critical Inquiry* 24 (1997): 82–132.
58. Bergius, *Dada Triumphs*, 137.
59. Ades, *Photomontage*, 10.
60. Ades, *Photomontage*, 10.
61. Lavin, *Cut with the Kitchen Knife*, 10.
62. See for example Hanne Bergius' (Bergius, *Dada Triumphs*, 164–178) and Maud Lavin's (Lavin, *Cut with the Kitchen Knife*, 19–25) for extensive interpretations.
63. Lavin, *Cut with the Kitchen Knife*, 24.
64. Höch will take this technique in an ironic twist into oil painting. The painting *Roma*, for example appears as a collage put together from fragmented material, but only simulates this impression.
65. Apollonio, *Futurist Manifestos*, 96.
66. Lavin, *Cut with the Kitchen Knife*, 37.
67. Lavin, *Cut with the Kitchen Knife*, 37.
68. Ades, *Photomontage*, 13.

69. Douglas Kahn, *John Heartfield: Art and Mass Media* (New York, Tanam Press, 1985).
70. Kahn, *Heartfield*, 120–121.
71. Kahn, *Heartfield*, 122.
72. Kahn, *Heartfield*, 125.
73. Ades, *Photomontage*, 10–11.
74. Picasso's *Still Life with Chair-Caning* is in general considered the first collage (Christine Poggi, *In Defiance of Painting: Cubism, Futurism, and the Invention of Collage* [New Haven: Yale UP, 1992], 1), and the nineteenth-century tradition of "ghost photography," where the existence of ghosts was suggested through a double exposure of the photographic plate, is a famous example for the early manipulation of photographic images.

CHAPTER 4

1. Carl von Clausewitz, *On War* (Princeton: Princeton UP, 1984), 117–121.
2. Dieter Görrisch, *Störsender von VHF bis Mikrowelle* (Franzis: Poing, 2004), 1.
3. Friedrich Kittler, *Gramophone, Film, Typewriter* (Stanford: Stanford UP, 1990), 1.
4. Steve Goodman, *Sonic Warfare: Sound, Affect, and the Ecology of Fear* (Cambridge: MIT Press, 2010), xiii–xiv.
5. Stan Gibilisco and Neil Sclater, *Encyclopedia of Electronics* (Blue Ridge Summit: Tab Professional and Reference Books, 1990), 627.
6. Michel Serres, *The Parasite* (Baltimore: Johns Hopkins UP, 1982), 19.
7. See, for example, Max Chop, "Nebengeräusche, Obertöne, Reinheit der Stimmung und Reinheit der Sprechmaschinen-Aufnahmen," *Phonographische Zeitschrift* 24 (1907): 594–595.
8. I take the notion of a "phonographic understanding" of sonic events from Kittler's assertion that the phonograph is a medium that is neutral to the recorded sound—i.e., it does not distinguish between sound and noise (Kittler, *Gramophone, Film, Typewriter*, 23). However, as I will outline, the parasitic noise distorts this neutrality, and I agree with Mark Katz that a "phonographic effect" dramatically changed music production (Mark Katz, *Capturing Sound: How Technology Has Changed Music* [Berkeley: U of California P, 2010]). Katz's focus, however, is mostly on practices of the music industries. In the following, I am more interested in the question how a "phonographic" understanding shaped the physical and epistemological view of the avant-garde on sound and noise.
9. For an overview of Futurist music and Russolo's *intonarumori*, see Robert Payton, "The Music of Futurism. Concerts and Polemics," *The Musical Quarterly* 62.1 (1976): 25–45.
10. Jonathan Sterne discusses in detail how practices of hearing significantly changed on the basis of technologies such as the stethoscope, headphone, etc. (Sterne, *The Audible Past: Cultural Origins of Sound Reproduction* [Durham: Duke UP, 2003]).

11. Luigi Russolo, *The Art of Noises* (New York: Pendragon, 1982), 23–30.
12. Raoul Hausmann, *Texte bis 1933*, 2 vols., ed. Michael Erlhoff (München: Edition Text + Kritik, 1982), 133–144.
13. Russolo, *Art of Noises*, 28.
14. Maria Zanovello Russolo, *Russolo, l'uomo, l'artista* (Milano: Cyril Corticelli, 1958), 18.
15. Payton, "Futurism," 25–26.
16. Payton, "Futurism," 28.
17. Franco G. Maffina, *Russolo/L'arte dei rumori 1913–1931* (Venezia: Archivio Storico delle Arti Contemporanee, 1977).
18. http://www.sfmoma.org/exhib_events/events/1459 (accessed 8 October 2012).
19. The recordings are on the CD Futurism and Dada Reviews.
20. Russolo, *Art of Noises*, 75–76.
21. Russolo, *Art of Noises*, 2.
22. Russolo, *Art of Noises*, 76.
23. Barclay Brown, "The Noise Instruments of Luigi Russolo," *Perspectives of New Music* 20.1–2 (1981–1982): 31–48.
24. Luciano Chessa, *Luigi Russolo and the Occult* (UMI Dissertation Services, 2005), 292.
25. Baines, Francis et al., "Hurdy-Gurdy," *The New Grove Dictionary of Music and Musicians*, Vol. 11 (London: Macmillan, 2001), 878–881.
26. Chessa, *The Occult*, 284–290.
27. Russolo, *Art of Noises*, 28.
28. Russolo, *Art of Noises*, 12.
29. Brown, "Noise Instruments," 42.
30. Carl Stahl, "Die Vermeidung von Misstönen," *Phonographische Zeitschrift* 103 (1909): 541–543.
31. Caleb Kelly, *Cracked Media: The Sound of Malfunction* (Cambridge: MIT Press, 2009), 85–116.
32. Kelly, *Cracked Media*, 114–115.
33. Kittler, *Gramophone, Film, Typewriter*, 23.
34. Katz, *Capturing Sound*, 2.
35. Katz, *Capturing Sound*, 2–3.
36. Katz, *Capturing Sound*, 211–221.
37. Russolo, *Art of Noises*, 37–40.
38. Helmholtz outlined his theory of acoustics in his groundbreaking study from 1863: Hermann v. Helmholtz, *On the Sensations of Tone* (New York: Dover, 1954). The distinction between sound and noise is, for Helmholtz, based on the different frequency pattern in a sonic event: "On what difference in the external means of excitement does the difference between noise and musical tone depend? The normal and usual means of excitement for the human ear is atmospheric vibration. The irregularly alternating sensation of the ear in the case of noises leads us to conclude that for these the vibration of the air must also change irregularly. For musical tones on the

other hand we anticipate a regular motion of the air, continuing uniformly, and in its turn excited by an equally regular motion of the sonorous body, whose impulses were conducted to the ear by the air" (Helmholtz, *Sensation of Tone*, 8).
39. Russolo, *Art of Noises*, 24.
40. Russolo, *Art of Noises*, 75–80.
41. Russolo, *Art of Noises*, 78–80.
42. Russolo, *Art of Noises*, 80.
43. Murray Campbell, "Timbre," *The New Grove Dictionary of Music and Musicians*, vol. 25 (London: Macmillan, 2001), 478.
44. Helmholtz, *Sensations of Tone*, 10.
45. Peter Hansen, *An Introduction to Twentieth Century Music* (Boston: Allyn and Bacon, 1971), 6–8.
46. Robert J. Payton, *The Futurist Musicians. Francesco Balilla Pratella and Luigi Russolo* (Ph.D. diss., University of Chicago, 1974), 1; Brown, "Noise Instruments," 48.
47. Russolo, *Art of Noises*, 27.
48. Russolo, *Art of Noises*, 72–73.
49. Russolo, *Art of Noises*, 80.
50. Russolo, *Art of Noises*, 24.
51. As Michael Kirby points out, Russolo did in practice not fulfill his dogma of a nonmimetic art. His compositions such as "reveil de la capitale" referred back to the dynamic of the modern metropolis, imitating the noises of an awakening city (Michael Kirby, *Futurist Performance with Manifestoes and Playscripts* [New York: PAJ Publications, 1986], 40).
52. Kirby, *Futurist Performance*, 177–178.
53. Stefan Rieger, *Schall und Rauch. Eine Mediengeschichte der Kurve* (Frankfurt am Main: Suhrkamp, 2007), 7–16. Also Robert Brain points out that the graphical method of nineteenth-century life science influenced the avant-garde understanding of phonetics and acoustics (Brain, "Genealogy of *Zang Tumb Tumb*": Experimental Phonetics and the Invention of Free Verse and Modernist Sound Art," *Grey Room* 43 [Spring 2011]).
54. Kittler, *Gramophone, Film, Typewriter*, 24–25.
55. This score was published for the first time in the Futurist journal *Lacerba* and illustrated a text about a Futurist musical notation by Russolo. In this article Russolo develops a new mode of notation that abolishes the notational system based on note-heads. While he keeps the system of pitch and measures (his score is written in 3/4 time and he uses G and F clefs), the duration and pitch of a sound is indicated by a line running horizontally and diagonally through the grid of the staff (*linea-nota*). This introduction of a "note-line" is the basic difference to the traditional notational system. He introduces this line in order to represent a complete transgression through the spectrum of microtonal steps that lie between the individual tones and can be generated by the intonarumori (Russolo, *Art of Noises*, 68).

That Russolo is able to write down his compositions using the traditional grid of musical notation indicates that he did not completely abandon tonal structures. In fact, as the literature points out, this score remains more or less within the framework of established compositional standards for rhythm and harmony. In his article " 'A New Musical Reality.' Futurism, Modernism and 'The Art of Noise,' " *Modernism/Modernity* 3 (1994): 129–151, Robert Morgan acknowledges that in its use of time the score appears rather tame rhythmically (Morgan, "A New Musical Reality," 141), and Barclay Brown refers to the clearly harmonic intent of the score (Brown, *Noise Instruments*, 36). Significantly, in this score Russolo indicates some glissandi, which the *intonarumori* can produce particularly well. But several other voices of the *intonarumori* represent a continual, determined pitch, which also could have been written down in a traditional notation. In fact, as Mark Radice points out, the traditional system based on noteheads is able to indicate small divisions of the beat with a much greater accuracy than Russolo's system (Radice, " 'Futurismo.' Its Origins, Context, Repertory, and Influence," *The Musical Quarterly* 73.1 (1989): 13).
56. Russolo, *Art of Noises*, 67–73.
57. Russolo, *Art of Noises*, 67–68.
58. Laszlo Moholy-Nagy, "New Plasticism in Music. Possibilities of the Gramophone" *Broken Music. Artists' Recordworks*, ed. Ursula Block and Michael Glasmeier (Berlin: DAAD-Gelbe Musik, 1989) 54–56.
59. Moholy-Nagy, "New Plasticism," 56.
60. Kittler, *Gramophone, Film, Typewriter*, 16.
61. Moholy-Nagy, "New Plasticism," 56.
62. Ernst Mach, *Die Analyse der Empfindungen und das Verhältnis des Physischen zum Psychischen* (Fischer: Jena, 1900), 157–158.
63. Russolo, *Art of Noises*, 29.
64. Russolo, *Art of Noises*, 87.
65. Bernhard J. Dotzler, "Simulation," *Ästhetische Grundbegriffe*, ed. K. Barck et al., Vol. 5 (Stuttgart: Metzler, 2003), 509–533.
66. Dotzler, "Simulation," 509.
67. Russolo, *Art of Noises*, 29.
68. As Norbert Wiener—the founding father of cybernetics—points out, simulations do not have the function of representing reality in a mimetic fashion. Instead they produce something that is from a mathematical point of view equivalent to the real system, although it looks completely different (Dotzler, "Simulation," 517). Don Ingels, in the introduction to his book *What Every Engineer Should Know about Computer Modeling and Simulation* (New York: Marcel Dekker, 1985), also emphasizes that "to simulate is to assume the appearance or characteristics without assuming the identity or reality." He goes on to say that "simulation in the present context means exercising the model and obtaining some result" (Ingels, *Computer Modeling*, 4).
69. Russolo, *Art of Noises*, 24.

70. Russolo, *Art of Noises*, 28.
71. Russolo, *Art of Noises*, 50.
72. Douglas Kahn correctly points out that Russolo limits his observations of war to the mechanical noises and completely excludes any human uttering, and thus presents a completely dehumanized perspective on modern warfare (Kahn, *Noise, Water, Meat: A History of Sound in the Arts* [Cambridge: MIT Press, 1999], 63).
73. Russolo, *Art of Noises*, 49.
74. Russolo, *Art of Noises*, 50–51.
75. These observations about the importance of acoustics on the battlefields in the first part of the twentieth century are not unique to Russolo, but rather common motifs in war literature. Ernst Jünger writes: "Mit den Geräuschen des Krieges noch unvertraut, war ich nicht imstande, das Pfeifen und Zischen, das Knallen der eigenen Geschütze und das beißende Krachen der in immer kürzeren Pausen einschlagenden feindlichen Granaten zu entwirren und mir aus all dem ein Bild zu machen" (Ernst Jünger, *In Stahlgewittern* (Stuttgart: Klett Cotta, 1978), 30).

    Also Remarque reports: "Der Stellungskampf von heute erfordert Kentnisse und Erfahrungen, man muß Verständnis für das Gelände haben, man muß die Geschosse, ihre Geräusche und Wirkungen im Ohr haben, man muß vorausbestimmen können, wo sie einhauen, wie sie streuen und wie man sich schützt" (Erich Maria Remarque, *Im Westen nichts Neues* (Köln: Kiepenheuer und Witsch, 2002), 94).
76. Russolo, *Art of Noises*, 50–51.
77. I, however, would not argue that this inversion contradicts Kittler's abuse statement, but it underlines that modern societies, especially Futurist societies, are in a constant state of mobilization where, as Kittler states, "discos are preparing our youth for a retaliatory strike" (Kittler, *Gramophone, Film, Typewriter*, 140).
78. Russolo, *Art of Noises*, 84.
79. Russolo, *Art of Noises*, 33.
80. Russolo, *Art of Noises*, 81.
81. Quoted in Radice, "Futurismo," 13.
82. Also the Russian composer Prokof'ev describes the relative low volume of the noise-intoners (Julia Kursell, *Schallkunst: Eine Literaturgeschichte der Musik in der frühen russischen Avantgarde* [Munich: Wiener Slawistischer Almanach, 2003], 131).
83. Hugo Ball, *Flight Out of Time: A Dada Diary* (New York: Viking Press, 1974), 57.
84. The third chapter discusses Dada poetry in detail, especially its relationship to human language and articulation.
85. Richard Huelsenbeck, *Dada Almanach* (Berlin: Erich Reiss, 1920), 106.
86. Robert Motherwell, ed., *The Dada Painters and Poets: An Anthology* (Cambridge: Harvard UP, 1979), 25.
87. The writer George Hugnet, for example, remembered that the Dadaists produced a variety of noises on stage by beating on bowls, cans, and other

utensils (Georges Hugnet, *L'aventure Dada, 1916–1922* (Paris, Galerie de l'Institut, 1957), 21). (See also: Huelsenbeck, *Dada Almanach*, 106.) Huelsenbeck also made his drum a central component in his poetry readings (Richard Huelsenbeck, *Wozu Dada: Texte 1916–1936*, ed. H. Kapfer (Gießen: Anabas, 1994), 47).
88. Kirby, *Futurist Performance*, 16.
89. Richard Huelsenbeck, *Dada siegt!* (Berlin: Malik, 1920), 20.
90. Motherwell, *Dada Painters and Poets*, 26.
91. For the Futurists, war is the highest state of conflict a human society can achieve. As Jeffrey Schnapp points out, the Futurists were not simply sympathetic with objects of the modern world such as engines, but recognized these machines as dangerous adversaries that had to be controlled (Jeffrey Schnapp, "Propeller Talk," *Modernism/Modernity* 1.3 [1994]: 161).
92. This account of Futurist art is in accordance with the Futurist ideology in general, but for Huelsenbeck this conception of Futurist art can be traced back to the writings of the Futurist painter Boccioni. Huelsenbeck acknowledged that the entire Dada circle in Zurich read the manifestos of the Futurist painter (Huelsenbeck, *Dada Almanach*, 5). It is central for Boccioni's aesthetics that the representation of movement and simultaneous events in painting has not only an analytic or mimetic purpose, but also demands an active participation of the spectator (Hansgeorg Schmidt-Bergmann, *Futurismus: Geschichte, Ästhetik, Dokumente* (Reinbek bei Hamburg: Rowohlt, 1993), 303).
93. It can be argued that this vitalistic appreciation of noise that finally resolves a difference between performers and audience is inspired by a Nietzschean distinction between the Apollonian and the Dionysian. In fact, Nietzsche is a great influence for Hugo Ball's poetics.
94. Harriet Watts, ed., *Dada and the Press* (New Haven: G. K. Hall, 2004), 49.
95. Watts, *Press*, 49.
96. Inez Hedges, *Languages of Revolt: Dada and Surrealist Literature and Film* (Durham: Duke UP, 1983), 43; Stephen C. Foster and Rudolf E. Kuenzli, eds., *Dada Spectrum: The Dialectics of Revolt* (Madison: Coda Press, 1979), 4; Peter Bürger, *Theory of the Avant-Garde* (Minneapolis: Minnesota UP, 1984), 50.
97. Watts, *Press*, 97.
98. This document is part of the Raoul Hausmann estate in the Berlinische Galerie. The Archival Signature is BG-RHA 1755.
99. BG-RHA 1755.
100. BG-RHA 1755.
101. BG-RHA 1755.
102. BG-RHA 1755.
103. Sungook Hong, *Wireless: From Marconi's Black-Box to the Audion* (Cambridge: MIT Press, 2001), 186.
104. Hong, *Wireless*, 186–188.
105. Hong, *Wireless*, 156.
106. BG-RHA 1755.

107. BG-RHA 1755.
108. "Versuch einer kosmischen Ontographie" (BG-RHA 1757).
109. The archival signature of the letter is: BG-RHA 1079.
110. Greg Armbruster, *The Art of Electronic Music* (Quill: New York, 1984), 4.
111. Armbruster, *Electronic Music*, 4–7.
112. Joel Chadabe, *Electric Sound: The Past and Promise of Electronic Music* (Upper Saddle River: Prentice-Hall, 1997), 5.
113. Chadabe, *Electric Sound*, 6.
114. Hong, *Wireless*, XIV.
115. Moholy-Nagy, "New Plasticism," 54.
116. Hausmann, *Texte*, II, 141–142.
117. Hausmann, *Texte*, II, 142.
118. Moholy-Nagy, "New Plasticism," 54.
119. Moholy-Nagy, "New Plasticism," 54.
120. For a short history of color music see: Kenneth Peacock, "Instruments to Perform Color-Music. Two Centuries of Technological Experimentation," *Leonardo* 21.4 (1988): 397–406.
121. Armbruster, *Electronic Music*, 27.
122. Hausmann, *Texte*, II, 142–143.
123. Hausmann, *Texte*, II, 143.
124. John H. Girdner, "The Plague of City Noises," *The North American Review* 163.478 (1896): 296–304.
125. Girdner, *City Noises*, 297–298.
126. Russolo, *Art of Noises*, 29.

Chapter 5

1. Filipp Tommaso Marinetti and Pino Masnata, "La Radia," ed. Douglas Kahn and Gregory Whitehead, *Wireless Imagination: Sound, Radio, and the Avant-Garde* (Cambridge: MIT Press, 1992), 265–268.
2. Lorenzo Mango provided a documentation of Marinetti's quest for a tactile art, *Alla scoperta di nuovi sensi*, which also contains the relevant sources such as the manifestos on tattilismo.
3. Hausmann, Texte *bis 1933*, vol. II, ed. Michael Erlhoff (München: Edition Text + Kritik, 1982), 24–30.
4. Hannah Höch, *Eine Lebenscollage. (1921–1945) Vol. 2*, ed. R. Burmeister and E. Fürlus (Ostfildern-Ruit: Hatje, 1995), 25.
5. Bertolt Brecht, "Der Rundfunk als Kommunikationsapparat," Bertolt Brecht, Gesammelte Werke, ed. Elisabeth Hauptmann, vol. 8 (Frankfurt am Main: Suhrkamp, 1967), 127–134.
6. Friedrich Kittler, *Gramophone, Film, Typewriter* (Stanford: Stanford UP, 1999), 96–97.
7. Michel Serres, *The Parasite* (Baltimore: Johns Hopkins UP, 1982), 15.
8. In fact, Marinetti formulated the extension of human sensibility already in 1913 in the manifesto "Destruction of Syntax" (Umbro Apollonio, *Futurist*

Manifestos [London: Thames and Hudson, 1970], 95–106) as an explicit goal of Futurism. "Futurism is grounded in the complete renewal of human sensibility brought about by the great discoveries of science" (Apollonio, *Futurist Manifestos*, 96). Marinetti's tactilism can be recognized as the most concrete enactment of this announcement.
9. Lorenzo Mango, *Alla Scoperta di Nuovi Sensi: Il Tattilismo Futurista* (Napoli: La città del sole, 2001), 7.
10. Filippo Tommaso Marinetti, *Critical Writings*, ed. Günther Berghaus (New York, Farrar, Straus and Giroux, 2006), 370.
11. Marinetti, *Critical Writings*, 370.
12. Marinetti, *Critical Writings*, 370.
13. A central problem in his writings is that Marinetti constructs, celebrates, but at the same time negates something like a Futurist tradition.
14. Less metaphorically, Marinetti also mentions—in both manifestos—a sculpture in which Boccioni mixed a variety of materials with different tactile qualities (like china or hair) as his main source of inspiration (Marinetti, *Critical Writings*, 375–377). Marinetti understands this sculpture as one of his major inspirations for developing a tactile art. More significantly, in both manifestos he refers to a night in 1917 as the primal scene of inspiration. On this night he was crawling in a dark trench and had to orient himself without any light (Marinetti, *Critical Writings*, 377).
15. Marinetti, *Critical Writings*, 370–371.
16. Marinetti, *Critical Writings*, 372.
17. Marinetti, *Critical Writings*, 372.
18. Certainly, the entire scene has highly erotic and sexual connotations. Marinetti is naked in the sea and the girl is looking at his little boats. One is attempted to recognize the remarks of the girl as a pickup line, but this intimate communication fails, perhaps because Marinetti does not recognize the intention of the girl, perhaps because the girl uses the wrong channel, namely visual-acoustic codes and not tactile signs.
19. Marinetti, *Critical Writings*, 371.
20. Marinetti, *Critical Writings*, 371.
21. Marinetti, *Critical Writings*, 371.
22. Marinetti, *Critical Writings*, 371–372.
23. Marinetti, *Critical Writings*, 372.
24. Marinetti, *Critical Writings*, 372.
25. Most prominently in the first Futurist manifesto, Marinetti claims that hatred of women, family, and love are central to the Futurist program. More directly, he targets love, family, and romantic relationships in "Against *Amore* and Parliamentarianism" from the manifesto "War, the World's Only Hygiene": "We scorn woman conceived as the sole ideal, the divine reservoir of *Amore*, the woman-poison, woman the tragic trinket, the fragile woman, obsessing and fatal, whose voice, heavy with destiny, and whose dreaming tresses reach out and mingle with the foliage of forests drenched in moonlight. We despise horrible, dragging Amore that hinders the march

of man, preventing him from transcending his own humanity, from redoubling himself, from going beyond himself and becoming what we call *the multiplied man*" (Marinetti, *Selected Writings*, 72). This quotation exhibits the misogynistic attitude of Italian Futurism. Nonetheless, these controversial claims are not simply directed against the entire female population, but attack a certain bourgeois understanding of gender roles. The Futurist attack on women has to be seen as part of rebellion against determined gender roles. Just so, Marinetti sides with the suffragettes, because they would liquidate traditional gender formations. Certainly, equal opportunities for women are not the primary intent of the manifesto of tactility. Marinetti does not want to integrate romantic notions of love into Futurism. He literally wants to replace silent whispers with "hands-on" activities.

26. Marinetti, *Critical Writings*, 372–373.
27. Marinetti, *Critical Writings*, 372–373.
28. Marinetti, *Critical Writings*, 372–373.
29. Marinetti, *Critical Writings*, 373.
30. Marinetti, *Critical Writings*, 374.
31. Marinetti, *Critical Writings*, 378.
32. Marinetti, *Critical Writings*, 374. Hausmann refers to this tactilist in his text "Présentismus," where he sees in Marinetti's tactilism a mere "sadism" for entertaining the Futurists. He describes the tactilist experiments as reminiscent of Roman gladiatorial games and adds that Marinetti's new sensory aesthetics does not contribute to a renovation of art and sensibility (Hausmann, *Texte*, II, 28).
33. Marinetti, *Critical Writings*, 378.
34. Marinetti, *Critical Writings*, 378.
35. Günther Berghaus, *Italian Futurist Theatre 1909–1944* (Oxford: Clarendon Press, 1998), 136–137.
36. Marinetti, *Selected Writings*, 121.
37. Michael Kirby, *Futurist Performance with Manifestoes and Playscripts* (New York: PAJ Publications, 1986), 20.
38. Marinetti, *Selected Writings*, 121.
39. Kirby, *Futurist Performance*, 255.
40. Marinetti, *Critical Writings*, 400–407.
41. Marinetti, *Critical Writings*, 401–402.
42. Marinetti and Masnata, "La Radia," 265–268.
43. Marinetti, *Teatro*, 634.
44. F.T. Marinetti, *Teatro*, ed. Jeffrey Schnapp (Milano: Mondadori, 2004), 634.
45. Kirby, *Futurist Performance*, 292.
46. Kirby, *Futurist Performance*, 293.
47. Marinett, *Teatro*, 633.
48. Marinetti, *Teatro*, 636.
49. While most of Marinetti's *sintesi* represent experiments with sound, noise, and silence, *Violetta e gli aeroplani* (Marinetti, *Teatro*, 638–656) is a radio

play about Giunco, a heroic boy and his girlfriend Violetta, that is based on dialogue and that unfolds a narrative in which the sound effects are used as realistic elements that support the story. In my discussion, I focus on Marinetti's abstract or formal radio plays, because they adapt the antihermeneutic and nonrepresentational aesthetic the he also developed in his radio manifesto.

50. In his radio manifesto Marinetti describes the proper use of the radio as a self-referential exhibition of the radiophonic features themselves: "La Radia shall be...a pure organism of radio sensations" (Marinetti and Masnata, "La Radia," 267).
51. Serres, *Parasite*, 7.
52. Dominik Schrage, *Psychotechnik und Radiophonie. Subjektkonstruktionen in artifiziellen Wirklichkeiten 1918–1932* (München: Fink, 2001), 9.
53. McLuhan, *Understanding Media*, 299.
54. Serres, *Parasite*, 7.
55. Serres, *Parasite*, 38–39.
56. Hausmann, *Texte*, I, 28.
57. Hausmann, *Texte*, II, 50–57.
58. Hausmann, *Texte*, II, 24–30.
59. This highly theoretical undercurrent—which runs through Hausmann's texts from the early twenties on—is connected to and at the same time hidden by polemical strategies that accuse the Weimar bourgeoisie of conserving outdated aesthetic and ethical values. Hausmann's text "Trommelfeuer der Wissenschaft" is a good example of a polemic that combines scientific discussion and sociopolitical criticism. In this text, he criticizes the society of the late Weimar Republic by means of analyzing the physiology of Albert Einstein (Hausmann, Texte, II, 156–161).
60. Hausmann, *Texte*, II, 28.
61. Hausmann, *Texte*, II, 27.
62. Hausmann, *Texte*, II, 24.
63. Hausmann publishes two other texts that are connected to this concept of Présentismus: "Die Absichten des Theater 'Pré'" (Hausmann, *Texte*, II, 58–59) and "Zweite präsentistische Deklaration" (Hausmann, *Texte*, II, 85–87).
64. Hausmann, *Texte*, II, 26.
65. Hausmann, *Texte*, I, 179–185.
66. Hausmann, *Texte*, II, 7–11.
67. Benjamin, "The Work of Art," 237–239.
68. Benjamin, "The Work of Art," 224. See also my discussion of the historical determinacy of the senses in the work of Russolo in Chapter 4.
69. Laszlo Moholy-Nagy, *Painting, Photography, Film* (Cambridge, MA: MIT Press, 1967)
70. Moholy-Nagy, *Photography*, 29.
71. "A more perfect, because scientifically grounded, performance is promised by Optofonetik. The bold imagination of the Dadaist Raoul Hausmann,

has been responsible for the first steps toward a future theory" (Moholy-Nagy, *Photography*, 22).
72. In 1913 the engineer Fournier E. E. d'Albe presented the discussion of an Optophone in the journal *Electrician* (Fournier E. E. d'Albe, "A Reading Optophone," *The Electrician* (London), 24 October 1913: 102–103). This invention is in fact an extension of a design that he had presented in 1912 in the German *Physikalische Zeitschrift*. This earlier optophone translated light intensities into sounds and "enabled totally blind persons to discover the whereabouts of windows, lights and bright objects by the ear alone" (d'Albe, "Reading Optophone," 102). The device from 1913 was able to transform printed text into sounds. Here, a light was projected through a rotating metal disk with eight dots that let pass light with different frequencies. These different light values enter a transparent film with the printed text on it, and finally, with the help of a selenium cell, the light intensity projected through the film is converted into a sound. The light varies in accordance with the dots through which light passed. The shape of letters only let through a certain part of the eight dots; accordingly, an individual letter can have a different sound. It is also interesting that d'Albe suggests a similar construction to Hausmann's apparatus when he mentions that the optophone connected to a keyboard makes an excellent musical instrument (d'Albe, "Optophon," 103).
73. Christian Ries, *Sehende Maschinen. Eine kurze Abhandlung über die geheimnisvollen Eigenschaften der lichtempfindlichen Stoffe und die staunenswerten Leistungen der sehenden Maschinen* (Hubers: Diessen, 1916).
74. Hausmann, *Texte*, II, 28.
75. Hausmann, *Texte*, II, 28.
76. Hausmann, *Texte*, II, 28.
77. Ernst Marcus, *Das Problem der excentrischen Empfindung und seine Lösung* (Berlin: Sturmverlag, 1918).
78. Marcus, *Excentrische Empfindung*, 7–8.
79. Marcus, *Exzentrische Empfindung*, 7.
80. Marcus, *Exzentrische Empfindung*, 68.
81. This immediacy of perception, which Marcus at first assigns to tactility, is not an exception but rather the standard form of contact to objects. More precisely, Marcus elaborates why the sense of touch is in no sense different from "transsomatic" forms of perception. "Es ist zunächst ein vollkommener Irrtum, daß [das] Tastgebilde—im Gegensatz zum optischen—ein intrasomatisches, am Nervenende lokalisiertes Gebilde sei. Es wird vielmehr ursprünglich transsomatisch außerhalb oder unterhalb des tastenden Fingers, daher als Oberfläche eines Fremdkörpers empfunden (die gegenteilige Behauptung widerstreitet der Erfahrung)" (Marcus, *Exzentrische Empfindung*, 70).
82. Ernst Marcus, "Die Zeit- und Raumlehre Kants: (Transzendentale Aesthetik). In Anwendung auf Mathematik und Naturwissenschaft;" *Ausgewählte Schriften*, ed. Gottfried Marin and Gerd Hergenlübe, Vol. 2 (Bonn: Bouvier: 1969), 572.

83. In the preface to the *Exzentrische Empfindung* Marcus highlights the importance of subjectivity in Kant's philosophy for his own account (Ernst Marcus, *Exzentrische Empfindung*, 5).
84. The reliance on the ether for explaining eccentric sensations follows the same logic as the explanation of the propagation of electromagnetic waves through the medium of the ether. In both cases a medium is presupposed because in the scientific opinion it is not possible to think about perception or waves without a medium. For Marcus—in accordance with the ether theory of the nineteenth century—ether is the matrix in which absolute relations between objects and absolute inertia becomes possible. "Das Äthermeer ist in *wirklicher* Ruhe in Relation zum absolut ruhenden geometrischen Raume, daher in wirklicher Ruhe in Relation zur Allheit der bewegten Körper" (Ernst Marcus, "Die Zeit- und Raumlehre Kants," 562). This belief did remain in the discourse even after Einstein's theory of general relativity for the purpose of explaining— at least hypothetically—the propagation of radio waves. An example is Artur Fürst's explanation of radiotechnology: "Einstein gelangt denn auch in seiner Relativitätstheorie zu einer Weltauffassung, die das Vorhandensein des Äthers leugnet. Dennoch dürfen wir uns seiner für die Erörterung der hier zu beschreibenden technischen Vorgänge weiter bedienen, da er eine bequeme Erklärung aller Phänomen ermöglicht. Die Behauptung, es gäbe einen Weltäther, ist eine Hilfshypothese, aber eine verzüglich brauchbare" (Artur Fürst, *Im Bannkreis von Nauen: Die Eroberung der Erde durch die drahtlose Telegraphie* (Stuttgart: Deutsche Verlagsanstalt, 1922), 14).
85. Especially central here: is Karl Koelsch, *Das spierelige Wesen der Wellen in Anwendung auf Licht und Farben* (Hannover, Helwig, 1922).
86. See, for example, Johannes Zacharias, *Die wirklichen Grundlagen der elektrischen Erscheinungen. Aufklärungen über den Magnetismus durch neue Versuche* (Berlin: Julis Bohnes Verlag, 1906).
87. Zacharias, *Grundlagen*, 86.
88. Koelsch, *Wesen*. 30.
89. BG-RHA 1757.
90. Hausmann, *Anfang*, 43.
91. See my discussion of Hausmann's optophonetic poetry in chapter 2.
92. Hausmann, *Texte*, II, 72.
93. The inventors Massole, Vogt, and Engl optimized the "Lichttonverfahren" by developing a photocell covered with potassium, which was much more responsive than the selenium cell.
94. Hausmann, *Texte*, II, 71–72.
95. Corinna Müller, *Vom Stummfilm zum Tonfilm* (München: Fink, 2003), 199.
96. Siegfried Kracauer comments on this technology as follows: "Der schmale Streifen ist nach dem Urteil der Fachleute eine Photographie der Schallwellen, in die er wieder zurückgewandelt wird. . . . Die Eingeweihten werden genau Bescheid wissen. Jedenfalls übertrumpft die Esoterik der

Technik heute bereits die eleusinischen Mysterien" (quoted from: Müller, *Tonfilm*, 199).
97. In a letter to Henri Chopin (quoted in Jacques Donguy, "Machine Head. Raoul Hausmann and the Optophone," *Leonardo* 34.3 (2001): 217–220), Hausmann mentions that he was in close contact with filmmakers such as Vogt who worked with the "Lichttonverfahren" (Donguy, "Machine Head," 217).
98. Ernst Ruhmer, *Das Selen und seine Bedeutung für die Elektrotechnik mit besonderer Berücksichtigung der drahtlosen Telephonie* (Berlin: F. & M. Harrwitz, 1902). In a letter to Henri Chopin, Hausmann states that he still owns a copy of this book (Donguy, "Machine Head," 217).
99. Hausmann, *Texte*, II, 173.
100. Hausmann, *Texte*, II, 54.
101. Anonymous, "Vorschlag zu einem direct schreibenden Phonographen" *Phonographische Zeitschrift* (15 Dezember, 1901): 315.
102. Ruhmer, *Selen*, 38–45.
103. Hausmann, *Texte*, II, 53.
104. In this sense, it also differs from the calculation machine that Hausmann developed in the thirties with Daniel Broido. This calculation machine employed a light cell, but the cell was only used for a very simple switching mechanism that moved the display mechanism to the next numerical position. In fact, this construction was not an actual calculation machine and certainly not a computer, as Hausmann still in 1966 had claimed (Hausmann, Texte, II, 214). This device was only able to multiply or combine several factors through a simple multiplication table. The complex switching mechanism, which included the photocell, was merely just for representing the result not for the calculation. I actually regard this device as a point of change in Hausmann's understanding of optophonetics, where he started to abandon his "ether dreams" and to explore the structure of light rays, which led to his post Weimar work in photography.
105. Hausmann, *Texte*, II, 143.
106. In his text "Die überzüchteten Künste" Hausmann gives a detailed description of this machine (Hausmann, *Texte*, II, 143–144); another detailed description of the machine can be found in Erlhoff, *Dadasoph*, 142–145.
107. As Michael Erlhoff notes: "so genau interessierte ihn die Maschine eben doch nicht. Sie zerlegte die Einzelheiten, um dann verknüpfen zu können: Differenzierung und Integration als notwendige Voraussetzung von umfassender Sensation. Das war es, was er suchte" (Erlhoff, *Dadasoph*, 145). In fact, Hausmann had great trouble patenting his machine. Initial attempts failed, because the patent office in Berlin did not see any use for the optophone and declined the patent. Only in 1935, when in exile, was Hausmann able to patent a similar device that he had redesigned as a calculating machine together with the engineer Daniel Broido (Erlhoff, *Dadasoph*, 212). This apparatus, however, did not operate with different colors, but with a slot system that projected constellations of light rays

(that corresponded to numerical values) onto a photocell. The patent is reproduced in Erlhoff, *Dadasoph*, 297–312.
108. Hausmann, *Texte*, II, 53.
109. Moholy-Nagy, *Photography*, 23
110. Moholy-Nagy, *Photography*, 23.
111. Hausmann, *Texte*, II, 55. In his discussion of the communication and perception of bees Hausmann draws from the work of the biologist Karl v. Frisch. Frisch became important through his analysis of the "bee dance" as a communicative device for the bees and contributed groundbreaking work to the understanding of the sensory perception of bees. He for example emphasized that although bees are color-blind they are able to perceive ultraviolet light (Karl von Frisch, *The Dancing Bees: An Account of the Life and Senses of the Honey Bee* (London: Methuen, 1954), 66). Frisch also asserts that bees are unable to discriminate between sounds (Frisch, *Honey Bee*, 29). Hausmann's speculation that acoustic sensations are crucial for the perception of the bees (Hausmann BG-RHA 1757, 59) (he assumes that the bee's eye processes acoustic as well as visual impressions) differs from the results of Frisch's research.
112. Ina Blom, "The Touch through Time. Raoul Hausmann, Nam June Paik and the Transmission Technology of the Avant-Garde" *Leonardo* 34.3(2001): 209–215.
113. Hausmann, *Texte*, I, 183.
114. Marcus understands human experience as a Fata Morgana projected into the outside world (Marcus, *Exzentrische Empfindung*, 15) and recognizes the perspectival changes in perception as similar to the stroposcopic effect of the cinematic film: "Man denke ferner z.B. daran, wie sich eine heranfahrende Lokomotive mit der Annäherung zu vergrößern scheint. Aber sie vergrößert sich nicht, sondern das optische Gebilde verändert sich mit der Annäherung des Körper-Korrelats, eine Veränderung, die auch der Kinematograph durch fortwährenden Wechsel der Bilder zur Darstellung bringt" (Marcus, *Exzentrische Empfindung*, 14–15).
115. BG-RHA 1757, 28.
116. For Hausmann, the ability of electric media to construct immediate contact over long distances is not simply a model for explaining human communication or perception, but he also believes that human perception itself will become capable of immediate communication: "Für diesen Weg der Erweiterung der Organfunktionalität ist auch der Ausspruch Professor Ayrton's nur eine Andeutung; er sagte 1906: 'Einst wird kommen der Tag, wenn wir alle vergessen sind, wenn Kupferdrähte, Guttaperchahüllen und Eisenband nur noch im Museum ruhen, dann wird der Mensch, der mit dem Freunde zu sprechen wünscht und nicht weiss, wo er sich befindet, mit elektrischer Stimme rufen, welche allein jener hört, der das gleichgestimmte elektrische Ohr besitzt'" (Hausmann, *Scharfrichter*, 176).
117. Hausmann, *Texte*, II, 27.
118. McLuhan, *Understanding Media*, 43.

119. Blom, "Touch Through Time," 212.
120. McLuhan, *Understanding Media*, 249.
121. Hausmann, *Texte*, II, 28.
122. Hausmann, *Texte*, II, 55.
123. Hausmann BG-RHA 1757, 2.
124. Kittler, *Gramophone, Film, Typewriter*, 96–97.
125. Brecht, "Kommunikationsapparat," 129.

CONCLUSION

1. Friedrich Kittler, *Discourse Networks 1800/1900* (Stanford: Stanford UP, 1990), 208.
2. Franz Kafka, "The Cares of a Family Man," *The Complete Stories* (New York: Schocken Books, 1971), 427–429.
3. Wolf Kittler, "Schreibmaschinen, Sprechmaschinen: Effekete technischer Medien Im Werk Franz Kafkas, "*Franz Kafka. Schriftverkehr*, ed. Wolf Kittler and Gerhard Neumann (Freiburg: Rombach, 1990), 75–163.
4. Kittler, "Schreibmaschinen, Sprechmaschinen," 158–160.
5. Kafka, "Cares of a Family Man," 428.
6. Kafka, "Cares of a Family Man," 428.
7. Kafka, "Cares of a Family Man," 428.
8. Kafka, "Cares of a Family Man," 429.
9. Kafka, "Cares of a Family Man,"429.
10. Carl Schmitt, *Theory of the Partisan: A Commentary on the Concept of the Political* (East Lansing: Michigan State UP, 2004).
11. Schmitt, *Partisan*, 3.

Bibliography

Ades, Dawn, *Photomontage* (New York: Pantheon Books, 1976).
Anonymous, "Vorschlag zu einem direct schreibenden Phonographen," *Phonographische Zeitschrift* (15 Dezember, 1901), 315.
Apollonio, Umbro, *Futurist Manifestos* (London: Thames and Hudson, 1970).
Armbruster, Greg, *The Art of Electronic Music* (Quill: New York, 1984).
Arp, Jean, *Collected French Writings* (London: Calder & Boyars, 1974).
Asendorf, Christoph, "Parabeln und Hyperbeln: Über die Kodierung von Kurven," *Über Schall: Ernst Machs und Peter Salchers Geschoßfotografien*, ed. Christoph Hoffmann and Peter Berz (Göttingen: Wallstein Verlag, 2001), 357–380.
Baader, Johannes, *Oberdada. Schriften, Manifeste, Flugblätter, Billets, Werke und Taten*, ed. Hanne Bergius, Norbert Miller and Karl Riha (Giessen: Anabas, 1977).
Backes-Haase, Alfons, *Kunst und Wirklichkeit: Zur Typologie des DADA-Manifests* (Frankfurt am Main: A. Hain, 1992).
Baines, Francis et al., "Hurdy-Gurdy," *The New Grove Dictionary of Music and Musicians*, vol. 11 (London: Macmillan, 2001), 878–881.
Ball, Hugo, *Flight out of Time: A Dada Diary* (New York: Viking Press, 1974).
Barthes, Roland, *Mythologies* (London: Paladin, 1972).
Baudrillard, Jean, *The Gulf War Did Not Take Place* (Bloomington: Indiana UP, 1995).
Benjamin, Walter, "The Work of Art in the Age of Mechanical Reproduction," *Illuminations*, ed. Hannah Arendt (New York: Harcourt, Brace and World, 1968), 219–253.
Benn, Gottfried, "Probleme der Lyrik," *Essays und Reden* (Frankfurt am Main: Fischer, 1989).
Bense, Max, *Einführung in die informationstheoretische Ästhetik: Grundlegung und Anwendung in der Textheorie* (Reinbek: Rowohlt, 1969).
Benson, Timothy, "Conventions and Constructions. The Performative Text in Dada," *Dada. The Coordinates of Cultural Politics*, ed. Stephen C. Foster (New York: Hall, 1996).
Berghaus, Günther, *Italian Futurist Theatre, 1909–1944* (Oxford: Clarendon Press, 1998).
Berghaus, Günther, *The Genesis of Futurism: Early Career and Writings, 1899–1909* (Leeds: The Society of Italian Studies, 1995).

Bergius, Hanne, *"Dada Triumphs!" Dada Berlin, 1917–1923: Artistry of Polarities. Montages, Metamechanics, Manifestations* (New Haven: G. K. Hall, 1996).
Bergius, Hanne, *Das Lachen Dadas: Die Berliner Dadaisten und ihre Aktionen* (Gießen: Anabas, 1989).
Berz, Peter and Christoph Hoffmann, eds, *Über Schall: Ernst Machs und Peter Salchers Geschoßfotografien* (Göttingen: Wallstein Verlag, 2001).
Beyerchen, Alan, "Clausewitz, Nonlinearity, and the Unpredictability of War," *International Security* 17.3 (1992–93): 59–90.
Biro, Matthew, *The Dada Cyborg: Visions of the New Human in Weimar Berlin* (Minneapolis: Minnesota UP, 2009).
Blom, Ina, "The Touch through Time. Raoul Hausmann, Nam June Paik and the Transmission Technology of the Avant-Garde," *Leonardo* 34.3 (2001): 209–215.
Bohn, Willard, *Italian Futurist Poetry* (Toronto: Toronto UP, 2005).
Bolle, Kees W., "Myth: An Overview," *The Encyclopedia of Religion*, ed. M. Eliade, vol. 10 (New York: Macmillan, 1987), 261–273.
Brain, Robert, "Genealogy of *Zang Tumb Tumb*: Experimental Phonetics and the Invention of Free Verse and Modernist Sound Art," *Grey Room* 43 (Spring 2011): 88–117.
Braun, Marta, *Picturing Time: The Work of Etienne-Jules Marey (1830–1904)* (Chicago: Chicago UP, 1992).
Brecht, Bertolt, "Der Rundfunk als Kommunikationsapparat," *Gesammelte Werke*, ed. Elisabeth Hauptmann, vol. 8 (Frankfurt am Main: Suhrkamp, 1967), 127–134.
Brown, Barclay, "The Noise Instruments of Luigi Russolo," *Perspectives of New Music* 20.1–2 (1981–1982): 31–48.
Brown, Stephen, "Michel Serres, Science, Translation, and the Logic of the Parasite," *Theory, Culture and Society*, 19.3 (2002): 1–27.
Budiansky, Stephen, *Battle of Wits: The Complete Story of Codebreaking in World War II* (New York: The Free Press, 2000).
Bürger, Peter, *Theory of the Avant-Garde* (Minneapolis: Minnesota UP, 1984).
Campbell, Murray, "Timbre," *The New Grove Dictionary of Music and Musicians*, vol. 25 (London: Macmillan, 2001), 478.
Campbell, Timothy, "Vital Matters. Sovereignty, Milieu, and the Animal in Futurism's Founding Manifesto," *Annali d'Italianistica* 27 (2009): 157–174.
Campbell, Timothy, *Wireless Writing in the Age of Marconi* (Minneapolis: Minnesota UP, 2006)
Campbell, Timothy, "'Infinite Remoteness.' Marinetti, Bontempelli, and the Birth of Modern Italian Visual Culture," *MLN* 120 (2005): 111–136.
Carey, Sarah, "Futurism's Photography: From fotodinamismo to fotomontaggio," *Carte Italiane*, 2.6 (2010): 221–217.
Caws, Mary Ann, *Manifesto: A Century of Isms* (Lincoln: U of North Nebraska P, 2001).
Chadabe, Joel, *Electric Sound: The Past and Promise of Electronic Music* (Upper Saddle River: Prentice-Hall, 1997).

Chessa, Luciano, *Luigi Russolo and the Occult* (UMI Dissertation Services, 2005).
Chop, Max, "Nebengeräusche, Obertöne, Reinheit der Stimmung und Reinheit der Sprechmaschinen-Aufnahmen," *Phonographische Zeitschrift* 24 (1907): 594–595.
Clausewitz, Carl von, *On War* (Princeton: Princeton UP, 1984).
d'Albe, Fournier E.E., "A Reading Optophone," *The Electrician* (24 October 1913): 102–103.
Demetz, Peter, *The Air Show at Brescia* (New York: Farrar, Strauss, and Giroux, 2002).
Demetz, Peter, "Varieties of Phonetic Poetry: An Introduction," *From Kafka and Dada to Brecht and Beyond*, ed. R. Grimm et al. (Madison: U of Wisconsin P, 1982).
Derrida, Jacques, "Subverting the Signature. A Theory of the Parasite," *Blast Unlimited* 2 (1990): 16–21.
Doherty, Brigid, "'See: We Are All Neurasthenics!' or, The Trauma of Dada Montage," *Critical Inquiry* 24 (1997): 82–132.
Donguy, Jacques, "Machine Head. Raoul Hausmann and the Optophone," *Leonardo* 34.3 (2001): 217–220.
Dotzler, Bernhard J., "Simulation," *Ästhetische Grundbegriffe*, ed. K. Barck et al., vol. 5 (Stuttgart: Metzler, 2003), 509–533.
Drucker, Johanna, *The Visible Word: Experimental Typography and Modern Art, 1909–1923* (Chicago: U of Chicago P, 1994).
Eco, Umberto, *The Open Work* (Cambridge, MA: Harvard University Press, 1989).
Eco, Umberto, *Apocalittici e Integrati: Comunicazioni di Massa e Teoria della Cultura di Massa* (Milano: Bompiani, 1964).
Eisenstein, Sergej, "The Dramaturgy of Film Form (The Dialectical Approach to Film Form)," *The Eisenstein Reader*, ed. R. Taylor (London: British Film Institute, 1998), 93–110.
Elder, R. Bruce, *Harmony and Dissent: Film and Avant-garde Art Movements in the Early Twentieth Century* (Waterloo: Wilfrid Laurier UP, 2008)
Erlhoff, Michael, *Raoul Hausmann, Dadasoph: Versuch einer Politisierung der Ästhetik* (Hannover: Zweitschrift 1982).
Foster, Stephen C. and Rudolf E. Kuenzli, ed., *Dada Spectrum: The Dialectics of Revolt* (Madison: Coda Press, 1979)
Frisch, Karl von, *The Dancing Bees: An Account of the Life and Senses of the Honey Bee* (London: Methuen, 1954).
Fuller, Matthew, *Media Ecologies: Materialist Energies in Art and Technoculture* (Cambridge, MA: MIT Press, 2005).
Fürst, Artur, *Im Bannkreis von Nauen: Die Eroberung der Erde durch die drahtlose Telegraphie* (Stuttgart: Deutsche Verlagsanstalt, 1922).
Gane, Nicholas and Stephen Sale, "Interview with Friedrich Kittler and Mark Hansen," *Theory, Culture and Society* 24.7–8 (2007): 323–329.
Gibilisco, Stan and Neil Sclater, *Encyclopedia of Electronics* (Blue Ridge Summit: Tab Professional and Reference Books, 1990).

Girdner, John H., "The Plague of City Noises," *The North American Review* 163.478 (1896): 296–304.
Goddard, Michael and Jussi Parikka, "Editorial," *The Fibreculture Journal* 17 (2011): 1–5.
Goodman, Steve, *Sonic Warfare: Sound, Affect, and the Ecology of Fear* (Cambridge: MIT Press, 2010).
Görrisch, Dieter, *Störsender von VHF bis Mikrowelle* (Franzis: Poing, 2004).
Grice, Malcom L., *Abstract Film and Beyond* (Cambridge, MA: MIT Press, 1977), 17–19.
Hansen, Peter, *An Introduction to Twentieth Century Music* (Boston: Allyn and Bacon, 1971).
Haraway, Donna, "A Cyborg Manifesto: Science, Technology, and Socialist-Feminism in the Late Twentieth Century," *Simians, Cyborgs and Women: The Reinvention of Nature* (New York: Routledge, 1991), 149–181.
Hausmann, Raoul, *Scharfrichter der bürgerlichen Seele: Raoul Hausmann in Berlin, 1900–1933*, ed. Eva Züchner (Berlin: Hatje, 1998).
Hausmann, Raoul, *Texte bis 1933*. 2 vols., ed. Michael Erlhoff (München: Edition Text + Kritik, 1982).
Hausmann, Raoul, *Am Anfang war Dada* (Gießen: Anabas, 1980).
Hayles, N. Katherine, *How We Became Posthuman: Virtual Bodies in Cybernetics, Literature, and Informatics* (Chicago: Chicago UP, 1999).
Hayles, N. Katherine, ed., *Chaos and Order: Complex Dynamics in Literature and Science* (Chicago: Chicago UP, 1991).
Hedges, Inez, *Languages of Revolt: Dada and Surrealist Literature and Film* (Durham: Duke UP, 1983).
Helmholtz, Hermann von, *On the Sensations of Tone* (New York: Dover, 1954).
Henderson Dalrymple, Linda, "Vibratory Modernism. Boccioni, Kupka, and the Ether of Space," *From Energy to Information: Representation in Science and Technology, Art, and Literature*, ed. Bruce Clarke and Linda Dalrymple Henderson (Stanford: Stanford UP, 2002), 126–149.
Herzfelde, Wieland and Raoul Hausmann, *Erste internationale Dada-Messe: Katalog* (Berlin: Kunsthandlung Dr. Otto Burchard, 1920).
Hiepe, Richard, *Die Fotomontage: Geschichte und Wesen einer Kunstform* (Ingolstadt: Stadttheater Ingolstadt, 1969).
Höch, Hannah, *Eine Lebenscollage (1921–1945)*, vol. 2, ed. R. Burmeister and E. Fürlus (Ostfildern-Ruit: Hatje, 1995).
Hofmannsthal, Hugo v., *Das Märchen der 672. Nacht. Das erzählerische Werk* (Frankfurt am Main: Fischer, 1999).
Hong, Sungook, *Wireless: From Marconi's Black-Box to the Audion* (Cambridge: MIT Press, 2001).
Huelsenbeck, Richard, *Dada-Almanach* (Berlin: Erich Reiss, 1920).
Huelsenbeck, Richard, *Dada siegt!* (Berlin: Malik, 1920).
Huelsenbeck, Richard, *Mit Witz, Licht und Grütze: Auf den Spuren des Dadaismus* (Hamburg: Nautilus. 1991).
Huelsenbeck, Richard, *Phantastische Gebete* (Berlin: Malik, 1920).

Huelsenbeck, Richard, *Wozu Dada: Texte, 1916–1936*, ed. H. Kapfer (Gießen: Anabas, 1994).
Hugnet, Georges, *L'aventure dada, 1916–1922* (Paris: Galerie de l'Institut, 1957).
Ingels, Don M., *What Every Engineer Should Know about Computer Modeling and Simulation* (New York: Marcel Dekker, 1985).
James, William, *Psychology* (New York: Henry Holt, 1908).
Jünger, Ernst, *In Stahlgewittern* (Stuttgart: Klett Cotta, 1978).
Kafka, Franz, "The Cares of a Family Man," *The Complete Stories* (New York: Schocken Books, 1971), 427–429.
Kahn, Douglas, *Noise, Water, Meat: A History of Sound in the Arts* (Cambridge: MIT Press, 1999).
Kahn, Douglas, *John Heartfield: Art and Mass Media* (New York, Tanam Press, 1985).
Kandinsky, Wassily, *Concerning the Spiritual in Art* (New York: Dover, 1977).
Katz, Mark, *Capturing Sound: How Technology Has Changed Music* (Berkeley: U of California P, 2010).
Kelly, Caleb, *Cracked Media: The Sound of Malfunction* (Cambridge: MIT Press, 2009).
Kern, Stephen, *The Culture of Space and Time, 1880–1918* (Cambridge, MA: Harvard University Press, 1983).
Kirby, Michael, *Futurist Performance with Manifestoes and Playscripts* (New York: PAJ Publications, 1986).
Kittler, Friedrich, *Optical Media: Berlin Lectures 1999* (Cambridge: Polity, 2010), 118.
Kittler, Friedrich, *Gramophone, Film, Typewriter* (Stanford: Stanford UP, 1999).
Kittler, Friedrich, *Discourse Networks 1800/1900* (Stanford: Stanford UP, 1990).
Kittler, Friedrich, "Rockmusik: Ein Missbrauch von Heeresgerät," *Appareils et Machines a Représentation. MANA. Mannheimer Analytica* 8 (1988): 87–101.
Kittler, Friedrich, "Im Telegrammstil," *Stil: Geschichte und Funktionen eines kulturwissenschaftlichen Diskurselements*, ed. Hans-Ulrich Gumbrecht and Karl Ludwig Pfeiffer (Frankfurt am Main: Suhrkamp, 1986).
Kittler, Wolf, "Schreibmaschinen, Sprechmaschinen: Effekte technischer Medien im Werk Franz Kafkas," *Franz Kafka: Schriftverkehr*, ed. Wolf Kittler and Gerhard Neumann (Freiburg: Rombach, 1990), 75–163.
Koelsch, Karl, *Das spierelige Wesen der Wellen in Anwendung auf Licht und Farben* (Hannover, Helwig, 1922).
Krämer, Sybille, "Writing, Notational Iconicity, Calculus: On Writing as a Cultural Technique," *MLN* 118.3 (2003): 518–537.
Kuenzli, Rudolf, "The Semiotics of Dada Poetry" *Dada Spectrum: The Dialectics of Revolt*, ed. Stephen. C. Foster and Rudolf. E. Kuenzli (Madison: Coda Press, 1979), 51–70.
Kursell, Julia, *Schallkunst: Eine Literaturgeschichte der Musik in der frühen russischen Avantgarde* (Munich: Wiener Slawistischer Almanach, 2003).
Lavin, Maud, *Cut with the Kitchen Knife: The Weimar Photomontages of Hannah Höch* (New Haven and London: Yale UP, 1993).

Lawton, Anna, "Futurist Manifestoes as an Element of Performance," *Canadian-American Slavic Studies* 19.4 (1985): 473–491.
Lessing, Gotthold Ephraim, *Laokoon oder über die Grenzen der Malerei und Poesie* (Stuttgart: Reclam, 1964).
Lista, Giovanni, *Futurism and Photography* (London: Estorick Collection, 2001).
Lista, Giovanni, "The Activist Model or, The Avant-Garde as Italian Invention," *South Central Review* 13.2/3 (1996): 13–34.
Luhmann, Niklas, *The Reality of Mass Media* (Stanford: Stanford UP, 2000).
Mach, Ernst, *Die Analyse der Empfindungen und das Verhältnis des Physischen zum Psychischen* (Fischer: Jena 1900).
Maffina, Franco G., *Russolo/L'arte dei rumori, 1913–1931* (Venezia: Archivio Storico delle Arti Contemporanee, 1977).
Mango, Lorenzo, *Alla Scoperta di Nuovi Sensi: Il Tattilismo Futurista* (Napoli: La città del sole, 2001).
Marcus, Ernst, *Das Problem der excentrischen Empfindung und seine Lösung* (Berlin: Sturm-Verlag, 1918).
Marinetti, Filippo Tommaso, *Critical Writings*, ed. Günther Beghaus (New York, Farrar, Straus and Giroux, 2006).
Marinetti, Filippo Tommaso, *Teatro*, ed. Jeffrey Schnapp (Milano: Mondadori, 2004)
Marinetti, Filippo Tommaso, *Filippo Tommaso Marinetti e il Futurismo*, ed. Luciano de Maria (Milano: Mondadori, 2000).
Marinetti, Filippo Tommaso, *Mafarka the Futurist: An African Novel* (London: Middlesex UP, 1997).
Marinetti, Filippo Tommaso, *Selected Writings*, ed. Robert W. Flint (New York: Farrar, Strauss and Giroux, 1971).
Marx, Karl and Friedrich Engels, *Collected Works*, vol. III (New York: International Publishers, 1975).
Marinetti, Filipp Tommaso and Pino Masnata, "La Radia," *Wireless Imagination: Sound, Radio, and the Avant-Garde*, ed. Douglas Kahn and Gregory Whitehead (Cambridge: MIT Press, 1992), 265–268.
Matthews, E. Bernard, *An Introduction to Parasitology* (Cambridge: Cambridge UP, 1998).
McLuhan, Marshall, *Understanding Media* (Cambridge, MA: MIT Press, 1994).
Moholy-Nagy, Laszlo, "New Plasticism in Music. Possibilities of the Gramophone," *Broken Music. Artists' Recordworks* (Berlin: DAAD-Gelbe Musik, 1989) 54–56.
Moholy-Nagy, Laszlo, *Painting, Photography, Film* (Cambridge, MA: MIT Press, 1967)
Morgan, Robert P., "'A New Musical Reality.' Futurism, Modernism and 'The Art of Noise'." *Modernism/Modernity* 3 (1994): 129–151.
Morgenstern, Christian, *Werke und Briefe: Kommentierte Ausgabe*. ed. M. Cureau (Stuttgart: Urachaus, 1990).

Mosso, Angelo, *Fatigue* (New York: G.P. Putnam's Sons, 1904).
Motherwell, Robert, ed., *The Dada Painters and Poets: An Anthology* (Cambridge: Harvard UP, 1979).
Müller, Corinna, *Vom Stummfilm zum Tonfilm* (München: Fink. 2003).
Nietzsche, Friedrich, *The Birth of Tragedy and the Case of Wagner* (New York: Random House 1967).
Orban, Clara, *The Culture of Fragments: Words and Images in Futurism and Surrealism* (Amsterdam and Atlanta: Rodopi, 1997).
Payton, Robert, "The Music of Futurism. Concerts and Polemics," *The Musical Quarterly* 62.1 (1976): 25–45.
Payton, Robert J., *The Futurist Musicians: Francesco Balilla Pratella and Luigi Russolo* (Ph.D. diss., University of Chicago, 1974).
Peacock, Kenneth, "Instruments to Perform Color-Music. Two Centuries of Technological Experimentation," *Leonardo* 21.4 (1988): 397–406.
Perloff, Marjorie, *The Futurist Moment. Avant-Garde, Avant Guerre, and the Language of Rupture* (Chicago: Chicago UP, 2003).
Philipp, Eckhard, *Dadaismus: Einführung in den literarischen Dadaismus und die Wortkunst des 'Sturmkreises'* (München: Fink, 1980).
Pinch, Trevor J. and Karin Bijsterveld, "'Should One Applaud?' Breaches and Boundaries in the Reception of New Technology in Music," *Technology and Culture* 44.3 (2003): 536–559.
Poggi, Christina, *Inventing Futurism: The Art and Politics of Artifical Optimism* (Princeton: Princeton UP, 2009).
Poggi, Christine, *In Defiance of Painting: Cubism, Futurism, and the invention of Collage* (New Haven: Yale UP, 1992)
Postman, Neil, *Amusing Ourselves to Death: Public Discourse in the Age of Show Business* (London: Penguin, 1985).
Prasad, Rama, *The Science of Breath and the Philosophy of the Tattvas* (London: Theosophical Publishing Society, 1894).
Puchner, Martin, *Poetry of Revolution: Marx, Manifestos, and the Avant-Gardes* (Princeton: Princeton UP, 2006), 13.
Radice, Mark A., "'Futurismo.' Its Origins, Context, Repertory, and Influence," *The Musical Quarterly* 73.1 (1989): 1–17.
Regnani, Gerado, "Futurism and Photography: Between Scientific Inquiry and Aesthetic Imagination," *Futurism and the Technological Imagination*, ed. Günther Berghaus (Amsterdam: Rodopi, 2009), 177–199.
Remarque, Erich Maria, *Im Westen nichts Neues* (Köln: Kiepenheuer und Witsch, 2002).
Richter, Hans, "The Film as an Original Art Form," *The Film Culture Reader*, ed. P. Adams Sitney (New York: Prager, 1970).
Rieger, Stefan, *Schall und Rauch. Eine Mediengeschichte der Kurve* (Frankfurt am Main: Suhrkamp, 2007).
Ries, Christian, *Sehende Maschinen: Eine kurze Abhandlung über die geheimnisvollen Eigenschaften der lichtempfindlichen Stoffe und die staunenswerten Leistungen der sehenden Maschinen* (Hubers: Diessen, 1916).

Riha, Karl, "fmsbwtözäu pggiv-..?mü. Raoul Hausmanns optophonetische Poesie,"*Raoul Hausmann*, ed. K. Bartsch and A. Koch (Graz: Droschl, 1996), 31–42.
Riha, Karl and Jörgen Schäfer, eds., *DADA Total: Manifeste, Aktionen, Texte, Bilder* (Stuttgart: Reclam, 1994).
Ruhmer, Ernst, *Das Selen und seine Bedeutung für die Elektrotechnik mit besonderer Berücksichtigung der drahtlosen Telephonie* (Berlin: F. & M. Harrwitz, 1902).
Russolo, Luigi, *The Art of Noises* (New York: Pendragon, 1982).
Russolo, Luigi, *L'arte dei rumori* (Milano: Edizioni Futuriste di Poesia, 1916).
Russolo, Maria Zanovello, *Russolo, l'uomo, l'artista* (Milano: Cyril Corticelli, 1958).
Salaris, Claudia, "Marketing Modernism. Marinetti as Publisher," *Modernism/Modernity* 1.3 (1994): 109–127.
Schivelbusch, Wolfgang, *The Train Journey: The Industrialization of Time and Space in the 19th Century* (Berkeley: U of California P, 1986).
Schmidt-Bergmann, Hansgeorg, *Futurismus: Geschichte, Ästhetik, Dokumente* (Reinbek bei Hamburg: Rowohlt, 1993).
Schmitt, Carl, *Theory of the Partisan: A Commentary on the Concept of the Political* (East Lansing: Michigan State UP, 2004).
Schnapp, Jeffrey, "Crash," *Modernism/Modernity* 6.1 (1999): 1–49.
Schnapp, Jeffrey, "Propeller Talk," *Modernism/Modernity* 1.3 (1994): 153–178.
Schrage, Dominik, *Psychotechnik und Radiophonie. Subjektkonstruktionen in artifiziellen Wirklichkeiten, 1918–1932* (München: Fink 2001).
Schreber, Daniel Paul, *Memoirs of My Nervous Illness* (New York: New York Review of Books, 2000).
Schröter, Jens and Alexander Böhnke, eds., *Analog/Digital—Opposition oder Kontinuum? Zur Theorie und Geschichte einer Unterscheidung* (Bielefeld: transcript, 2004).
Serres, Michel, *Hermes: Literature, Science, Philosophy* (Baltimore: Johns Hopkins UP, 1982).
Serres, Michel, *The Parasite* (Baltimore: Johns Hopkins UP, 1982).
Shannon, Claude, *Mathematical Theory of Communication* (Urbana: University of Illinois: 1949).
Siegert, Bernhard, "Cacography or Communication? Cultural Techniques in German Media Studies," *Grey Room* 29 (2007): 26–47.
Spörl, Uwe, "Manifest," *Reallexikon der deutschen Literaturwissenschaft*, vol. II (Berlin and New York: de Gruyter, 2000), 535–537.
Stahl, Carl, "Die Vermeidung von Misstönen," *Phonographische Zeitschrift* 103 (1909): 541–543.
Sterne, Jonathan, *The Audible Past: Cultural Origins of Sound Reproduction* (Durham: Duke UP, 2003).
Strate, Lance, "A Media Ecology Review," *Communication Research Trends* 23.2 (2004): 1–48.
Taylor, Seth, *Left-Wing Nietzscheans: The Politics of German Expressionism, 1910–1920* (Berlin and New York: de Gruyter, 1990).

Tisdall, Caroline and Angelo Bozolla, *Futurism* (New York: Thames and Hudson, 1977).
Tzara, Tristan, *Seven Dada Manifestos and Lampisteries* (London: Calder, 1977)
Virilio, Paul, *The Vision Machine* (Bloomington and Indianapolis: Indiana UP, 1994).
Virilio, Paul, *War and Cinema: The Logistics of Perception* (New York: Verso, 1989).
Watts, Harriet, ed., *Dada and the Press* (New Haven: G. K. Hall, 2004).
Winthrop-Young, Geoffrey, *Kittler and the Media* (Cambridge: Polity Press, 2011).
Zacharias, Johannes, *Die wirklichen Grundlagen der elektrischen Erscheinungen: Aufklärungen über den Magnetismus durch neue Versuche* (Berlin: Julis Bohnes Verlag, 1906).

INDEX

absolute film, 83, 92–4
abstract film, 14, 92–4
abstract painting, 92–4
abuse, 2–15, 18–19, 24–5, 28, 37, 42–3, 46, 50, 55, 57, 66, 79–83, 90–2, 95, 98, 103, 106, 111, 114–15, 125, 127, 129, 133–4, 144–5, 152, 171–2, 176–7, 186, 204
acceleration, 2, 4, 10–11, 26–9, 43, 49–52, 55, 59, 61, 85, 88, 118, 121, 146, 176
acoustics, 4, 14, 60–1, 76, 110–26, 130, 134–9, 141, 147, 155–8, 163, 165–8, 171, 176, 182, 201–2, 204, 207, 213
advertisement, 4, 20–1, 28–9, 39, 42, 45, 47, 51, 73, 92, 95, 97, 103–6, 152, 187
afterimages, 64
aleatoric, 66
alphabet, 55, 72, 74, 195
amplification, 10, 13–14, 34, 59, 109–15, 119, 125, 129–38, 140, 176
anarchy, 128
anthropology, 4, 79, 135, 145, 160, 169, 183
antidadaism, 41–2
Apollonian, 63–4, 191
Arbeiter Illustrierte Zeitung (AIZ), 102
Armstrong, Edwin Howard, 134
articulation, 14, 58, 63, 65, 76–9, 127, 195, 204

art of noise, 10, 14, 110–12, 116–32, 135, 137–8, 140–1, 176, 183, 192, 201–6, 220
artwork essay, 8, 73, 81–2, 88, 92, 144, 161–2, 184, 189, 195–8, 209, 215
atoms, 4, 49–50, 149, 182
Audion, 136
autonomy, 10, 101
avant-garde, xi–xiii, 1–15, 17–20, 43–6, 56, 81–2, 107, 109–11, 122, 130, 132–5, 138–41, 143–6, 172–3, 175–9, 185–6, 194, 197, 200

Baader, Johannes, 36–8, 70–3, 95, 190, 215
Balla, Giacomo, 46
Ball, Hugo, xiii, 17, 31, 34–7, 45–6, 60–70, 126–7, 129, 189, 191, 194, 195, 204–5, 215
ballistics, 88–90
Barthes, Roland, 24–5, 188, 215
Bauhaus, 162
Benjamin, Walter, 8, 73, 81–2, 88, 92, 144, 161–2, 184, 189, 195–8, 209, 215
Benn, Gottfried, 20, 23, 187, 215
Benson, Timothy, 44, 189–90, 215
Bergius, Hanne, 42, 44, 96–7, 185, 190, 199, 215–16
Berlin, 1–2, 14, 36–40, 43, 62, 65–6, 70, 83, 92–8, 106, 132–3, 162–4, 175, 193
Berliner Illustrirte Zeitung, 95, 98, 100

binary code, 155–8, 161
Biro, Matthew, 96, 186, 199, 216
Birth of Tragedy, 63–4, 194, 221
Boccioni, Umberto, 46, 82, 85–9, 91, 93, 106, 194, 197, 205, 207, 218
Bohr, Niels, 4
bourgeoisie, 6, 10, 29, 31, 34–5, 38, 43, 47, 93, 103–4, 208–9
Bragaglia, Anton Giulio and Arturo, 82–3, 89–91, 93, 106–7
Brecht, Bertolt, 144, 172, 206, 214, 216
Bredow, Hans, 9, 145, 172
Brinkmann, Walter, 168
Broido, Daniel, 1–2, 9, 135, 165, 181, 199, 212
Brownian motion, 10, 49, 182
bruitism, 61, 69, 109, 111, 126–30
Bürger, Peter, xii, 11, 181, 184, 205, 216

Cabaret Voltaire, 31, 62, 65, 69–70, 128, 189, 194
Cage, John, 9, 115
Cahill, Thaddeus, 136
calculating machine, 1–2, 167, 181, 212
Cangiullo, Francesco, 153–6
central organ, 163, 170
channel, 4–8, 10, 13, 17–18, 21, 27–8, 30–1, 33, 42–3, 46, 58, 60–2, 80, 105, 112, 126, 131, 136, 139–40, 148, 159, 169, 172, 176–7, 207
chaos, 63–4, 73, 98, 103, 105, 111, 118, 132, 138, 140, 183, 185
chronophotography, 81, 84–9, 91, 106–7, 197
church service, 62–3
cinema, 2, 50, 53, 57, 79, 81–2, 86, 89, 91, 93–4, 152, 154, 173, 192, 213
circuit, xi, 8, 11, 13, 18, 29, 58–60, 83, 98, 109, 134, 136, 139, 141, 158, 166–7, 183

Clausewitz, Carl von, 109, 185, 200, 216–17
Clavilux, 137
cohabitation, 18
collage, 1–2, 6, 14, 37, 45, 69, 72, 79, 81–3, 92–102, 105–6, 133, 146, 176, 186, 198, 200
color pianos, 166–7
communication theory, 4, 183
Communist Manifesto, 17–18, 31, 189
complexity, 4–5, 35, 48, 52, 54, 62, 71, 79–80, 86, 110, 118, 120, 122–3, 130–2, 138, 140, 167, 176, 178, 182–3, 185
Corra, Bruno, 93
cryptography, 4, 76
curves, 85, 88, 91, 121, 131, 197, 198
Cut with the Kitchen Knife, 98, 101

Dada-Almanach, 66–7, 182, 189–90, 194, 204–5, 218–19
Dadaco, 79
"Dadadegie," 72–4, 77, 79
Dada Rundschau, 83, 99–101
Dadasoph, 1, 72, 133, 138, 144, 164, 172, 175, 199
Dada, xi–xiii, 1–2, 6–11, 13–15, 17–19, 28–46, 60–83, 88, 92–111, 126–33, 138–40, 143–6, 161–4, 169, 172, 175–8, 182, 185–6, 189–90, 193, 195, 204–5, 209
Daguerre, Louis-Jacques-Mandé, 81, 84, 89
D'Albe, Fournier E.E., 162, 165–6, 210, 217
De Forest, Lee, 134, 136
deictic, 60, 69
Demetz, Peter, 78–9, 192, 217
Der Dada, 70–1, 103–4
Dionysian, 62–5, 111, 205
discourse network, 7, 10, 12–13, 66, 80, 184–5
disruption, xii, 4, 155

Doherty, Brigid, 96, 185, 193, 196, 199, 217
Dotzler, Bernhard, 122, 203, 217
Drucker, Johanna, 50, 191, 194, 217
dynamism, 82, 84–94, 99, 106–7
Dynamophone, 136

Ebbinghaus, Hermann, 10
Ebert, Friedrich, 100–1
eccentric perception, 163, 169, 171, 211
Eco, Umberto, 19, 183, 187, 217
ecstasy, 64
Eggeling, Viking, 83, 93
Einstein, Albert, 4, 144, 164, 168, 182, 188, 209, 211
Eisenstein, Sergei, 56, 193, 217
electrical engineering, 5, 109, 134–8, 141, 164, 166
electricity, 28, 58, 134, 164, 170–1, 194
Electrola, 135
electromagnetism, 7, 11, 28, 85, 109, 134–5, 144–5, 168–70, 193, 211
Elektrophon, 137
endoscope, 2, 165
enharmonic notation, 121
entropy, 10, 12, 29–30, 46, 62, 93, 95, 97–9, 196
Erlhoff, Michael, 72–3, 78, 181, 195–6, 201, 206, 212–13, 217
ether, 14, 85, 135, 141, 143–5, 154–9, 163–4, 168–73, 177, 179, 193, 211–12

Fantastic Prayers, 60, 68–9, 194–5, 218
fascism, 8, 143–4, 172, 175
feedback, 10, 14, 79–80, 96, 105, 107, 110–11, 118–22, 126, 129–34, 138, 140–1, 144, 172, 176
Le Figaro, 2, 19–22
film, 8–9, 13–14, 27, 51, 53–7, 82–3, 86, 91–4, 105–7, 121, 144, 162, 165, 192–3, 210, 212

"fmsbw," 74–9, 195–6
frequency, 75–6, 91, 115, 132, 136, 165–6, 168, 183, 195, 201, 210
Freud, Sigmund, 161
friction, 102, 109, 185
Friedländer, Salomo, 162
Fuller, Matthew, 3, 182, 217
futurism, xi–xiii, 2, 6–9, 13–15, 17–28, 33, 38–9, 43–62, 65, 79, 81–93, 95–6, 105–7, 109–14, 118, 122–32, 137, 139–40, 143–8, 151–4, 158–61, 172, 175–8, 182, 185–8, 192, 194, 197, 202–8

Gesamtkunstwerk, 6, 151
Ghosts before Breakfast, 94
Ginna, Arnaldo, 93
Girdner, John H., 139–40, 206, 218
glissando, 122, 124–5, 138, 203
Goddard, Michael, 3, 182, 218
gramophone, xii, 2, 4, 8, 49, 110–14, 117, 121–2, 132–40, 144, 149–51, 165, 176
graphic method, 88, 91, 121, 197, 202
Greek drama, 64–5
Grosz, George, 95, 97–8, 103, 193
Gsell, Paul, 87

haptic, 144, 149, 161–2, 169–71
Hausmann, Raoul, xiii, 1–2, 6, 8–14, 17, 36–7, 40–6, 60–2, 65–6, 70, 72–9, 95–8, 105–6, 111, 132–41, 143–6, 160–73, 175–6, 179, 181–2, 184, 190, 195–6, 199, 201, 205–6, 208–14, 218
Heartfield, John, 14, 36, 83, 95–8, 102–6
Helmholtz, Hermann von, 4, 58, 116–17, 130, 138, 140, 182, 201–2, 218
Henderson, Linda, 85, 88, 193–4, 197–8, 218
hermeneutics, 10, 13, 45–6, 53–4, 57, 62, 132, 144–5, 171, 178, 209

Herzfelde, Wieland, 36, 103–4, 199, 218
Hitler, Adolf, 143, 154, 172, 175
Höch, Hannah, 14, 36, 83, 95–103, 199, 206, 218
Hofmannsthal, Hugo von, 45, 191, 218
Hörbiger, Hanns, 160
host, xii, 3–6, 9, 13–15, 19, 33, 35, 42, 79–80, 82, 96, 147, 152, 158, 172–3, 176, 178, 183
Huelsenbeck, Richard, 9, 11, 17, 31–6, 40, 46, 60–2, 65–70, 127–33, 140, 182, 189–90, 194–5, 204–5, 218–19
hurdy-gurdy, 113
hybrid, 24, 72, 92, 96, 102, 171, 186
hypersensitivity, 144–5, 150

identity, 11, 178, 203
imaginary, 24, 43, 82, 86, 90, 121–2, 171, 197
indexicality, 5, 14, 23, 82, 93, 107, 120, 134, 139
information theory, 4, 10, 12, 46, 75–6, 139–40, 150, 183
infrastructure, 27–8, 152
interruption, 5, 7, 52, 80, 113, 145
intonarumori, 110, 112–18, 120, 123–7, 136, 176, 200, 203
intuition, 49, 57, 88
irritation, xii, 4–14, 18, 23, 32–3, 56, 59, 68, 74, 79, 90, 94, 97, 106, 123, 125–6, 132, 139, 146, 158, 163, 172, 175–8

James, William, 58, 194, 219
Janco, Marcel, 65

Kafka, Franz, 177–9, 192, 214, 219
Kahn, Douglas, 102–3, 106, 186, 189, 200, 204, 206, 219–20
Kant, Immanuel, 160, 162, 164, 211
"Karawane," 63, 66–70
Katz, Mark, 115, 200–1, 219

Kelly, Caleb, 9, 115, 184, 186, 210, 219
Kern, Stephen, 26, 188, 219
Kittler, Friedrich, 7, 9–13, 52–3, 81–2, 115, 121–2, 125, 145, 172, 176–7, 184–5, 191–2, 196–8, 200–6, 214, 217, 219
Kittler, Wolf, 177, 214, 219
Koelsch, Karl, 164, 211, 219
"K'perioum," 77, 79
Krämer, Sybille, 72–3, 195, 219
kymograph, 91

Lacan, Jacques, 121, 197
language, xii, 9, 14, 24–5, 32, 35, 39–40, 45–70, 75–80, 126–7, 148, 158, 189, 196–7
Laocoon, 87
Lavin, Maud, 99, 101
Lichtspiel Opus 1, 93
life sciences, 88, 121, 131
lines of force, 82, 86, 89, 96, 197
longitudinal wave, 134–5
Luhmann, Niklas, 19, 21, 187, 190
Lumière, Auguste and Louis, 82

Mach, Ernst, 89, 91, 122, 198, 203, 220–1
Mafarka, 19, 47, 147, 187, 191, 220
magazines, 1, 72, 95, 102–3, 199
Mager, Jörg, 137
magic, 2, 61–2, 94
magic bishop, 62
Magic Flute, 70
Mallarmé, Stéphane, 50
Marconi, Guglielmo, 2, 143, 169–70
Marcus, Ernst, 160, 162–4, 169–71, 210–11, 213, 220
Marey, Étienne-Jules, 81, 84–9, 106–7, 198
Marinetti, F.T., xii–xiii, 2, 6, 8, 10–14, 17, 19–28, 32, 36, 45–62, 65, 80–1, 83–4, 86–7, 96, 99, 110, 126–30, 141, 143–62, 169, 172, 175, 179, 181–2, 185–9, 191–4, 196–7, 206–9, 220

masks, 64–5
mass media, xii, 1, 6, 8, 13, 18–22, 27, 29–30, 36, 42–4, 66, 79, 81, 83, 94–5, 98–102, 105, 126, 158, 170, 173, 176, 187
materiality, 3, 13, 48–9, 51–4, 58, 73, 80, 110, 117, 119, 122, 133–4
McLuhan, Marshall, 3, 76, 159, 170, 182, 209, 213–14, 220
media ecology, 2–6, 18, 26–8, 112, 143–6, 164, 172–3, 177, 182
media a priori, 12–13
media theory, 3, 7, 10, 12, 15, 19, 81, 121, 122, 182, 183, 185
Méliès, Georges, 2, 82, 86, 94
meta-semiotics, 73–4
Meyer, Raimund, 44, 189
micro tones, 91, 118, 120, 138, 202
military, 2, 5–9, 11, 51–2, 55, 69, 81, 83, 109, 125–6, 128, 145, 153, 155, 172, 184, 186
mimicry, 10, 83, 102–6
modernism, xi, 20, 45–6, 48, 50, 70, 103, 193
modernity, xii, 4, 6, 11–12, 25–8, 30, 50, 65, 80, 83, 101, 111, 124, 139
Mondrian, Piet, 137
montage, 53–6, 71, 73, 82–3, 95–106, 185–6
morse code, 2, 53, 158
Mosso, Angelo, 89, 198, 221
musical notation, 91, 117, 121, 202–3
Mussolini, Benito, 172, 175
Muybridge, Eadweard, 81, 84–6, 88–9, 106–7
mystical, 22–4, 46, 62–3, 65–6
myth, 4, 22–6, 146
mythology, 4, 13, 18, 22–6, 43, 64

Nachrichtentechnik, 138
nervous system, 8, 57–9, 62, 139, 150–2, 163–4, 170, 210

networks, 7, 10–14, 18, 27–8, 43, 46, 51–2, 57–9, 62, 66, 76, 80, 97, 109, 136, 144, 159, 169–70, 172, 176, 179, 185
news of the day, 2, 19–23, 95
newspaper, xii, 2, 4, 8–9, 19–22, 27–8, 30–2, 35–7, 44, 72–3, 79, 92, 95, 101–2, 146, 173, 176
Niépce, Nicéphore, 81, 84, 89
Nietzsche, Friedrich, 63–5, 194, 205, 221
Nike of Samothrace, 20, 23
noise intoner, 8, 110, 112–13, 116, 120, 122, 125–6, 136, 204
noisescape, 110–11, 119, 126, 128
noise, xi, 2, 4–8, 10, 12–14, 22, 33, 35, 39–40, 42, 44–6, 53, 58–9, 63, 65, 70, 79, 98, 107, 109–41, 145, 148–9, 156–8, 171, 176, 182, 186, 192, 193, 197, 200–6, 208
non-linearity, 178–9, 183, 185
nonsense, xii, 29–30, 36, 41–2, 45, 55, 68–9, 74, 78, 103, 160, 177
Noske, Gustav, 100–1
note-line, 91, 121, 131, 150, 202–3

Odradek, 175, 177–9
"OFFEA," 74–5, 165
onomatopoeias, 52–3, 55, 59, 68–9, 192
optical unconscious, 161
optophone, 2, 162, 166–9, 171, 181, 210, 212, 217
optophonetics, 1, 76, 78, 135, 137, 144–6, 160, 162, 164–9, 171, 175, 181, 210–12, 217
oscillator, 136

Paik, Nam June, 9
painting, 27, 46, 85–9, 92–3, 95–6, 105, 197, 199, 205
panoptic view, 81, 83, 99, 101–2

parasite, xi–xiii, 2–7, 12–15, 17–19,
    23–5, 28–31, 33–8, 40, 43, 46,
    51–2, 59, 62, 68, 70, 73–4,
    78–81, 83, 95–6, 109, 114,
    117–18, 131, 133–4, 138–9,
    143, 145–7, 158–9, 162, 171–3,
    175, 177–9, 183
parasitic noise, 5, 42, 109–10, 115,
    117–18, 121–2, 126, 128, 133,
    138–41, 200
Parikka, Jussi, 3, 182, 218
parole in libertà, 32, 46, 48, 50–1, 53,
    55, 59, 61, 143, 146, 149–50,
    153–4, 192, 197
partisan, 178–9, 186
passatism, 24, 27, 84, 161
performance, xi, 6, 9, 20–1, 30, 32–3,
    35, 37–8, 41, 58, 60–2, 66,
    68–9, 76–7, 107, 110–12, 115,
    119, 125–32, 136, 138–9, 141,
    152–4, 158–9, 167, 172–3,
    176–7, 194, 196, 209
performativity, 44–60
Perloff, Marjorie, 17, 55, 186–7, 193,
    221
phonograph, 2, 10, 13, 144–5, 162,
    165–7, 210–13
Phonographische Zeitschrift, 110, 114,
    166, 200–1, 212, 215, 217, 222
photo cell, 1, 6, 8, 13, 144–5, 162,
    165–7, 210–13
photodynamism, 89–91
photography, xiii, 13–14, 54, 81–97,
    100, 105–7, 162, 165
physics, 1, 9–10, 84, 94, 111, 160,
    168, 185
physiological sound, 137
physiology, 8, 10–11, 26, 46, 57, 59,
    62, 64, 78–9, 84–5, 88–9, 97,
    121, 137, 143–5, 150–2, 154–5,
    158, 161–4, 172–3, 176, 195,
    197–8, 209
poetics, 2, 8, 18, 46–53, 56–9, 61–2,
    65–6, 75–80, 165, 185, 189,
    192, 197, 205

poetry, xii, 2, 8, 10, 14, 18, 20, 31–2,
    34, 45–81, 88, 92, 105–7, 111,
    126–31, 144–6, 152–4, 158,
    165, 176, 183, 185, 189, 192–8,
    204–5, 211
Popées electriques, 47
poster poems, 74–6, 79, 196
posthumanism, 3, 11, 126, 184, 186
Postman, Neil, 3, 19, 182, 187, 221
Pratella, Francesco Balilla, 112
Présentismus, 143, 160–2, 181,
    208–9
primal instinct, 62
primal language, 66, 127, 129
psychophysics, 10, 58, 176, 185

radio, 2, 6–9, 12–15, 28, 59, 76, 111,
    136–8, 140–1, 143–6, 151,
    153–9, 164, 170, 172–3, 176–9,
    194, 208–9, 211
radio plays, 153–9, 172
radio *sintesi*, 154–9, 172, 208
radio tube, 9, 14, 111, 134, 136–8,
    140–1, 175
randomness, 10, 45, 52, 66, 69, 74–5,
    80, 99, 120, 157
reaction, 6, 17, 33, 35, 41, 46, 61,
    107, 110–11, 125–6, 131–2,
    152–4, 163, 176
rheotome, 136
rhythm, 21, 93–4
Richter, Hans, 83, 93–4, 199, 221
Rieger, Stefan, 121, 198, 202, 221
Riegl, Alois, 162
Ries, Christian, 162, 210, 222
Rodin, Auguste, 87–8
Roi Bombance, 47
Ruhmer, Ernst, 165–7
Russolo, Antonio, 112
Russolo, Luigi, 6, 8–11, 14, 61, 91,
    110–28, 130–3, 136–8, 140–1,
    149–50, 176, 182–3, 192,
    200–6, 209, 222
Rutherford, Ernest, 4
Ruttman, Walter, 93

Salcher, Peter, 89, 198, 221
Schikaneder, Emanuel, 69–70
Schivelbusch, Wolfgang, 26, 57, 188, 193, 222
Schmitt, Carl, 179, 214, 222
Schnapp, Jeffrey, 26, 51, 53, 185, 187–8, 191–2, 205, 208, 220, 222
Schönberg, Arnold, 137
Schopenhauer, Arthur, 64
Schulz, Frank, 40–2, 132, 190
Schwitters, Kurt, 78
science, 4, 9, 11, 82, 84, 86, 88–91, 121, 131, 160, 171, 175, 185, 202, 207
sculpture, 46, 92, 96, 146, 198, 207
semiotics, 46, 62, 66, 71–4, 79, 119, 122, 165
senses, 8, 13–14, 49, 53–61, 78–80, 87–8, 93, 98, 110, 115, 119, 120, 123–5, 137, 141, 144, 146–72, 175, 185, 192–3, 201, 206–13
sensitivity, 49, 80, 124, 138, 144–6, 150–1, 161–2, 167
serate, 21, 125, 128–30, 152, 154
Serner, Walter, 131–2
Serres, Michel, xii, 4–7, 10, 17, 25, 30, 33, 40, 73, 109, 130, 139, 145, 159, 177–8, 182–4, 189, 195, 200, 206, 209, 222
Shannon, Claude, E., 4–5, 183, 222
signal, 5, 8, 60, 76, 109, 111, 121, 134, 136, 138–41, 145, 154–9, 165, 176–7
simulacrum, 83
simulation, 13, 90, 102, 110, 121–6, 140, 203
singing arc lamp, 167
sintesi, 154–7, 208
sirens, 63, 65, 116, 126
Sophocles, 65
sound, 2, 6, 9–11, 14, 35, 41, 48, 53, 60, 62–3, 65–7, 76, 78, 107, 109, 110–27, 130, 132–41, 144, 149–50, 155–7, 162, 165–9, 186, 192, 196, 200–3, 208–10, 213
sound film, 165
sound-on-film system, 165
sound-noise, 14, 114–20, 123, 130, 140, 149
sound pickup, 11, 114–15, 133–5, 144, 165
sound poetry, 60, 63, 65, 76, 126, 189, 195
specter, 17, 28–9, 31
speed, 13, 25–8, 44, 50–4, 58–9, 82, 89, 120, 146, 150, 182, 188, 192
stage, 14, 20, 33, 35–6, 39, 60, 62–3, 68–70, 125, 128–9, 131, 133, 152–8, 172–3, 176, 185, 204
static film, 105–7
Sterne, Jonathan, 11, 184, 200, 222
stimulation, 6, 23, 29, 58, 130–1, 147, 153, 156–8, 163, 172, 196
Stockhausen, Karlheinz, 9
Stravinsky, Igor, 112
Student of Prague, 86
subjectivity, 11–12, 28, 45, 49–51, 58–9, 63–4, 79–80, 96, 103, 122, 126, 131, 139, 144, 147, 159, 163–4, 169–73, 185, 211
subversion, 3, 6–9, 12–15, 18, 28, 33, 38, 43–4, 60, 62, 68, 83, 92–4, 96–8, 102–7, 126, 133, 145–6, 152, 176, 179
surveillance, 53, 81, 101, 192
synesthesia, xii, 1, 60, 76, 93, 121, 135, 137, 144, 164–6, 169, 171, 196
synthesizer, 117
synthetic theater, 153–4

tactilism, 143–52, 159–60, 185, 206–8
tactilist, 148–51, 159, 169, 208
tactility, 14–15, 49, 106–8, 143–52, 159–60, 162–3, 169–71, 185, 192, 197

Tato, 83, 197
telegram style, 46, 59
telegraph, 2, 4, 8, 14, 25–7, 32, 46, 50–3, 57–9, 62, 76–9, 155, 158
telephone, 8, 58, 111, 136, 154, 161, 166–7
telharmonium, 135–6
theater, xi, 2, 20, 47, 62, 65, 82, 107, 131, 144, 146, 151–4, 158, 173, 176, 194
theory of relativity, 1, 4, 144, 164, 182, 211
theremin, 137
Theremin, Lev, 137
timbre, 110, 116–20, 123, 138, 140, 176
trajectory, 91, 124
transversal wave, 133–5
trauma, 57–9, 97, 185, 193
typography, 21, 45–6, 50, 66, 68, 70–1, 74–5, 79, 81
Tzara, Tristan, 29, 34, 38, 44, 79–80, 131–2, 194, 196, 223

Ullstein Verlag, 95, 98

vacuum tube, 9, 14, 111, 114, 134–8, 140–1, 175
Varèse, Edgar, 125
variety theater, 2, 62, 82, 146, 149, 152–3, 158, 176
Venice, 27
vers libre, 47–8

vibrations, 57–8, 85, 87–8, 114, 118, 133–6, 138–9, 163, 165, 167–8, 170–1, 192–3, 201–2
Virilio, Paul, 53, 81, 87, 192, 196, 198, 223
visuality, xiii, 1–2, 6, 45, 57, 71–2, 74, 76, 81, 83, 85–7, 89, 92–6, 98–9, 105, 107, 121, 145, 147, 150–1, 163, 165–6, 168–71, 176, 197–8, 207, 213
voice, 2, 61, 63, 78, 115, 117, 126–7, 129–30, 134, 175, 194
Volksempfänger, 154

war, 2, 4–5, 7–8, 11, 26–7, 30–2, 34, 37, 39, 54, 58–9, 76, 81–2, 84, 97–8, 100, 105, 109, 112, 122–6, 128–30, 139, 145, 172, 179, 184–5, 190, 193, 204–5
Welteislehre, 160
Wilfred, Thomas, 137
writing, 48, 60, 72–4, 79, 96, 99, 122, 162, 165–7

x-rays, 85, 151

yogic breathing, 79

Zacharias, Johannes, 164, 211, 223
Zola, Émile, 47
Zurich, 30–2, 34, 36–40, 60, 62, 68, 92, 94, 106, 111, 126, 128, 132, 195, 205

GPSR Compliance

The European Union's (EU) General Product Safety Regulation (GPSR) is a set of rules that requires consumer products to be safe and our obligations to ensure this.

If you have any concerns about our products, you can contact us on

ProductSafety@springernature.com

In case Publisher is established outside the EU, the EU authorized representative is:

Springer Nature Customer Service Center GmbH
Europaplatz 3
69115 Heidelberg, Germany

www.ingramcontent.com/pod-product-compliance
Lightning Source LLC
LaVergne TN
LVHW012100070526
838200LV00074BA/3766